PASSIONS AND DECEPTIONS

PASSIONS AND DECEPTIONS

THE EARLY FILMS OF ERNST LUBITSCH

Sabine Hake

PRINCETON UNIVERSITY PRESS   PRINCETON, NEW JERSEY

Library of Congress Cataloging-in-Publication Data

Hake, Sabine, 1956–
Passions and deceptions : the early films of
Ernst Lubitsch / Sabine Hake.
p.   cm.
Includes bibliographical references and index.
ISBN 0-691-03197-5 (CL)—ISBN 0-691-00878-7 (PB)
1. Lubitsch, Ernst, 1892–1947—Criticism and
interpretation. 2. Silent films—Germany—History
and criticism. I. Title.
PN1998.3.L83H35   1992
791.43'0233'092—dc20   92-1189

A shorter version of chapter 7 was first published as
"So This Is Paris—A Comedy of Misreading," in
Journal of Film and Video 40,
no. 3 (Summer 1988): 3–17.

This book has been composed in Galliard

Princeton University Press books are printed on
acid-free paper and meet the guidelines for
permanence and durability of the Committee on
Production Guidelines for Book Longevity
of the Council on Library Resources

Printed in the United States of America

10 9 8 7 6 5 4 3 2 1

10 9 8 7 6 5 4 3 2 1
(Pbk.)

FOR MY PARENTS,

Edeltraud and Günter Hake ————————————————

Contents

Illustrations

PASSIONS AND DECEPTIONS

Introduction

IN GENERAL, critics either have remained indifferent or have resorted to the most conventional approaches when they are confronted with the films of Ernst Lubitsch. Though film theory has become increasingly sophisticated, there seems to be little understanding of and even less appreciation for what are frequently regarded as nothing more than formulaic sex comedies without redeeming value. However, it is precisely because of their alleged shallowness, artificiality, and cynicism that these films continue to challenge the established rules of criticism. The films of Lubitsch, and the earlier ones in particular, seem to resist traditional value judgments, because their profundity lies hidden under sleek surfaces or is lightened by the pleasures of style. They undermine the basic rules of the classical narrative cinema by dissolving the distinctions between form and content, narrative and representation. And they defy those critical approaches that regard narrative as the primary site of meaning production in film. In order to better understand these qualities, criticism must draw attention to the insurmountable difference between filmic and critical language, a problem that, although it haunts all writing about film, is especially noticeable vis-à-vis the early Lubitsch films and their oscillation between conformism and subversion.

To this day, the critical reception of Lubitsch films lacks the diversity of theoretical perspectives that have made the writings on Hitchcock (to name the most obvious example) so challenging and productive. Short of this diversity, his work falls prey to the equally charged positions of the detractor and the fan. Most critics assume a position somewhere between these extremes. Those searching for hidden messages and higher truths tend to defend the later, warmer Lubitsch, playing down or rejecting his chilling obsession with form; or they approach the problem by introducing further distinctions. For instance, Dwight MacDonald, in reviewing *Trouble in Paradise*, praises the film's style as being "as close to perfection as anything I have ever seen in the movies" but at the same time dismisses its story as "banal—and quite unimportant."[1] By distinguishing between form and content, he tries to come to terms with the film's ambiguity but, at the same time, resorts to problematic value judgments like "perfection" and "unimportance." Ultimately, MacDonald's assessment reveals nothing less than the anxiety of visual pleasure and, as its corollary, the widespread re-

[1] Dwight MacDonald, *Dwight MacDonald on Movies* (Englewood Cliffs, N.J.: Prentice-Hall, 1969), 84.

sistance to theories that focus on a film's effects rather than its "inherent" values.

Conversely, critics who are susceptible to notions of "style"—and style in this context means an excess of filmic means, a foregrounding of formal strategies, a self-reflective use of the medium—reject such moralistic earnestness. Their enthusiasm, and their close attention to formal qualities, have produced a more impressionistic writing style that, despite the lack of an explicitly theoretical framework, captures the atmosphere of the films quite effectively. Describing the experience of watching a Lubitsch film, many admirers have turned to metaphors and, rather appropriately, found an inexhaustible reservoir of images in the language of the body. With the suggestive term "Lubitsch touch," the tactile register was introduced. Variations have subsequently been presented in terms of Richard Corliss's Lubitsch "caress"[2] and Andrew Sarris's Lubitsch "grasp."[3] Other critics have invoked more gruesome analogies. Jean Mitry, for instance, compares Lubitsch's sense of precision to "a surgeon's bistoury lancing an abscess."[4] Again others have turned to the offerings of the restaurant, thus also introducing a wider range of bodily pleasures. Under the heading "Champagne Pearls," Michael Esser mentions various champagne brands, comparing *Kohlhiesel's Daughters* to Henkel Piccolo, *The Merry Jail* to Mumm Magnum, and *Passion* and *Deception* to Dom Perignon.[5] Such a suggestive play on "spirits" recalls Sarris's remark that, in the later films, "the Lubitsch champagne is beginning to be diluted with vinegar from the well-stocked cupboard of Billy Wilder."[6] In favor of more solid nutrition, French critic Jean George Auriol uses expressions like "spicy," "frothy," "tasty," and "creamy" to describe the concoctions of delightful nothingness created by "le maître" Lubitsch.[7] And describing his famous ellipses, François Truffaut proclaims: "In the Lubitsch Swiss cheese each hole winks."[8] Given Lubitsch's many filmic reflections on culinary pleasures, and the relation-

[2] Discussing *The Shop around the Corner*, Corliss writes: "The famed Lubitsch touch is here more of a caress; rarely does a visual effect call attention to the director instead of the situation." In *Talking Pictures: Screenwriters in the American Cinema 1927–73* (Woodstock, N.Y.: Overlook Press, 1974), 172.

[3] Andrew Sarris, intro. to William Paul, *Ernst Lubitsch's American Comedy* (New York: Columbia University Press, 1983), x.

[4] Jean Mitry, qtd. in Herman G. Weinberg, *The Lubitsch Touch: A Critical Study*, 3d. rev. ed. (New York: Dover, 1977), 144.

[5] Michael Esser, "Champagnerperlen," *Zitty* (Berlin), February 1984.

[6] Sarris, "Ernst Lubitsch: American Period," in *Cinema: A Critical Dictionary. The Major Film-Makers*, vol. 2, ed. Richard Roud (New York: Viking Press, 1980), 649. Sarris is referring to the films after *Ninotchka* and *Bluebeard's Eighth Wife*.

[7] Jean George Auriol, "Chez Ernst," *La revue de cinéma* 17 (September 1947).

[8] François Truffaut, "Lubitsch Was a Prince," in *The Films in My Life*, trans. Leonard Mayhew (New York: Simon & Schuster, 1975), 51.

ship between food and sexuality in particular, such metaphors help to illuminate similarly elusive pleasures in the cinema. They draw attention to the ability of style to be affirmative in the worst sense—as the reproduction of formulas, as the repetition of the eternal same—and, at the same time, to serve as a vehicle for subversive strategies and self-reflective moments. Unfortunately, these suggestive metaphors also reinforce the widespread prejudice that the Lubitsch films do not deserve a more rigorous terminology. Here Andrew Sarris's question "as to whether Ernst Lubitsch . . . is worthy of all this attention"[9] unwittingly admits to the continuing resistance to critical approaches that could liberate the films from the fetters of morality and good taste.

From the beginning, Lubitsch criticism has been characterized by a remarkable degree of coherence and continuity. Ever since the first reviews appeared in trade journals, newspapers, and popular magazines, critics have tried to assess the films within the context of American cinema and its audiences. Some scholars (Grafe, Patalas, Prinzler) have discovered similar continuities in the work itself. Their emphasis on the structural qualities of the Lubitsch films often goes hand in hand with a pronounced skepticism about the films' social referentiality. As the British critic Raymond Durgnat, one of the few to argue in this vein, notes about Lubitsch in the thirties, "The Lubitsch comedy survives the Depression without difficulty. . . . The condition of such lightness is all the assumptions of privilege, money, or their equivalent, impudence. But Lubitsch uses the paraphernalia of high society in an almost abstract way . . . so that his films, while pointedly indifferent towards social egalitarianism, relate to no particular class code, nor even fun morality . . . but to a hedonistic magnanimity whose cynicism is not unkindly and which is the reverse of snobbish."[10] The majority of American critics has focused on the dramatic changes in Lubitsch's popularity, thus emphasizing the discontinuities. To that end, they have conceived a narrative of rise and decline not dissimilar to the three-act structure of the classical drama. With the Great Depression as America's great moment of truth, *Trouble in Paradise* is usually presented as the turning point in relation to which all earlier and later films are assigned their place. However, the critical assessment of the pre-1932 and post-1932 films has varied considerably over the years. During the thirties and forties, most reviewers rejected Lubitsch's post-1932 films as cynical, formulaic, and overly refined. Rather ironically, these were often the same characteristics—the worldliness, the irony, the sophistication—that had made his comedies look innovative and provocative in the twenties. Preference for

[9] Sarris, intro. to Paul, *Ernst Lubitsch's American Comedy*, x.

[10] Raymond Durgnat, *The Crazy Mirror: Hollywood Comedy and the American Image* (New York: Horizon Press, 1970), 119.

the early (American) Lubitsch still predominates in historical surveys, works on film genres, and studies explicitly concerned with film and society. For instance, Gerald Mast, in a book on film comedy, writes: "The rise of the comedy of Capra coincided with the decline of the comedy of Lubitsch. And this simultaneity was no accident. With the depression at their backs and World War II staring them in the face, Americans demanded entertainment that would help them affirm their own beliefs, ideals, and mission."[11] Measured against such demands, Lubitsch's thirties comedies indeed seem like escapist entertainment. But that could be said about most film comedies of the period.

With the rise of author criticism, the films of the late thirties and early forties have become the focus of critical attention. Seen as the work of a mature directorial personality, these films are valued more for their philosophical implications than their formal qualities. Accordingly, the earlier films are dismissed as yet-unrefined, preliminary sketches. Some American scholars have pursued this line of argument, usually in the context of one-director studies (Poague). While they have drawn attention to the previously ignored films of the forties, which show Lubitsch as a romantic and a humanist, they have also confirmed the classical Hollywood cinema (i.e., the cinema of the thirties and forties) as the ultimate standard against which all other films are measured, including his earlier ones. This approach is based on, and contributes to, a monolithic view of film history according to which differences represent signs of imperfection and deviance.

There are obvious reasons for the conflation of oeuvre and film history. Extending over thirty-five years, Lubitsch's body of work intersects with great changes in the technology and aesthetics of cinema. Not surprisingly, the distinction between silent and sound films, and pre-1932 and post-1932 films, can be found in most comprehensive accounts of his career. When it comes to evaluating the films' artistic quality or social relevance, however, critics often structure their arguments around the notion of cultural difference, thus foregrounding Lubitsch's work in two different national cinemas. In so doing, they not only separate rather artificially the foreign from the familiar and the affirmative from the subversive, but also confuse the significance of a particular film with its participation in these scenarios of

---

[11] Gerald Mast, *The Comic Mind: Comedy and the Movies* (Indianapolis: Bobbs-Merrill, 1973), 259. See also Andrew Bergman, *We're in the Money: Depression America and Its Films* (New York: New York University Press, 1971), esp. 57–69. As for Lubitsch's work in the forties, the assessments are even less favorable; note Whittemore's scathing remark about *To Be or Not to Be*: "For Lubitsch there is a laugh in everything. Laughter is salutary, but it is difficult to laugh at suffering on a world scale." In Don Whittemore, "Ernst Lubitsch," *Passport to Hollywood. Film Immigrants: Anthology*, ed. Don Whittemore and Philip Alan Cecchettini (New York: McGraw-Hill, 1976), 157.

difference. The same problem occurs when Lubitsch is alternatively characterized as the eternal German, the well-adjusted immigrant, the subversive immoralist, and the mercenary conformist. To be sure, categories like nationalism/internationalism and conformism/marginality are crucial for understanding Lubitsch's marginal position as a Jew in Germany and an immigrant in the United States. At times, however, critics use these categories to conceal an underlying feeling of betrayal or resentment. Lubitsch, they claim, was someone who tried to obscure his otherness through an outspoken commercialism and, closely related to that, an overly strong investment in filmic style. Accusations like these have accompanied the critical reception of his films since he emerged as a major German director in the late teens. Even after Lubitsch had already left Germany, the left-liberal members of the Weimar intelligentsia continued to claim him for the project of an emancipatory, if not revolutionary cinema. This is evidenced by Herbert Ihering's bitter reaction to *The Patriot*: "It is about time that Jannings and Lubitsch get out of Hollywood and make contact with the real world"[12] or by Rudolf Arnheim's speculations after a screening of *Broken Lullaby*: "Lubitsch is a terrible example for the waste of art in our times. . . . Just imagine what kind of films he would create for us if he smoked his cigars in Moscow, and not in Hollywood."[13]

Making similar claims about Lubitsch's adaptability, the British critic John Russell Taylor praises him as "the model of the émigré who assimilated completely into the Hollywood community";[14] someone, in other words, whose healthy commercialism prevailed over the artistic aspirations of less adaptable directors imported from Europe. John Baxter, however, expresses a very different opinion in his account of Hollywood in the thirties: "Ernst Lubitsch, in retrospect, seems like a director who never adequately adjusted to the necessities of the American cinema. His style and approach were those of Germany, and without the sophistication of European audiences he found himself forced increasingly to talk down to his public."[15] Consequently, Baxter excludes Lubitsch from his list of great di-

[12] Herbert Ihering, *The Patriot* (1929), reprinted in *Lubitsch*, ed. Hans Helmut Prinzler and Enno Patalas (Munich: J. Bucher, 1984), 158. All translations are mine unless noted otherwise.

[13] Rudolf Arnheim, "Rapprochement in Oel" (1932), in *Kritiken und Aufsätze zum Film*, ed. Hans Helmut Diederichs (Munich: Hanser, 1977), 263.

[14] John Russell Taylor, *Strangers in Paradise. The Hollywood Emigrés 1933–1950* (New York: Holt, Rinehart and Winston, 1983), 21.

[15] John Baxter, *Hollywood in the Thirties* (New York: A. S. Barnes, 1968), 42. Also see his chapter on Lubitsch in *The Hollywood Exiles* (New York: A. S. Barnes, 1968), 27–57. In a different context, John Belton has utilized the European/American distinction for a comparison between Lubitsch's cynicism and the all-American warmth of Frank Borzage, the "other" director of *Desire*: "Where Lubitsch's winking visual puns and conceits reveal a view of the world that is deeply cynical in outlook, Borzage's innocent, unblinking eye and visual sim-

rectors which includes such "mediocre" talents as Lewis Milestone and Victor Fleming. Even Andrew Sarris resorts to this nationalist and, ultimately, conformist rhetoric by incorporating the entire range of positions in a short essay on Lubitsch. He begins by emphasizing the similarities between the German and American films but then continues: "Unlike Lang and Murnau, therefore, Lubitsch is much more an American director than a German director, and must be evaluated accordingly. . . ." Having proven Lubitsch's adaptability to mainstream culture, he then introduces the notion of cultural exchange—"Lubitsch was the last of the genuine Continentals let loose on the American continent"—only to conclude, very surprisingly, with the image of the eternal outsider: "It was as if Lubitsch had never come to these shores with his expansive smile, his cigar and his gourmet tastes."[16]

More recently, a number of critics have tried to move beyond such evaluative categories and interpret cultural difference as an operating principle within the films rather than a dividing line between them. Linking the internationalism of the silent cinema to the absence of strong national traits in Lubitsch's work, Leo Braudy argues: "To a sympathetic eye, therefore, Lubitsch's easy transition from Germany to Hollywood casts him as the archetypal director of the silent period, whose art, because it is not tied to a specific national language, is therefore beyond nation, national cultures, and national politics entirely—a truly international artist."[17] Braudy draws attention to the discursive function of difference in film as well as criticism. Even the occasional romanticizing of silent cinema does not diminish his contribution. For Braudy identifies a way of leaving behind the polemics about Lubitsch's national identity and focusing on the historical conditions that influenced his formation as a filmmaker. As will be argued in this study, the silent cinema indeed remained the determining influence throughout his career and was largely responsible for his playful exploration, rather than fearful affirmation, of cultural difference.

Attending to the problem of difference from the side of style, Braudy also introduces the notion of an expatriate consciousness. It is precisely the lack of strong national ties that, in his view, accounts for the importance of style as a marketable commodity and a method of self-reflection: "The question of Lubitsch's style is crucial to thinking about the role of an expatriate consciousness in film-making because style is precisely the most

---

plicity make him seem naive by contrast." In *The Hollywood Professionals: Howard Hawks, Frank Borzage, Edgar G. Ulmer* (London: Tantivy, 1974), 76.

[16] Sarris, "Ernst Lubitsch: American Period," 643, 644, and 649. Dwight MacDonald (see n.1), on the other hand, claims that Lubitsch, even after nine years in Hollywood, was "still more Teutonic than American . . ." (82).

[17] Leo Braudy, "The Double Detachment of Ernst Lubitsch," *Modern Language Notes* 98, no. 5 (December 1983): 1072.

marketable and most portable evidence of talent or genius anyone in films has."[18] Consequently, Braudy sees Lubitsch's ironic detachment as a strategy of cultural adjustment. Irony ignores national boundaries and creates a truly international atmosphere. More specifically, it must be seen as a discursive strategy that "embraces the audience as a co-conspirator of interpretation, and accomplice to the director's and the camera's knowingness."[19] Braudy's definition of the American comedies applies equally to the German period. After all, Lubitsch's position as the outsider, including that of the Jew, inspired, across the decades and across the continents, a unique perception of the self in relation to external reality that remains the distinctive mark of his authorship.

The convictions and tenets of author-oriented criticism not only inform the more cursory references to Lubitsch. They also characterize the first monographs on the director. It was Herman G. Weinberg, a personal friend, film critic, and filmmaker himself, who initiated Lubitsch scholarship in the United States. His *The Lubitsch Touch* (1968) gives a more or less chronological account of Lubitsch's entire career and, at least at the time, provided a rich though not always reliable source of information. Mixing biography and filmography, the study relies to a large degree on anecdotes and amusing gossip from the set and the front office; yet it also offers lengthy appraisals of a few selected films (on others, note the dismissive "Let us pass over *Desire, Angel,* and *Bluebeard's Eighth Wife* . . ."[20]). Not surprisingly, in spite of Weinberg's obvious sympathies for Lubitsch the person, *The Lubitsch Touch* contributed to the continuing neglect of Lubitsch's films.

The situation changed dramatically when, beginning in the early sixties, a number of French critics associated with the film journal *Cahiers du cinéma* "discovered" the classical Hollywood cinema and its leading directors (Ford, Huston, Hawks, Welles). Their films became the subject of numerous critical articles and enthusiastic reviews. The *Cahiers* critics introduced the notion of *auteur* as a kind of organizing principle for identifying the creative forces in the cinema; with few exceptions, these were thought to converge in the figure of the director. Meant as a polemical intervention rather than a fully developed theory, *Cahiers*'s "politique des auteurs" produced a special Lubitsch issue (No.198/1968)[21] as well as several mono-

---

[18] Ibid., 1075.

[19] Ibid., 1078.

[20] Weinberg, *The Lubitsch Touch,* 155. The appendix comprises interviews with two of Lubitsch's main screenwriters, Walter Reisch and Samson Raphaelson, tributes by several collaborators, brief evaluations by contemporary critics, excerpts from the screenplay of *Ninotchka*, and a number of texts written by Lubitsch himself, some of which are translated from the German.

[21] Even *Cahiers du cinéma*'s special Lubitsch issue (no. 198, February 1968), despite its ide-

graphs that discussed Lubitsch's major films in the context of recurring themes, stories, and stylistic characteristics.[22] What has since then become known as *auteurism* was largely responsible for introducing key concepts from literary criticism into the study of popular films and filmmakers. Rejecting the sharp distinction between high and low culture, the *Cahiers* critics elevated the representatives of the entertainment industry to artists in their own right. Their passion for the cinema, even their polemical declarations and idiosyncratic tastes, may have been occasionally marred by exaggerated views on film authorship. But their writings also paved the way for other approaches to Hollywood cinema, including the structuralist and ideology-critical approaches that were developed by Jean-Louis Comolli, Jean Narboni, and others in a direct response to *auterism*. To this day, French scholarship on Lubitsch is characterized by a style of writing that combines witticisms and striking formulations with profound observation and insight. Considerable attention is given to Lubitsch's play with, and implication in, the mechanisms of commodity culture. Critics like Jean-Loup Bourget, Jean Domarchi, and Bernard Eisenschitz have not only examined in great detail the intricate relationship between narrative structure and visual representation, but have also drawn attention to the explosive mixture of elegance and rationality that distinguishes many Lubitsch films —a very French combination after all.

After the introduction of auteurist criticism to the United States, and with its subsequent elevation to "author theory" in the writings of Andrew Sarris, Lubitsch eventually acquired the status of a "classic." The numerous retrospectives organized in Europe and the United States over the past

---

ology-critical approach, confirmed the old prejudice that Lubitsch was a superficial director interested only in creating an imaginary fairy-tale world, populated by operetta characters and artificial to the core. In "Lubitsch était un prince," Truffaut compares the films to childhood fantasies, and Jean Domarchi, in "Homme de partout," draws attention to Lubitsch's calculated commercialism without acknowledging its ironic subtext. Commenting on the *Cahiers* issue, and the politically charged atmosphere of the late sixties in which it was published, E. Ann Kaplan has suggested that Lubitsch's preference for "light" genres (as opposed to the more serious Westerns by Ford or the action-packed gangster films by Lang) as well as his fascination with the paraphernalia of class society (aristocracy, conspicuous wealth) may have prevented more thorough studies on the director. See "Lubitsch Reconsidered," *Quarterly Review of Film Studies* 6.3 (Summer 1981): 305–12.

[22] See, for instance, Mario Verdone, *Lubitsch* (Lyon: Serdoc, 1964); Bernard Eisenschitz, "Lubitsch (1892–1947)," in *Anthologie du cinéma* (Paris: l'Avant-scène du cinéma, 1968); Guido Fink, *Ernst Lubitsch* (Florence: la nuova Italia, 1977); Jacqueline Nacache, *Lubitsch* (Paris: Edilic, 1987); Bernard Eisenschitz and Jean Narboni, *Ernst Lubitsch* (Paris: Cinémateque Française, 1985). The most recent contribution to Lubitsch scholarship is Jean-Loup Bourget and Eithne Bourget, *Lubitsch ou la satire romanesque* (Paris: Stock, 1987). While there is certainly more to be learned from the French writings on Lubitsch, this study focuses on his American and German reception, thus in a way mirroring the moves made by Lubitsch himself.

twenty years,[23] the inclusion of his name in film histories, anthologies, and encyclopedias,[24] and, last but not least, his becoming a dissertation topic bear witness to this process.[25] Here author criticism has helped to eliminate the cruder aspects of biographism in works on film directors, and it has shifted the critical focus to the films themselves, and to mise-en-scène in particular. But the almost exclusive attention to questions of style has come at the expense of those approaches that place less emphasis on "quality" or "creativity": genre criticism, historical criticism, and political criticism. The controversy over Lubitsch's later and, presumably, more mature films reveals the implications of this work-oriented film criticism. Claiming these films for a humanist cinema, critics have praised their emotional warmth and social relevance. Yet, in the process, the use of style as a form of distanciation has been neglected or completely ignored. Characteristic of this approach is Leland Poague's *The Cinema of Ernst Lubitsch: The Hollywood Films* (1977). The book opens with the statement: "The more one studies Lubitsch the clearer it becomes that form really does follow function, and

[23] Examples include the 1965 retrospective of early Lubitsch films organized by the Venice Film Festival, a small 1967 retrospective (which traveled to Paris in 1967 and to New York in 1968), the 1968 retrospective at the Museum of Modern Art in New York (the Weinberg book was published in conjunction with that event), the 1983 Conference on "Space Frame Narrative. Silent Cinema 1916–26" organized at the University of East Anglia in Norwich, the 1983 "Festival du cinéma Juif" organized by the Cinémateque Française in Paris, and the large 1984 Lubitsch retrospective at the International Berlin Film Festival, not to mention numerous small retrospectives in major European and American cities.

[24] Aside from the monographs mentioned in this chapter, references to Lubitsch can also be found in *The National Society of Film Critics on Movie Comedy*, ed. Stuart Byron and Elisabeth Weis (New York: Grossman/Viking, 1977) 70–75; Charles Higham, *Warner Brothers* (New York: Charles Scribner's Sons, 1975) 18–28; Stuart Kaminsky, *American Film Genres: Approaches to a Critical Theory of Popular Film* (Dayton, Ohio: Pflann, 1974); Richard Koszarski, *Hollywood Directors 1914–40* (New York: Oxford University Press, 1976); and David Robinson, *Hollywood in the Twenties* (London: Methuen, 1973).

[25] Jan-Christopher Horak's "Ernst Lubitsch and the Rise of Ufa, 1917–1922" (M.S. thesis, Boston University, 1975) contains a comprehensive and well-informed survey of the German films, with a strong emphasis on Ufa studio politics. Robert William Mills's "The American Films of Ernst Lubitsch—A Critical History" (Ph.D. diss., University of Michigan, 1976), on the other hand, sets out to "designate Lubitsch's stature as a figure of great and somewhat neglected importance in the history of the American cinema . . ." (8). In fact, his study contains little more than a sketchy survey of Lubitsch's American career and conceals the lack of a critical perspective through lengthy quotations from secondary sources. Two years later, Robert Carringer and Barry Sabath published a complete filmography/bibliography, *Ernst Lubitsch: A Guide to References and Resources* (Boston: G. K. Hall, n.d.), in the well-known G. K. Hall series. Apart from a biographical sketch and a brief summary of Lubitsch's career, the work contains detailed plot synopses of all films (including unverified stage and film credits), an extensive bibliography, and a complete list of the holdings (film prints, screenplays, stills, newspaper clippings) of most international film archives. For an earlier filmography, see also Theodore Huff, "An Index to the Films of Ernst Lubitsch," *Sight and Sound Index Series* 9 (January 1947).

the function of Lubitsch's later films became increasingly the expression of an other-centred, if not self-effacing, humanism."[26] Influenced by auteurism ("auteurism as a working hypothesis") and New Criticism, the thirteen readings emphasize story and character development, recurring themes and motifs and relate them to what is perceived as Lubitsch's humanist message. To be sure, Poague's earnestness provided a much-needed counterweight to Weinberg's ineffectual anecdotes but, with his belief in fixed meanings, also seemed strangely disconnected from the developments in film theory at that time. By contrast, William Paul's *Ernst Lubitsch's American Comedy* (1983) offers a more systematic approach that is based on the author's close attention to questions of filmic representation. Despite an obvious preference for "the emotional riches of his later films, films that represent his greatest achievement,"[27] Paul avoids the common practice in studies on "light" genres of either denigrating or defending the subject under investigation. His introductory comment, "Lubitsch's art is profoundly meaningful precisely because it is profoundly comic,"[28] rejects all attempts at searching for a "deeper meaning" that would limit insights from the outset. In this spirit, Paul examines the changing function of irony and metaphor, the struggle between narrative and counter-narrative strategies, and the gradual disappearance of a strong authorial voice in the Lubitsch comedies of the thirties and forties. *Lubitsch* (1984), a German anthology edited by Hans Helmut Prinzler and Enno Patalas, does not

---

[26] Leland A. Poague, *The Cinema of Ernst Lubitsch: The Hollywood Films* (South Brunswick, N.Y.: A.S. Barnes, 1978), 148. Under headings like "Time and the Man" or "Frivolity and Responsibility," Poague interprets the films against and through one another (e.g., *The Marriage Circle* and *The Shop around the Corner*) and uses this deliberately ahistorical method in order to unmask Lubitsch as a humanist at heart. Despite his limitation to Lubitsch's American films, and despite an obvious lack of interest in their formal qualities, Poague claims in the introduction: "Thus, despite the limitations of this study, I believe that I understand Lubitsch more thoroughly than he has been understood before" (7). Conceived as a "close analysis rather than casual value judgments," and a "workable compromise between criticism and meta-criticism," Poague's study reveals its shortcomings all too easily once it is exposed to close scrutiny. The author frequently invites the reader to join him in speculating along and beyond the margins of the films as if they were case studies from the practice of a real-life marriage counselor. Note Poague's diagnosis of the Stock marriage in *The Marriage Circle*: "We assume, I believe, that their marriage started on the right foot, as a genuine expression of trust, affection, and shared goals, which somewhere along the line went sour and degenerated to the point of game-playing" (24) or his comments on Sonia and Danilo in *The Merry Widow*: "In other words, we see how easily even bright people can fall into emotional and perceptual traps, with only the slightest help from circumstance" (61).

[27] Paul, *Ernst Lubitsch's American Comedy*, 8. Discussing nine sound films, including *The Shop around the Corner*, *To Be or Not to Be*, *Heaven Can Wait*, and *Cluny Brown*, Paul reevaluates the work of Lubitsch in the context of thirties film comedy and relevant sociopolitical developments; hence chapter headings like "The Anarchic Touch," "The Return to Order," "Love and Politics," and "The Transcendental Vision."

[28] Ibid., 7.

offer a more theoretical perspective either. Rather, by participating in the exchanges between films and audiences, and by "explaining a few rules of the game without assuming the role of a judge,"[29] the contributing authors try to accommodate the films and their fleeting qualities through a collage of images and texts, as it were. With its comprehensive introduction by Prinzler, a provocative essay on style by Frieda Grafe, and a collection of highly opinionated film reviews, the anthology simulates, on the level of critical discourse, what its authors repeatedly describe as a unique characteristic of all Lubitsch films: the refusal of closure and the engagement of the reader/spectator in a productive, ongoing dialogue. In this group, Frieda Grafe and Enno Patalas deserve special mention, because they belong among the few German film critics who since the seventies have offered consistently interesting work on Lubitsch.

While most critics agree on Lubitsch's status as a major, even if somewhat neglected or unfashionable, Hollywood director, the assessment of his status has been the reason for many heated arguments. In the process, Lubitsch's unmistakable filmic style—that is, precisely those authorial interventions that distinguish the film *auteur* from the *metteur-en-scène* (to invoke another auteurist concept)—has become more of a liability than a mark of distinction. This situation has proven especially devastating for a body of work that has always achieved its best effects through that which resists immediate accessibility: irony, travesty, and self-reflectivity. With the notable exceptions mentioned above, the present state of Lubitsch criticism has done little to shed more light on the tensions between norm and difference, and between co-optation and subversion that characterize most of the films. As a result, their equally ambiguous participation in the pleasures of seeing and knowing, desiring and experiencing, remains closed to critical inquiry as well. This study wants to change such attitudes and perceptions.

All monographs on Lubitsch have been informed by auteurism and its basic tenets. Seen from the perspective of recent developments in poststructuralist theory, especially with its proclamations on "the death of the author" (Foucault), the differences, say, between Poague's literary framework and the visual analyses of Paul seemed less important. Their (explic-

---

[29] The book was published in conjunction with the major Lubitsch retrospective at the 1984 Berlin Film Festival. Profusely illustrated, *Lubitsch* opens with three pieces: a socio-biographical survey by Prinzler, the transcript of a television program on Lubitsch by Patalas, and a brilliant analysis of Lubitsch's commodity fetishism by Frieda Grafe. These are followed by a number of primary texts from the twenties (reviews by Ihering, Kerr, Pinthus), recollections by several Lubitsch collaborators, and brief film reviews of all his films by a very diverse group of contributors, including feminist critics (Uta Berg-Ganschow, Claudia Lenssen), film directors (Helma Sanders-Brahms, Rosa von Praunheim, Robert Van Ackeren), and actors (Hans Zischler). For a critical reveiw, see Jochen Brunow, "Ein Steinbruch," *epd Film* 5 (1984): 3.

itly or implicitly) stated belief in traditional notions such as originality, quality, and continuity places them firmly within the American reception of auteurism and explains their lack of interest in structuralist and post-structuralist ideas. However, it is precisely this insistence on the author as a figure of integration and integrity that has allowed them to neglect two important characteristics of the Lubitsch film: the emphasis on sexual difference and the active participation of the spectator. Surprisingly, while questions of gender and spectatorship are of central significance for those critical methods that have challenged auteurism, they have had virtually no impact on Lubitsch criticism. Since the early eighties, the name of Lubitsch has more or less disappeared from scholarly debates; the few articles and conference papers on the influence of industrial practices on Lubitsch's work in the thirties only confirm this impression.[30] More general trends in film studies have undoubtedly contributed to the critical neglect of Lubitsch. These include a distinct lack of interest in directed-oriented studies; the continuing disregard for "light" genres like comedy or musical; a noticeable shift in historical research to early silent cinema and the forties; and a greater concern for the contextual and intertextual relationships of cinema. However, that does not explain the particular fate of Lubitsch criticism. There can only be speculation about why Lubitsch has remained of such little interest to structuralist, poststructuralist, psychoanalytic, and feminist film critics. While the films of Hitchcock have been studied in great detail from almost all new theoretical perspectives (Rothman, Nichols, Bellour, Modleski), thus initiating a kind of meta-discourse on film criticism, the work of Lubitsch seems to offer few theoretical challenges. While the work of Ford or Hawks has lent itself as easily to traditional auteurist approaches as to its structuralist variations (Wollen), Lubitsch was perhaps too little of an auteur in the heroic sense to inspire comparable revisions. While Lang's films have provided a testing ground for the most advanced poststructuralist concepts (Humphries), Lubitsch's preoccupation with "frivolous" themes either prompted a rejection of his films on ideological grounds or encouraged scholarship in the spirit of affirmation. And while the films of von Sternberg proved very useful in testing psychoanalytically informed theories of spectatorship (Studlar), Lubitsch's American comedies have often been regarded as too superficial for similar excursions into the unconscious. The problem of sexual difference has been largely ignored by Lubitsch scholarship or, at best, been discussed in the context of humanistic notions of reconciliation and tolerance. In the first works on the representation of women in the Hollywood film, critics have

---

[30] I am referring here to William O. Huie, Jr., "Style and Technology in *Trouble in Paradise*: Evidence of a Technicians' Lobby?," *Journal of Film and Video* 39, no. 2 (Spring 1987): 37–51 and to several papers presented at the 11th Ohio University Film Conference, October 1989, and the 1990 Society for Cinema Studies Conference in Washington, D.C.

focused exclusively on the problem of sociosexual stereotypes. Arguing in
that vein, Marjorie Rosen has questioned the degree of emancipation attributed to the uninhibited heroines of Lubitsch's sophisticated comedies.
While he often portrayed "superficially radical, sexually demanding fe-
males," Rosen argues, "Lubitsch nevertheless encumbered them with dolt-
ish or unattractive characteristics. At once they became less threatening,
relinquishing any real challenge to the sociosexual status quo."[31] Conversely, Molly Haskell has praised Lubitsch for the complexity of his
women figures. For Haskell, they possess both sense and sensuality, the
quintessential qualities of the American girl and the European woman.[32]
However, more recent developments in feminist film criticism of the eighties have bypassed Lubitsch. In light of the many theoretical studies on the
problem of representation and sexual difference, this lack of interest seems
inexplicable. Even E. Ann Kaplan repeats the earlier accusations of misogyny, arguing that "Lubitsch's approach to sexuality was such as to make
him of little interest to feminists."[33] She does not take into account that
eroticism in the cinema, and particularly in the cinema of Lubitsch, may
not be exclusively determined by character development or plot construction, but also by more complex structures of identification and pleasure.
One needs only to point to the great emphasis on spectatorship that Lubitsch's films share with psychoanalytic approaches to female desire in the
cinema.

Clearly, then, the present state of Lubitsch scholarship is unacceptable.
The current prejudices against Lubitsch not only prevent the adequate assessment of his silent and early sound films but also virtually cast a veil of
mystery over his German films. Critics may acknowledge them as important precursors, but they do so with terms like "crude" and "yet unrefined,"
thereby using the Hollywood film of the thirties and forties as the ultimate
standard of evaluation. As long as the "early Lubitsch" remains this unknown entity referred to with the apologies that only legitimate such neglect, "the whole Lubitsch" remains inaccessible as well. Only a return to
the early German films—and, implicitly, only the recognition of their prevailing influence—provides the critical framework that is necessary for an
intervention in improving the present state of Lubitsch scholarship.

The following study offers both a general introduction to Lubitsch's
early work and a number of close textual readings. Its main purpose is to
fill the gaps left by previous studies, to complement their findings, and to
compensate for the glaring discrepancy between the films' complex visual

[31] Marjorie Rosen, *Popcorn Venus: Women, Movies and the American Dream* (New York:
Coward, McCann & Goeghegan, 1973), 130–31.

[32] See Molly Haskell, *From Reverence to Rape: The Treatment of Women in the Movies*, 2d. ed.
(Chicago: University of Chicago Press, 1987), 86–87 and 96–102.

[33] Kaplan, "Lubitsch Reconsidered," 306.

strategies and the almost exclusive emphasis on narrative analysis in the critical literature on the subject. While most American scholars have focused on Lubitsch's later films, the present study concentrates on his silent and early sound films. This different emphasis is to a large degree motivated by the desire for a more complete account of Lubitsch's work. But beyond that, it is based on the assertion that the silent German cinema must be seen as the dominating influence—an influence that manifests itself in the preference for specific genres, themes, characters, and, above all, in the close attention paid to style.

As is to be expected, this study is based on and structured around the notion of authorship. The early Lubitsch films, it argues, are characterized by recurring visual and narrative strategies. Accordingly, the following chapters will attempt to identify and interpret these strategies as the filmic representation of a problematic, a configuration, a manifestation. On the one hand, this set of core themes and ideas—the authorial vision in the traditional sense—is to be understood as the unique expression of one creative individual, the film director. On the other, this particular configuration also reflects, through the means of cinema, the encounter between a socioculturally determined biography and the new medium of film at a particular historical juncture. My emphasis is not so much on what is being represented—the hidden message, the ultimate truth—but on under what conditions the formation of a style takes place and what effects it produces. To find answers to these questions, the present study combines traditional methods of auteurist criticism, including biographical evidence, with more overarching concerns, especially those relating to the problem of sexual and cultural difference. Moreover, there will be some consideration of the technological and cultural changes that accompanied the emergence of the classical narrative cinema to which Lubitsch contributed so significantly. Each film will be discussed as part of a negotiation involving different modes of representation, narration, and spectatorship; a process that intersects with the conditions of production in two different national cinemas and technologies of film; finally, a process that is associated with a certain name: Lubitsch—here to be understood both as an author or oeuvre in the traditional sense and as a problematic activated in and by the films.

Passions and Deceptions consists of two parts: an introductory survey of Lubitsch's work in the silent and early sound cinema (1914–32) and five close readings of films from that period. While the choice of a particular historical framework or specific films is always difficult—and hardly ever divorced from personal preferences—several factors contributed to the study's conception and scope. Previous works on Lubitsch have focused on the later American films and their distinctly humanist perspective. What is needed at this point is a study that, by focusing on the earlier German and American films, complements the findings of other scholars and, at the same time, opens up new critical perspectives. For similar reasons, the strong emphasis on the German period, especially in the introductory survey, was necessary to draw attention to its determining influence on Lubitsch's development as a filmmaker. The five close readings, finally, were conceived in such a way that they foreground the characteristics that link, rather than separate, the German from the American films, and the silent from the sound films. Other alternatives—to limit the study to the German films or the silent films, respectively—would have made it possible to concentrate on other, perhaps equally important, films from the silent period. However, that would have contained the films within specific film historical categories (e.g., national cinemas, silent/sound film) and thus obfuscated their transgressive, international qualities. Under these conditions, the study's cutoff points are a compromise between theoretical and practical considerations. A close reading of Lubitsch's one-reelers would have required a more thorough discussion of early cinema, and its different relationship between narrative and spectacle in particular. Conversely, the inclusion of his later films would have called for more explicitly historical or sociological approaches, including a critical assessment of the changes in American society and a reevaluation of the relationship between comedy and politics. Both possibilities were beyond the scope of this study. By beginning the close readings with *The Oyster Princess*, this study acknowledges the connection between the rise of the feature-length film and the notion of authorship in the cinema. By ending with *Trouble in Paradise*—*Design for Living* or *Angel* could have been chosen instead—the close readings draw attention to the changing role of film in society. Accordingly, in the mid-thirties, Lubitsch's daring pronouncements on the human condition, his preoccupation with style, and his pervasive sense of irony disappeared and gave way to a more direct involvement with his stories and characters. In a sense, romance and commitment took the place of eroticism and critical reserve; *Ninotchka* symbolizes these changes. However, no value judgments should be derived from these transformations. The present study only limits itself to the early films in order to do justice to their actual contribution to the history of film, to provide a new critical framework for Lubitsch's later films, and to explore the dynamics of continuity and change that make all his films part of an ongoing process.

With these aims, the introductory part documents Lubitsch's work in the four major phases: the early German silent film (1914–18), German silent film (1918–23), American silent film (1923–29), and early American sound film (1929–32). It discusses the films in relation to studio politics, audience reception, and generic conventions. Special attention will be given to Lubitsch's collaboration with actors, scenarists, and set designers. Examples from a number of films will be used to illustrate the ways in which new visual and narrative strategies are introduced into the framework of respective genres, thereby changing their meaning in turn. More-over, the introductory survey also examines how the films negotiate the forces of convention and subversion: through the representation of differ-ence along the lines of gender, class, and nationality; through changing subject-object relationships; through the triangulation of desire between looking, dancing, and consumption; and, most of all, through the identi-fication of a position of ironic detachment.

In light of the discussions on notions like authorship and biography, it may seem unproductive to begin this study with references to an individual biography. For the same reasons, it may seem unnecessary to trace Lu-bitsch's career chronologically through almost three decades and describe the intersections between an emerging directorial style and the history of cinema. Such attempts are informed by the desire for a coherent narrative and invariably lead to specific problems, including the insistence on conti-nuity rather than change, and the emphasis on similarity rather than differ-ence. Nonetheless, the introductory chapter has its values insofar as it tries to place the qualities associated with a particular body of work within a larger historical context. The influences are manifold: the filmmaker's pref-erence for certain stories and characters; the impact of artistic innovations and cultural traditions; the contribution of screenwriters, cinematogra-phers, set designers, and actors. Other determining factors include studio politics, new technological developments, and, last but not least, the dra-matic changes in the social and cultural significance of the cinema and the concept of film authorship itself. As part of such configurations, chronol-ogy helps to reconstruct the links between recurring themes and the social contexts—be they related to class, race, or gender—that engender them, as actual experiences or as secret desires. Similarly, the scattered comments on spectatorship make it possible to reestablish the different "horizons of expectation" against which Lubitsch's films must be measured, if their meaning is not to be reduced to stylistic characteristics. With this in mind, the purpose of the introductory survey is to find a compromise between the often contradictory perspectives of film history and studies on author-ship.

The second part consists of five close readings that focus on one partic-ular film or a group of films. This combination of textual and contextual analysis makes it possible to provide detailed analyses while at the same time taking into account the larger framework in which Lubitsch's early films have to be situated. The films were chosen for their representative character, primarily in regard to genre, as well as for their usefulness in opening up new perspectives and identifying recurrent themes and motifs. Questions of "quality" were, though not irrelevant, secondary. *The Mar-riage Circle*, for instance, may ultimately be a "better" film than *So This Is Paris*, and *The Smiling Lieutenant* may offer more insights than *Monte*

Carlo, but this lack of concern for originality also allows for a greater emphasis on typicality. Within this framework, the five close readings approach each film from a slightly different perspective, depending on its unique qualities. The approaches include feminist and psychoanalytic film criticism as well as reception-oriented theories. Considerations of genre play only a minor part; the same is true for references to the film industry. This diversity originates in an unwillingness to impose on the films a one-dimensional, unified perspective that ultimately obliterates their differences as well as their similarities. Nonetheless, the five chapters do share important concepts and concerns. Above all, they draw attention to the strong emphasis on difference—of gender, class, and nationality—that not only governs plot construction and character development in the films but also determines the function of mise-en-scène, camera movement, and editing. They show how Lubitsch's presence as an author is perceivable through what is present as well as absent, that is, through what is accessible to representation and what requires more devious strategies of interpretation. But by approaching this central concern from a variety of critical perspectives, the chapters offer different points of view on the same problematic.

The first chapter takes three early German comedies, *The Oyster Princess* (1919), *The Doll* (1919), and *The Mountain Cat* (1921), and examines their playful investigation of the problem of femininity in the context of specific counter-narrative strategies. To this end, the notions of spectacle and the fantastic are introduced as conceptual guides through the jungle of sexual difference, pointing perhaps to other forms of pleasure in the cinema. The second chapter approaches *Passion* (1919) and *Deception* (1920) from two sides: the side of historical reception and the formal characteristics of set design and mass choreography. As will be argued, Lubitsch's period films function as a site for multiple inscriptions and acquire full meaning only in the conflation of film politics, German nationalism, and eroticism. In the third chapter, the close reading of *So This Is Paris* (1926) shows how desire emerges as the central problem of eroticism and, in a more fundamental sense, of hermeneutics as well. Since this question is tied to the presence of various spectators inside and outside of the film, all of which bring to bear their own perspectives on the filmic text, a number of concepts from reception theory will be used to distinguish between the forces of conformism and misogyny, on the one hand, and those of parody, on the other. Continuing with early sound film, the fourth chapter takes the musical *Monte Carlo* (1930) to examine how Lubitsch deals with the transition to sound, especially as regards the problematic association of music, woman, and narrative. The songs will be discussed for their important contribution to story development and characterization, followed by a few general remarks on the connections between music/sound and the feminine in Lubitsch's silent and early sound films. The fifth chapter on *Trouble in Paradise* (1932), finally, not only marks the end of the present study but will also deal exclusively with a film that may be characterized as both blatantly commercial and forcefully subversive. Using the motif of theft as a central metaphor of filmic representation, the film is described as a game with free-floating signifiers where "trouble in paradise" also means the crisis of commodity fetishism and of the sign as such.

The introductory survey and the five close readings explore certain narrative and visual strategies, perhaps even obsessions, that are associated with a particular name, two different national cinemas, and two periods in the history of cinema. It is in recognition of the inevitable blind spots in every critical enterprise that *Passions and Deceptions* relies on very different critical perspectives and makes use of diverse theoretical concepts. While its argument is based on a feminist approach to the representation of sexual difference, psychoanalytic and reception-oriented categories, as well as recent studies of silent cinema, are utilized at critical points. Instead of providing a fixed theoretical framework, these concepts will be used like catalysts, or as crystallization points, in the re-production of the effects brought forth by the films' very own sounds and images. Consequently, the existing conflicts between feminist film theory, psychoanalytic approaches, and reader-response criticism in this study will have to be overlooked.

This diversity, however, is organized around one central issue: the role of women and the function of sexual difference. All readings refer back, in one way or another, to the position occupied by woman as the agent and the agency of all narrative and visual strategies. Consequently, *Passions and Deceptions* not only sets out to challenge existing opinions about the early Lubitsch films but also attempts to change the prevalent view of Lubitsch as a director of little relevance to feminist film critics. To phrase it differently, the study strives at once to reclaim his films for the feminist project and expose them to a more theoretical approach. Lubitsch's filmic reflections on sexual difference can contribute to a better understanding of early cinema and its contribution to the formation of classical narrative cinema, especially as regards the complicated relationship of woman, narrative, and spectacle. That is why any exclusive emphasis on characterization and narrative motifs obscures, rather than illustrates, the significance of woman as a discursive agent. It indirectly confirms those critical assumptions about authenticity and identity that constitute the dominant discourse about sexual difference in the first place. With these implications, *Passions and Deceptions* tries to move away from the debate on the representation of women and concentrates instead on the more elusive configurations of woman and representation. Searching in the stories for signs of other meanings is only a first step; it has to be followed by a close examination of the affinities between sexual difference and filmic representation. As will be argued, the association between woman and spectacle, as well as the close links between the camera, the object, and the look, are residues of an earlier "cinema of attractions." Its influence remains present in the oscillation between conformism and subversion and the overarching sense of ironic detachment that lies at the basis of the films examined. The woman, in the process, comes to function as the discursive agent who negotiates these disparate influences and, at the same time, protects the claims of diversity: as a threat and a challenge. Under her influence, the boundaries between characters and objects dissolve. The animation of the inanimate world finds an equivalent in the objectification of the human world. This reversal leads at once to a confirmation and erosion of the dominant order. Moreover, Lubitsch's obsession with objects masks a rather insidious critique of humanism, including its masculinist bias and anthropocentric perspective. His rejection of psychology paves the way for a kind of enlightened eroticism that brings together different "filmic protagonists," including sets and props, lighting, camera work, and editing, for the dream a "materialist" cinema. What at first sight may look like a cool, intellectual play with objects, then, really points to an all-encompassing eroticism. This is the utopian vision behind the multileveled investigations of sexual difference. At the beginning of the process stands woman: as the marker of sexual difference and as the center around which all other systems of difference develop.

For purposes of clarification, some very broad definitions might be helpful at this point. As a rule, the term *narrative* is used to mean both a story and the telling of a story. It refers to a course of action propelled forward by dramatic events and the interaction between characters; its coordinating principle is psychological motivation. The spectacle, by contrast, defies narrative; in the context of this study, the term *spectacle* includes the display of the spectacular and the effect of specularity. It foregrounds the visual aspects of film and, because of its greater investment in mise-en-scène, disrupts temporal continuity and dramatic tension; its main objective is visual pleasure. Authorial inventions, finally, include all the visual and narrative strategies that work against the immediate appeal of a film, thereby making the spectator's participation a necessary and integral part of the narration. The interaction between author and spectator makes possible, and is made possible, by the pervasive sense of ironic detachment that cuts across the genres, styles, and periods of film history; its most subversive effects include meta-discursiveness and self-reflectivity. In the collaboration of these forces—narrative, spectacle, authorship, and spectatorship—irony emerges as the primary force that unmasks the characters' noble gestures and actions; that produces a critical distance between story and spectator, and camera and mise-en-scène; and that inevitably draws attention to the making of film's stories and the means of cinema.[34]

While *Passions and Deceptions* is geared toward readers from various academic fields, above all film studies and women's studies, it also hopes to address a more general readership interested in Lubitsch. For that reason, the following chapters try to present the material as clearly as possible while at the same time accommodating the need for a more rigorous approach. The introductory survey provides a historical framework for the general reader as well as the specialist, while the five close readings allow the films to determine the course of a critical argument. Here the informed reader is invited to use the footnotes for additional information on certain theoretical issues. Such a procedure seems most appropriate at this point in Lubitsch criticism. It is presented with the hope that the early films of Ernst Lubitsch might spark new interest among film scholars and film audiences, giving them pleasure as well as insights.

[34] This discussion of irony is influenced by another conservative theoretician of irony, Thomas Mann, especially his "Ironie und Radikalismus." See also the definition of Romantic irony as "transcendental buffoonery" (Friedrich Schlegel).

Part I

THE EARLY LUBITSCH—
AN OVERVIEW

One

From Comic Actor to Film Director, 1914–1918

THE circumstances that prompted Lubitsch to pursue a career in film were more or less typical of the early silent cinema. Acting aspirations brought him to the theater, and the promise of money brought him to the screen. But it was a growing dissatisfaction with the lack of artistic control that stood behind his most important decision, the move from acting to directing. Lubitsch's brief stage career was connected with Max Reinhardt and his famous repertory theater at the Deutsche Theater in Berlin. He was introduced to Reinhardt in 1910 by a mentor, the comic actor Victor Arnold, and immediately admitted into the ensemble. In the following years, Lubitsch played extras and bit parts, among them the second grave digger in *Hamlet* and Wagner in *Faust*, and he specialized in old-men parts, despite his young age.[1] Like other Reinhardt actors, among them Emil Jannings, Paul Wegener, and Conrad Veidt, he developed an interest in screen acting when it was still considered a profession of ill repute. Because of his distinctive physiognomy, Lubitsch concentrated on comic parts, appearing in variety shows and, after 1913, in short slapstick comedies. He gave his most memorable stage performance as the hunchback in Friedrich Freska's oriental pantomime *Sumurun*, a role that he played in the monumental Reinhardt production and his own film adaptation of *Sumurun* (1920, *One Arabian Night*).[2] The years in Reinhardt's ensemble had an enormous impact on Lubitsch's formation as a filmmaker. In later years, he would fre-

[1] A note on the procedure of naming: each time I mention a German film for the first time, I list the German title first, followed by the title used in American distribution. If a film was not distributed in the United States, the English translation appears in quotation marks. After that, I refer to English titles only. For the most part, I follow *Ernst Lubitsch: A Guide to References and Resources*, ed. Robert Carringer and Barry Sabath (Boston: G. K. Hall, n.d.). In cases of conflicting filmographic references, I follow Gerhardt Lamprecht, *Deutsche Stummfilme*, 9 vols. (Berlin: Deutsche Kinemathek, 1967–70) and Hans Helmut Prinzler and Enno Patalas, eds., *Lubitsch* (Munich: C. J. Bucher, 1984). These German film historians are probably more familiar with the early Lubitsch than Carringer and Sabath.

[2] Richard Riess's novel *Sumurun*, published shortly after the film's release, underscores the biographical references in Lubitsch's portrayal of the hunchback: "The hunchback left. He went back to the booth. Looking for his lute he touched its strings and composed a new song that he would later present on the market: a song about the love of Sumurun and Nur al Din, the trader from Basra. And about a beautiful woman with black curls who was insatiable in her desire . . ." In *Sumurun* (Berlin: Filmbuch-Verlag, 1920), 70.

quently speak of the invaluable insights he had gained into directing, and the dramatic use of mass choreography in particular, by observing Reinhardt during stage rehearsals.[3]

Lubitsch made his first film appearance as Moritz Abramowsky in the lost one-reeler *Die Firma heiratet* (1914, *The Perfect Thirty-Six*), directed by Carl Wilhelm.[4] If one can believe contemporary reviews, *The Perfect Thirty-Six* already contained the essential ingredients that would soon characterize Lubitsch's own store comedies, including the focus on deception as a narrative and visual motif. Not surprisingly, many reviewers criticized the sympathetic portrayal of salesmen who deceived their female customers by selling larger clothing sizes as smaller ones. Such professional behavior, they seemed to argue, represented a most shameless indulgence in the cult of appearances and contributed indirectly to the decline of traditional moral values. For *The Perfect Thirty-Six* dared to portray deception as an essential part of human existence, even glorifying its association with modern consumerism. In so doing, the film laid the basis for Lubitsch's later investigations of the relationship between appearance and truth, reality and simulation. During the years that followed, there was still a great variety in his roles and collaborations. Lubitsch appeared in a Max Mack film, *Robert und Bertram* (1915, "Robert and Bertram") whose provincial setting and sentimental story of two vagabonds had a somewhat restraining effect on his acting style. For *Fräulein Piccolo* (1915, "Miss Piccolo"), he worked together with Franz Hofer, who was known for melodramas and sentimental love stories. In his own films, Lubitsch would also play a cuckolded husband, an unsuccessful physician, the conductor of a women's chorus, a "Negerian" prince, and Satan himself. But the cultivation of a specific screen personality was the first step toward film authorship.

Gradually Lubitsch lost interest in old-men roles and, in a somewhat reverse order, entered the world of pubescent boys and eternal juveniles. Playing stock characters like Moritz or Meyer, he developed a screen persona that was as recognizable as that of French comic Max Linder or the Chaplin of the later Essanay and Mutual two-reelers (fig. 1). Though not stated openly, his characters are presumed to be Jewish, an assumption that is reinforced by the films' quintessential setting, the clothing store. They

[3] Reinhardt's acclaimed Shakespearean productions may also be responsible for Lubitsch's frequent references to this famous playwright. Examples include the two Shakespearean winter films *Kohlhiesel's Daughters* (1920) and *Romeo and Juliet in the Snow* (1920), Gary Cooper's reading of *The Taming of the Shrew* in *Bluebeard's Eighth Wife* (1938), the staging of *Hamlet* in *To Be or Not to Be* (1942), and Charles Boyer's *Richard III* quotes in *Cluny Brown* (1946). On Lubitsch's work under Reinhart and his early film acting career, see Michael Hanisch, *Auf den Spuren der Filmgeschichte: Berliner Schauplätze* (Berlin: Henschel, 1991), 257–331.

[4] According to Prinzler and Patalas, similar claims have been made about two lost (or nonexistent) films, *Die ideale Gattin* (1913, "The Ideal Wife") and *Meyer auf der Alm* (1913, "Meyer in the Alps").

1. Film advertisement

are young apprentices with names like Moritz Rosenthal, Moritz Apfelreis, Sally Pinkus, Sally Katz, Sally Pinner, or Sally Meyer. Following in the footsteps of Siegmund Lachmann of *Der Stolz der Firma* (1914, "The Pride of the Firm"), Lubitsch's antiheros usually arrive in Berlin from provincial places like Ravitch in Poznan. After a series of comic adventures, they conquer the nation's capital and the shop owner's daughter, convincing everyone through their irresistible charm and firm determination. Films from this series include (though unverified) *Arme Marie* (1915, "Poor Mary"), *Der G.m.b.H. Tenor* (1916, "Tenor Incorp.") and *Der Blusenkönig* (1917, "The Blouse King"); unfortunately, no copies of these films have survived. However, it is in *Doktor Satansohn* (1916, "Doctor Satanson"), the three-reeler directed by Edmund Edel, that the actor Lubitsch defines most clearly the parameters of his play with desire and its fulfillment. Playing a physician ("a specialist for beauty care and body culture") who promises his female patients eternal youth, provided that they never again kiss a man, Lubitsch appears in the film as a modern Mephistopheles figure. He controls the images and the process of imagination. When he appears in the older woman's mirror, and leaves behind his business card, the scene functions like an advertisement for a film. The woman becomes his first victim in a seduction scene that depends crucially on his presentation skills but that would not take place without the desire of the other, the spectator. When Lubitsch lays down the rules of the transformation process (i.e., the taboo of physical intimacy), he also establishes the play of closeness and distance that constitutes all identification processes in the cinema. The moment when the doctor presents the rejuvenated woman in his magic transformation box anticipates the display of Cesare by Dr. Caligari. But here, the doctor's creature is the product of her own desire, not of somnambulism; here the doctor's accomplishment leads to humorous confusions, not destruction and despair. The overall atmosphere remains one of knowing detachment. Lubitsch even maintains his urbane perspective in somewhat unusual settings. A later film, *Meyer aus Berlin* (1919, "Meyer from Berlin"), shows the typical Berlin Jew who suddenly finds himself confronted with the adversities of nature, in this case the Bavarian Alps. Again role-playing proves to be essential, even if the regional costume—lederhosen, Tyrolian hat, climbing rope, and ice pick—seems strangely out of place in the luxurious resort hotel. And again imagination proves to be a key for his survival in foreign places. This is evidenced by a dream sequence in which Lubitsch "climbs" a mountain, the Watzmann, by simply eliminating two zeroes when a sketch of the mountain and an altitude mark appear (through trick photography) over his bedstead.

Despite the commercial success of *The Pride of the Firm*, Lubitsch felt increasingly frustrated. He would later explain to Weinberg: "I was typed, and no one seemed to write any part which would have fitted me. After two successes, I found myself completely left out of pictures, and as I was unwilling to give up I found it necessary that I had to create parts for myself. Together with an actor friend of mine, the late Erich Schönfelder, I wrote a series of one-reelers which I sold to the Union Company. I directed and starred in them. And that is how I became a director. If my acting career had progressed more smoothly I wonder if I ever would have become a director."[5]

Dissatisfaction, then, was the driving force behind Lubitsch's first directorial efforts, the lost one-reeler *Fräulein Seifenschaum* (1915, "Miss Soapsuds") and the three-reeler *Schuhpalast Pinkus* (1916, "Shoe Salon Pinkus"). Assuming the roles of author-actor-director, Lubitsch soon found himself in a situation where he was producing films as if on a conveyor belt. His films had such charming titles as *Der Kraftmeyer* (1915, "The Muscle Man"),

[5] Ernst Lubitsch, letter to Herman G. Weinberg (10 July 1947), *The Lubitsch Touch: A Critical Study*, 3d. rev. ed. (New York: Dover, 1977), 284.

Der gemischte Frauenchor (1916, "The Mixed Ladies' Chorus") or *Käsekönig Holländer* (1917, "The Dutch Cheese King"), and they were often advertised in the following manner: "Theater owners! Get the one-reeler series with Ernst Lubitsch, the indefatigable film comedian. These comedies are a must for every program. Frantic laughter guaranteed. Projections Actien-Gesellschaft Union."[6] Unfortunately, no copies of these films have survived.

The focus on class difference, including the desire for social recognition, points to the strong influence of ethnic comedy. This genre provided Lubitsch with his formulaic stories and stock characters, and its playful investigation of different cultural traditions contributed significantly to the sense of disrespect that made his one-reelers so successful with German audiences. Jewish humor provided a main source of inspiration, as is evidenced by Lubitsch's self-deprecating acting style and the many references to the social and cultural milieu of the *Konfektion* (clothing manufacture); thus reviewers often described his films as "Jewish milieu piece[s]."[7] It would be difficult, and perhaps futile, to look for biographical evidence such as visits to the theater or family traditions that would point to direct influences. However, one can find many similarities between Lubitsch's humor and the diverse traditions that constituted Yiddish theater in the nineteenth century.[8] Its origins reach back to the Purim play, a religious holiday and a celebration of spring. While based on Bible stories, the Purim play always included clowns and fools whose irreverent jokes and slapstick scenes disrupted the well-known narratives and created an atmosphere of exuberance and bliss. The fool's sacrilegious attitude toward death and their unrestrained enjoyment of violence and destruction reveal the transgressive quality of the Purim play, both as regards the social order and moral conventions. Its characters resemble stock characters from the Italian commedia dell'arte, as well as the German *Hanswurst* and *Pickleher-ing* figures; similarities to the Shrovetide plays can also be found. At the same time, the cultural and religious traditions of Judaism distinguish the Purim plays in important ways. Instead of trying to imitate life, the plays were staged in a presentational fashion, a reaction to the religious prohibition against making images. With their flat painted backdrops, conventional symbols, and symbolic actions they stood closer to popular spectacles than to the emerging bourgeois theater. The use of Yiddish, a jargon deemed unfit for literary writing, further underscored the proximity to popular entertainment, to what might be called *shund* (trash). At the same

---

[6] Advertisement in *Lichtbild-Bühne* (12 June 1915).

[7] Argus, qtd. by Hanisch, *Auf den Spuren der Filmgeschichte*, 305.

[8] For an introduction to Yiddish theater, see Nahma Sandrow, *Vagabond Stars. A World History of Yiddish Theater* (New York: Harper & Row, 1977).

time, the limitation to a few Biblical episodes inevitably shifted the emphasis from dramatic configurations to questions of performance and style. Active audience participation was encouraged rather than quiet immersion in the characters' psychological dilemmas. This penchant for commentary has an equivalent in the Talmudic method of scholarship, that is, of an ongoing process of interpretation and reinterpretation. In the context of the Purim plays, the self-referential play with the inherited and the known served affirmative functions but also cultivated a taste for puns and double entendres, thus introducing a distinctly intellectual quality. With the emergence of Yiddish theater, these traditions provided the mold in which new social experiences could be expressed in a humorous form. One recurring motif, the move from the country to the big city, can be found in many Yiddish plays from the late nineteenth century. Industrialization and growing anti-Semitism in Russia resulted in large waves of Jewish migration. Forced to leave behind the old communities, Eastern Jews were confronted with the task of surviving in a non-Jewish world while at the same time maintaining their cultural identity. Lubitsch's store comedies restage this experience of the newly arrived immigrant in the urban spaces of Berlin. Similarly, Sally Pinkus and his accomplices combine character traits of the *shmendrik*, a stupid but shrewd young man, with the aggressive clumsiness of the *schlemihl*, who makes up for his social disadvantages through his knowledge of human foibles and the art of persuasion.

The presence of Jewish humor in the early comedies is closely linked to the awareness of difference. On the level of performance as well as in the choice of roles Lubitsch creates a distance and provides a framework that makes possible the expression of painful experiences. Humor provides a protective shield against social discrimination and a vehicle for dealing with ambivalent feelings about one's social, sexual, and ethnic identity. It allows for the recognition of sorrow and suggests its overcoming through the liberating power of laughter. Thus humor becomes a weapon in breaking down boundaries; it turns the recognition of otherness into a shared experience, rather than a reason for separation and isolation. Nonetheless, Lubitsch's references to Jewish culture remain problematic. For the popular appeal of his earliest films was also founded on the problematic conflation of ethnic and national characteristics—references to "the provinces" often concealed anti-Polish sentiments—and the heavily clichéd opposition of provincial and urban life-styles. By playing with stereotypes, Lubitsch made them available to critical analysis. But by using them, his humor also stayed within the logic of such distinctions. Not surprisingly, Nazi film historians would later use Lubitsch as a main target for their anti-Semitic slurs—and try to exclude him from the history of German film. Writes Oskar Kalbus: "Today it seems incomprehensible that movie audiences, during the hard war years, cheered an actor who always played with a brashness so alien to us."⁹ Such discriminatory explicitness has found a counterpart in more recent critical assessments that seek refuge in vague generalities. For instance, Charles Silver uses the expression "very Old World, very Jewish, very male"¹⁰ to describe Lubitsch's humor without specifying its implications. Other critics have deflected from the existence of an identifiable "Jewish style" by emphasizing the tension between European and American elements in his films. Here references to Lubitsch's Jewishness remain suspiciously absent. The fact that the early Lubitsch played stereotypical Jewish characters and that he used Jewish culture as an important point of reference would require a more detailed discussion of Jewish self-images and of what Sander Gilman has described, in a not unproblematic term, as "Jewish self-hatred."¹¹ Such a discussion is not possible in the context of this study. It must suffice to quote the film historian Lotte Eisner, who, in a statement indicative of her own middle-class prejudices against Eastern Jews, once described Lubitsch's early comedies as a combination of Berlin pragmatism, Huguenot wit, and the kind of cynical humor that she found prevalent among members of the Jewish petty bourgeoisie. According to Eisner, Lubitsch possessed a "Central European" vulgarity that revealed his family background in the *Konfektion*, and he never overcame "the vainglory of the *nouveau-riche*."¹² In a more provocative tone, but equally careless of his use of social and ethnic stereotypes, Jean-Louis Comolli has pointed to the contradictions in what he describes as Lubitsch's infatuation with money and power: "Thus one could say without exaggeration that *The Pride of the Firm* (and without doubt the entire series) is the most anti-Semitic body of work ever to be produced, if . . . Ernst Lubitsch had not been Jewish himself!"¹³ The wavering between self-mockery and self-contempt is most noticeable in the early one-reelers, but it also continues in the cool portrayal of the main protagonists and the foregrounding of filmic style that characterize the later films. Stylization, in this regard, marks the end point in a chain of displacements that is both socially and aesthetically motivated; a closer look at Lubitsch's biography only confirms this assertion.

During the early years of his career, Lubitsch's social background provided the main inspiration for the social settings of his films. Born in Berlin

⁹ Oskar Kalbus, *Vom Wesen deutscher Filmkunst*, vol. 1 (Altona-Bahrenfeld: Zigaretten-Bilderdienst, 1935), 27.

¹⁰ Charles Silver, *Marlene Dietrich* (New York: Pyramid, 1974), 91.

¹¹ For an insightful discussion, see Sander Gilman, *Jewish Self-Hatred. Anti-Semitism and the Hidden Language of the Jews* (Baltimore: The Johns Hopkins University Press, 1986), esp. the chapters "Toward a Philosophy of Language" and "Toward a Psychology of Language."

¹² Lotte Eisner, *The Haunted Screen*, trans. Roger Greaves (Berkeley: University of California Press, 1973), 79.

¹³ J.-L. C. [Jean-Louis Comolli], *Der Stolz der Firma*, *Cahiers du cinéma* 198 (February 1968): 31.

on January 29, 1892, as the child of German Jews of Polish-Russian background, Lubitsch grew up in the predominantly Jewish neighborhood of the Scheunenviertel where his father Simon Lubitsch owned a women's clothing store. After finishing school, he worked as an errand boy for a tailor but soon decided to enter the more exciting world of the theater and, later, the movies. In order to succeed, the apprentice-turned-actor only had to reinvent the characters and situations that were most familiar to him. Some critics (like Eisner) have suggested—and they have done so with dismissive overtones—that Lubitsch never really left the world of the "rag trade." And indeed, his films do contain elements of a fetishistic involvement with set and costume design. The sensual appeal of fabrics, of fashion as a form of self-expression and disguise, is an important part of Lubitsch's presentation of female stars, but it also informs his approach to the more immaterial "materials" of cinema. Frieda Grafe has commented on this duplicity of means: "Lubitsch's films are made like fashion and work like fashion. They are seductive. They arouse wishes and desires. He demonstrates from the inside, with the means of cinema, how susceptible we are to persuasion. He shows quite bluntly that this is what the cinema thrives on. Wishes and desires in industrial society are not natural, they are calculated."[14] It is precisely this fixation on consumer goods that forces so many characters to leave behind their humble origins and realize their almost self-destructive longing for social and economic success. In their opportunism, but also in their lack of self-confidence, Lubitsch's own petty bourgeois background provides a ubiquitous point of reference. The same holds true for the shifting perspectives assumed by the actor/narrator. Moving back and forth between the irony of the critical observer and the melancholia of the permanent outsider, Lubitsch reenacts the uncertainties associated with a social position at the margins: outside of the middle class and the working class, in opposition to the characteristics that traditionally constitute Germanness. Therefore his early comedies reveal a kind of class consciousness that prompted Enno Patalas to call them the most plebeian films ever made in Germany, with the term *plebeian* obviously referring to the problem of class position.[15]

[14] Frieda Grafe, "Was Lubitsch berührt," in Prinzler and Patalas, *Lubitsch*, 87.

[15] See Patalas, "Ernst Lubitsch: German Period," in *Cinema: A Critical Dictionary. The Major Film-makers*, vol. 2, ed. Richard Roud (New York: The Viking Press, 1980), 639–43. Not surprisingly, Lubitsch's career has often been analyzed in the context of class experience. The early years, especially, have been described in great detail by Friedrich Porges, Curt Riess, and Géza von Cziffra. In their sensationalist accounts of German film history, the young Lubitsch is described as the hero of real-life melodramas and comedies. Porges sketches the following scene: "Ernst's stomach made itself heard. It rumbled alarmingly. From now on, hunger would probably be a permanent companion." In "Der Jüngling aus der Konfektion," *Schatten erobern die Welt. Wie Film und Kino wurde* (Basel: Verlag für Wissenschaft, Technik und Industrie, 1946), 172. In the same vein, Riess ruminates about Lubitsch's unappealing

Lubitsch's preference for specific plot structures, his strong emphasis on style, and his pervasive sense of irony must also be situated within a particular historical context. During the teens and early twenties, Germany experienced dramatic social, political, economic, and cultural changes. The devastation of World War One, the collapse of the Wilhelmine Empire with the following years of hunger, unemployment, and political instability, and as the first step toward democratization, the founding of the Weimar Republic in 1919 made the transition from a traditional to a modern society particularly difficult. It is not surprising that Lubitsch's German films frequently refer back to this period—but not, as one might expect, as a time of liberation. For him, the advent of modernity remains linked to an experience of loss, both of the enlightened rationality and eroticism associated with the eighteenth century and the kind of turn-of-the-century sensibility according to which good manners and good taste are the expression of a genuine love for the world. These tastes and sentiments stand only in apparent opposition to the petty-bourgeois settings of the early comedies. Precisely because the world of luxury and privilege had never been accessible to Lubitsch personally was he able to capture its spirit and, on a more profound level, to salvage its dream of an ethics of form for the redemptive project that governed his entire work. The longing for that which transcends the realm of the necessary underlies his fascination with glamorous historical periods as well as his weakness for the aristocracy. Lubitsch's brand of conservatism, then, is conservative in the most positive sense of the word. (As some of the later films show [e.g., *That Uncertain Feeling*], it can also be oppressive to the point of mummification.)

Hans Helmut Prinzler has examined the affinities between Lubitsch's social background, his favorite screen roles, and his filmic style from the

---

physiognomy, only then to plumb the depths of his juvenile soul: "There is this short, stout young man burdened with an almost dreadful ugliness. A typical Berliner. With a mouth that is much too big, he is never at a loss for words. He cracks jokes about everything. Only few people will ever understand that he only jokes because he is afraid to be hurt . . . only his sad dark eyes show what really goes on in his soul." In *Das gab's nur einmal*, vol. 1 (Munich: Hanser, 1977), 69. And von Cziffra speculates on the relationship between Lubitsch, "the man with the big nose," and his attractive star Harry Liedtke: "Ugly Ernst envied handsome Harry for his looks and felt pity for him because of his lack of talent." In *Es war eine rauschende Ballnacht: Eine Sittengeschichte des deutschen Films* (Frankfurt am Main: Ullstein, 1987), 68. By and large, such film books can be passed over without much loss. However, if they are quoted by someone like Weinberg without acknowledgment of his sources, the call for scholarly ethics becomes more than a matter of good manners. To cite an example, Riess's description of the young struggling actor in Reinhardt's company (in the original German: "Er kann von hundert Mark Monatsgage einfach nicht existieren. Er muß einmal ein Mädchen ausführen können. Er muß sich einen neuen Anzug kaufen" (71)) appears in Weinberg's book in an almost literal translation: "He couldn't live on 100 marks a month. He would like to take a girl out occasionally, he'd like to buy a new suit." In *The Lubitsch Touch: A Critical Study*, 3d. rev. ed. (New York: Dover, 1977), 9.

viewpoint of social experience. The typical petty-bourgeois character in a Lubitsch film, he argues, tries to fulfill his social and economic ambitions but feels constantly threatened by the possibility of discrimination and decline. For the same reason, Lubitsch's acting style stands in a comic tradition that is based on instant results and that distinguishes itself through an unabashed calculation of all means. Unlike the filmmaker, the actor Lubitsch compensates for his lack of precision by producing a surplus of comic effects. He acts out the attitudes of the social climber through the body. Sometimes his distinctly physical acting style produces unexpected effects, for instance when he expresses confusion by scratching his head or when he shows sadness by sucking his thumb. These are gestures that evoke, against the claims of masculinity, the lost paradises of childhood. Prinzler writes: "He exhibits his role all too obviously. There are no elisions, no economy of means, no timing, but above all directness, frontal play. One can take pleasure in the Jewish charm of this clumsy, egotistical, cowardly, servile, ambitious social climber."[16] A superimposition in *The Pride of the Firm* identifies with almost shameless honesty the desires that stand behind such ambitions. Here the "before" and "after" of class mobility are projected onto each other in the double portrait of Siegmund Lachmann. He enters on the scene as a badly dressed shop assistant and is then magically transformed into an elegant businessman who does not even feel the need to hide his feelings of triumph and accomplishment. With implications reaching far beyond such individual success stories, these moments of transformation highlight Lubitsch's own goal as a filmmaker, that is, of achieving the most through increasingly less—truly an economy of representation.

On the other side of these scenarios of seduction, the spectators in the motion-picture theaters—the cinema's "customers," as it were—are called upon to respond like the women who frequent the films' stylish shoe salon and clothing stores. The analogy, again, is not coincidental. As the temples of modern society, the motion-picture theater and the department store provide the ideal setting for escapist fantasies and consumerist desires. Both address themselves especially to women: as the quintessential modern consumers, the foremost experts in questions of style, and as that group in society that is most open to, and most in need of, the play with other identities. Accordingly, in the moment that imagination triumphs as the driving force behind the desire for consumer goods, the hero in *Shoe Salon Pinkus* changes the store's name from "shoe shop" to "shoe palace," a promotional strategy that recalls the advancement of the flickers to "motion-

[16] Prinzler, "Berlin 29.1.1892—Hollywood 30.11.1947. Bausteine zu einer Lubitsch-Biografie," in Prinzler and Patalas, *Lubitsch*, 17. Ulrich Kurowski makes a similar point in "Zur Karriere des Ernst Lubitsch. Aufsteiger-Obsessionen," *Film + Ton-Magazin* 6 (June 1980): 56–61.

picture palace." Other sequences in the film investigate the profits that can be made through the conflation of advertisement and eroticism. Here the almost fetishistic approach to the techniques of cinema, which are also those of advertisement, spills over into the play with multiple levels of referentiality. For instance, Lubitsch's flirtation with other filmic styles inspires the documentary style used in the fashion-show sequence. Celebrating beautiful shoes as well as various filmic means, the sequence disrupts the flow of the narrative and culminates in a seemingly endless series of close-ups aimed at the prospective buyer/spectator. Sally Pinkus himself uses similar methods. He attracts the attention of the famous dancer Melitta Hervé (Else Kenter) by selling her shoe size six for size four; smaller feet, after all, are considered more attractive. Later he uses her dance soirées to announce that the dancers' shoes are for sale in his store. Such blatant self-advertisement in the film's diegetic space finds a continuation in the listing of those Berlin stores that donated their shoes for the production. In the end, the successful new store manager proposes marriage to the dancer who, in the meantime, has become a shareholder in the firm: "Why share?" Sally argues. "Just marry me and the money stays in the family." German critic Karsten Witte comments on such behavior: "Morally speaking, Sally Pinkus has to be characterized as a clever opportunist. But Lubitsch does not cast moral judgment, calling people either good or bad. They simply *are* good and bad; with this diagnosis Lubitsch causes a stir."[17]

Made for quick consumption, Lubitsch's early comedies flaunt their mode of production—literally and figuratively speaking. They openly acknowledge and take advantage of film's unique position between the commodity and the work of art. Their indebtedness to popular forms of entertainment—the folk play, the pantomime, the circus—is most obvious in the preference for exaggerated performance styles and dramatic situations and in the noticeable lack of concern for narrative continuity and psychological motivation. The early Lubitsch comedies share these characteristics with most German films made during the war years.[18] While the rapid expansion of the film industry required increasing standardization, including of the means of filmic representation, the fairground continued to be a strong influence, as is evidenced by the continuing appeal of the spectacular and the grotesque. The emergent classical narrative cinema produced its own pockets of resistance, so to speak. This also explains why many films from the teens appear surprisingly unaffected by the moral and aesthetic restraints that would soon become necessary with the cinema's ele-

[17] Karsten Witte, review of *Schuhpalast Pinkus*, in Prinzler and Patalas, *Lubitsch*, 125.
[18] On other German films from the period, see *Before Caligari: German Cinema 1895–1920*, ed. Paolo Cherchi Usai and Lorenzo Codelli (Pordenone: Le Giornate del Cinema Muto, 1990).

vation to middle-class culture. Profiting from the tension between economic expansion and creative innovation—a tension that also inspired the so-called "art films"—Lubitsch's early German films must therefore be described as first studies, preliminary designs and, in a sense, the blueprint for all later films, including perhaps their marks of imperfection.

Two

The German Feature Films, 1918–1922

DURING the war and postwar years, Lubitsch produced films at an almost frantic rate.[1] Determined to streamline the process of production, he began to look for collaborators and gradually surrounded himself with the artistic and technical elite of the German cinema. Scenarist Hanns Kräly (Hans Kraly), who had played a salesman in *The Perfect Thirty-Six*, was the first to be recruited to the Lubitsch team. Together they wrote a number of scenarios for one-reelers; after the success of *Shoe Salon Pinkus*, they decided to move on to three-reelers. Kräly worked with Lubitsch on all German films, followed him to Hollywood, and contributed greatly to the sophisticated flair of the Warner comedies. Similarly, from 1916 to 1922 the cinematographer Theodor Sparkuhl shot almost all the Lubitsch films, sometimes aided by Alfred Hansen. Lubitsch's collaboration with well-known stage designers like Kurt Richter, Ernst Stern, and Paul Leni profited from the creative atmosphere that characterized the German theater of the teens and twenties. Most of his films for Pagu (Projektions-Ag Union) were designed by Kurt Richter, who was equally skilled at creating intimate chamber-play settings and spectacular tableaux. The Austrian Ernst Stern, whose stage designs included Reinhardt's prestigious Shakespearean productions as well as the most recent Expressionist plays by Reinhard Goering, Georg Kaiser, Walter Hasenclever, and Fritz von Unruh, perfected his mixture of Jugendstil and orientalism in films like *The Mountain Cat* and *The Loves of Pharaoh*. The graphic artist and theater designer Leni, who in the twenties directed such quintessential "Expressionist" films as *Hintertreppe* (1921, *Backstairs*) and *Das Wachsfigurenkabinett* (1923, *Waxworks*), designed the sets for *Der Blusenkönig* (1917, "The Blouse King") and the detective farce *Der Fall Rosentopf* (1918, "The Rosentopf Case"); he also created the decoration for the prologue that accompanied the 1926 Berlin

[1] For a comprehensive survey of Lubitsch's German films, see Jan-Christopher Horak, "The Pre-Hollywood Lubitsch," *Image* 18, no. 4 (1975): 19–29; and N. Simsolo, "Ernst Lubitsch: periode allemande," *Revue du cinéma* 405 (May 1985): 75–82. For a few useful film synopses, see also Ilona Brennicke and Joe Hembus, *Klassiker des deutschen Stummfilms 1910–1930* (Munich: Wilhelm Goldmann, 1983).

premiere of *Forbidden Paradise*.[2] As a collaborator since 1917, Ali Hubert designed the costumes for all the period films; following Lubitsch to Hollywood, he again demonstrated his skilled use of historical detail in films like *The Student Prince* (1927) and *The Patriot* (1928).[3]

During the early teens, Lubitsch directed an average of five to eight one- and two-reelers per year. In 1915, Lubitsch and Ernst Mátray founded a short-lived film-production company, the Malu-Film, which folded after two films, the lost one-reelers *Aufs Eis geführt* (1915, "A Trip on the Ice") and *Zucker und Zimt* (1915, "Sugar and Spice"). The majority of Lubitsch films, however, were produced by Paul Davidson of Pagu and shot at the Union (and later Ufa) studios in Berlin-Tempelhof. Davidson's influential position in the film industry was based on a chain of theaters, the Union-Theater, that he had started in 1910 and that allowed him to contract stars like Asta Nielsen, Henny Porten, and Pola Negri for his growing film production; in 1917 Davidson became one of the two general directors for Ufa. Under his contract with Pagu, Lubitsch was sometimes loaned out to other studios, among others for the Argus production of Strindberg's *Rausch* (1919, *Intoxication*) and the Messter-Film production of the popular *Kohlhiesels Töchter* (1920, "Kohlhiesel's Daughters"). In both cases, the box-office appeal of Asta Nielsen and Henny Porten led to these special arrangements. Shortly before leaving Germany, Lubitsch got involved in the EFA (Europäische Film-Allianz) project and, because of his good business sense, was able to gain additional influence as coproducer of his last German films, *Das Weib des Pharao* (1921, *The Loves of Pharaoh*) and *Die Flamme* (1922, *Montmartre*). With two significant exceptions, Lubitsch gave up acting after his first feature film, *Die Augen der Mumie Mâ* (1918, *The Eyes of the Mummy*), from then on devoting all his energies to scriptwriting and directing. *The Eyes of the Mummy* announces Lubitsch's decision in its credit sequence, thus making his artistic ambitions an integral part of the promotional campaign: "He [Lubitsch] succeeds in persuading his boss and discoverer, Paul Davidson of Union Film, that he must now realize his artistic dreams in the creation of a great film drama. Davidson decides to risk a lot of money . . ." The rest, as the credits try to suggest, is history. Lubitsch's last film role, the singer/storyteller in *Sumurun*, reflects this transition through its peculiar position inside and outside of the narrative.

[2] See *Paul Leni: Grafik Theater Film*, ed. Hans-Michael Bock (Frankfurt am Main: Deutsches Filmmuseum, 1984), 252 and 258. In most filmographies, Kurt Richter is listed as the set designer for *Der Fall Rosentopf*.

[3] For memoirs by Lubitsch collaborators from the German period, see Ali Hubert, *Hollywood—Legende und Wirklichkeit* (Leipzig: E. A. Seemann, 1930); Emil Jannings, *Theater, Film—das Leben und ich* (Berchtesgaden: Zimmer und Herzog, 1951), esp. 115–32 and 157–91; Ernst Stern, *My Life, My Stage*, trans. Edward Fitzgerald (London: Victor Gollancz, 1951), esp. 178–87.

Similarly, the prologue of *Die Puppe* (1919, *The Doll*) makes a humorous comment on the art of filmmaking and, in a way, finalizes his decision to become a full-time director. Playing a magician or puppeteer, Lubitsch sets up a toy set that, through superimposition, turns into the film's "real" setting.[+] With this remarkable gesture, the filmmaker disappears forever behind the camera and sets the stage for more complicated configurations between narrator and main protagonists. As long as Lubitsch played the leading roles, his films were structured around a male protagonist. Once he gave up acting, women protagonists took over this position. The leading actresses, in a way, refined the acting styles and roles that were first introduced by Lubitsch, the actor, and consequently functioned as much as a figure of self-identification as they represented, in the more traditional sense, the object of male desire. Lubitsch's closeness to his female characters, both in role and performance style, reveals the identification of the Jewish male with the marginal position of women. It also points to a regressive narcissism that finds expression in the women's relationship to beautiful clothes and luxury items, as commodified versions of an all-encompassing eroticism. In that vein, the sympathetic portrayal of women in the later Lubitsch films is as much a result of his old-fashioned interpretation of sexual difference as it bears witness to a more complicated process of identification on the basis of an experience of difference.

At first glance, Lubitsch's feature-length comedies seem to continue in the tradition of the shoe salon one-reelers. However, as the films become more sophisticated, the old slapstick elements are relegated to comic subgenres like the rustic farce, as is evidenced by *Romeo und Julia im Schnee* (1920, "Romeo and Juliet in the Snow") and *Kohlhiesel's Daughters*. Both films take their inspiration from Shakespearean plays (*Romeo and Juliet*, *The Taming of the Shrew*), but they replace the noble protagonists and refined surroundings with simple German peasants and remote mountain villages. Increasingly, however, Lubitsch chooses urbane settings that allow him to display in great detail the chic fashions and elegant interior

---

[+] Freud has commented on the continuing influence of childhood fantasies on the daydreams of adults, and the artist's creative imagination in particular. One of the examples in "Creative Writer and Daydreaming" reads like an early Lubitsch comedy: "Let us take the case of a poor orphan to whom you have given the address of some employer where he may perhaps find a job. On his way he may indulge in a day-dream appropriate to the situation from which it arises. The content of his phantasy will perhaps be something like this: He is given a job, finds favor with his new employer, makes himself indispensable in the business, is taken into his employer's house, marries the charming young daughter of the house, and then himself becomes a director of the business, first as his employer's partner, and then as his successor." In Sigmund Freud, "Creative Writers and Day-Dreaming" (1907), *Standard Edition of the Complete Psychological Works of Sigmund Freud*, 24 vols., trans. and ed. James Strachey (London: The Hogarth Press, 1953–66), vol. 9, 148. Unless otherwise stated, references to Freud's work will be references to the *Standard Edition*.

designs that from then on characterize his protagonists as much as their relationships to one another. Beginning with *Wenn vier dasselbe tun* (1917, "When Four Do the Same"), geometric configurations provide the matrix for the new scenarios of human desire. With their three or four main participants, the stories are usually based on triangular and circular structures that generate and are generated by sexual desire. Eroticism becomes a stand-in for all desires, including the lust for money or power. But no matter how daring they are in their view of modern life-styles, these films—therein following the rules of the "well-made play"—end up confirming the status quo, even if it is a status quo "flawed" by the ongoing claims of desire. *When Four Do the Same*, for instance, begins with two couples: a father and his daughter, a female book dealer and her male shop clerk. The desire for personal freedom undermines the hierarchical structures of kinship and profession that constitute the original couples, just as the power of love leads to the formation of two new couples, the old lovers and the young lovers. This process creates tensions and misunderstandings but eventually results in a workable compromise between individual desire and social responsibility. Dismissing such parallel constructions as mechanistic, Werner Sudendorff notes: "Here the dramatic construction of Lubitsch's later comedies has been reduced to a naked framework. In this film the multiplication of gestures and the mildly ironic duplication of events have deteriorated into mechanistic entities that exist side-by-side but rarely interact with each other."[5] By describing *When Four Do the Same* as the expression of an "activism aimed into a void," Sudendorff draws a connection between the film's circular structure and its sociopolitical implications. He interprets duplication and circularity as characteristics of a conservative aesthetics that fetishizes formal concerns to the point of depletion and, in so doing, sacrifices their critical potential as well. While Sudendorff's critique may be accurate on the level of narrative analysis, it neglects the kind of "critical mass" that develops in the interaction of all filmic means, including the relationship among camera, narrator, and spectator, and that can easily turn conformism into parody and parody into a vehicle of social criticism.

Continuing along these lines, *Die Austernprinzessin* (1919, *The Oyster Princess*) must be regarded as the first Lubitsch comedy that shows a distinct filmic style. Reviewing the film four years after its release, Béla Balázs praised "[t]he director's undeniable, intentional self-irony. Here the comic mode already emanates from a directorial style that is founded on self-mockery. Film fashions and film manners, even filmic effects are unmasked,

⁵ Werner Sudendorf, review of *Wenn vier dasselbe tun*, in *Lubitsch*, ed. Hans Helmut Prinzler and Enno Patalas (Berlin: C. J. Bucher, 1984), 126.

and all that only through a slight touch of exaggeration."[6] In a similar vein, Wollenberg noted much later: "Lubitsch looked for an alternative. . . . He attempted screen comedy to equal stage comedy: comedies based on a logical story, carried by psychologically motivated characters. His natural sense of humor combined with his film sense in his production of *The Oyster Princess*. All three elements—story, superb acting and grand decor—blended together by Lubitsch's direction, combined in another international success."[7] With *The Oyster Princess* Lubitsch had come into his own.

In the following years, Lubitsch worked primarily in two genres, the period film and film comedy. His penchant for "solid entertainment" distinguished Lubitsch from contemporaries like F. W. Murnau and Fritz Lang, who clearly profited from his formal innovations but who also chose more ambitious projects and difficult subject matter. Again the hierarchy of the genres plays a crucial part in the critical assessment of their work. While the names of Lubitsch, Murnau, and Lang have come to represent the best of the classical German cinema, Murnau and Lang have received special attention as its foremost auteurs.[8] His talent for comic situations separated Lubitsch from the disturbing inner worlds of Murnau's *Schloss Vogelöd* (1921, "Vogelöd Castle") or *Nosferatu* (1921) and made him seem frivolous and superficial. Similarly, Lubitsch's playful approach to set design had little in common with Lang's claustrophobic spaces in *Die Spinnen* (1919–20, *Spiders*) or the architectural philosophy of *Der müde Tod* (1921, *Destiny*). The debates on film as art also seemed to have had little effect on Lubitsch. The movement toward a German art cinema inspired films like Paul Wegener's *Der Golem* (1914 and 1920, *The Golem*), *Der Student von Prag* (1913, *The Student of Prague*) in the version by Stellan Rye, and Robert Wiene's *Das Kabinett des Dr. Caligari* (1920, *The Cabinet of Dr. Caligari*) and was largely responsible for the growing international interest in German films after World War One. Lubitsch used similar techniques, and often collaborated with the same cinematographers and set designers that gave the so-called "Expressionist" films their distinct look, but his orientation remained strictly populist and commercial. Especially his period films—alternative terms like *historical film* or *costume drama* accommo-

---

[6] Béla Balázs, "Die Selbstironie des Films" (1923), *Béla Balázs Schriften zum Film*, vol. 1, ed. Helmut H. Diederichs (Munich: Hanser, 1982), 211. The text has been translated into English as "Self-Mockery on the Screen," *Hungarofilm Bulletin* 3 (1984): 16.

[7] H. H. Wollenberg, "Ernst Lubitsch," *Penguin Film Reviews* 7 (September 1948): 64.

[8] The standard histories of the German silent cinema are Lotte Eisner's *The Haunted Screen*, trans. Roger Greaves (Berkeley: University of California Press, 1973) and Siegfried Kracauer's *From Caligari to Hitler: A Psychological History of the German Cinema* (Princeton, N.J.: Princeton University Press, 1977). On Lang, see Frieda Grafe et al., *Fritz Lang* (Munich: Hanser, 1976). On Murnau, see Lotte Eisner, *Murnau* (Frankfurt am Main: Kommunales Kino, 1979) and, for a good discussion of the representation of sexuality, Janet Bergstrom, "Sexuality at a Loss: The Films of F. W. Murnau," *Poetics Today* 6 (1985): 185–203.

date his specularization of history only partially—appealed to audiences
through the sheer size of the sets and the splendor of the costumes. However, they also convinced through the suggestive mixture of public and
private histories; the term *period* refers precisely to the visual aspects of this
encounter of story and history.[9] The influence of Griffith films like *The
Birth of a Nation* (1915) or *Intolerance* (1916) on Lubitsch's approach to the
genre is highly probable. At the same time, *Orphans of the Storm* (1922), like
Passion, a film about the French Revolution, may have been inspired by
Lubitsch's period films which at the time enjoyed great popularity in
America. Both directors shared an unfailing sense of cinematic spectacle
but they also paid close attention to the dramatic interaction among characters; hence the frequent references to Griffith in articles on Lubitsch. At
times, Lubitsch's period films acquired a touch of orientalism or melodrama, as can be seen in *One Arabian Night* and *The Loves of Pharaoh* (fig.
2). At times, the comedies adopted elements from the fantastic and the
grotesque, as is evidenced by the Hoffmannesque atmosphere of *Die Puppe*
(1919, *The Doll*) or the Surrealist set designs in *Die Bergkatze* (1921, *The
Mountain Cat*). But for the most part, the intimate scale of ethnic comedy
and the choreographed splendor of the period film provided the framework against which the other films had to assert their uniqueness. Sometimes, however, Lubitsch was forced to comply with specific requests.
Asked to direct a promotional film for the new Ufa star Pola Negri, he
chose *Carmen* (1918, *Gypsy Blood*). While the film undoubtedly profited
from the popularity of the Bizet opera, its melodramatic story remained as
uncharacteristic for Lubitsch as the somber "street film" atmosphere of *Intoxication* and *Montmartre*, two other star vehicles that offered little opportunity for the usual visual puns.[10]

To a large degree, Lubitsch's work in the period film was motivated by
economic considerations. While he was establishing himself as a successful
director, the foundation of Ufa (Universum Film AG) in 1917 and the following structural reorganization of the film industry resulted in the merger
of many smaller film studios, including Davidson's Union-Ag. Under these
changed conditions, Lubitsch agreed to direct *Madame Dubarry* (1919, *Passion*) and, as a sequel, *Anna Boleyn* (1920, *Deception*), two films that gener-

---

[9] Alternative terms include *historical film*, *monumental film*, *costume film*, and *costume drama*.
The term *period film* (*historischer Ausstattungsfilm*), however, seems to accommodate best the
dimensions of the genre in its interpretation by Lubitsch, including the strong emphasis on
spectacle, the highly personalized approach to history, and the mixing of history and eroticism.

[10] Balázs praises *Montmartre*'s "classical style. " In *Schriften*, vol. 1, 167. For other enthusiastic
reviews, see B. E. Lüthge, "*Rausch*," *Film-Kurier* (3 August 1919), reprinted in Prinzler and
Patalas, *Lubitsch*, 131–32 and Herbert Ihering, "*Die Flamme*," *Berliner-Börsen-Courier* (12 September 1923), reprinted in Prinzler and Patalas, *Lubitsch*, 145–46.

2. *One Arabian Night*

ated a lot of revenue for the studio and established the period film as a highly profitable enterprise. Ufa used the period films to strengthen its position on the international market, where they impressed audiences and critics through their technical perfection and spectacular designs. For German audiences, the genre also offered a convenient way of escaping into a more glorious past, as Pola Negri notes in her memoirs: "One of the reasons [for the success of *One Arabian Night*] was certainly because its intensely romantic oriental fatalism was precisely the kind of escapism a war-weary people craved for."[11] Gregor and Patalas have characterized the period film as sensational, opportunistic, and exploitative, thereby also criticizing Lubitsch for his involvement with the genre: "His ambivalent relationship to power is most evident in *One Arabian Night* where the themes of the historical film are represented in the guise of a fantastic pantomime. This bloody ballad of tyranny, jealousy, denunciation, and double

[11] Pola Negri, *Memoirs of a Star* (Garden City, N.Y.: Doubleday, 1970), 39. Like Lubitsch, Negri left Germany in the early twenties, succeeded in Hollywood as a European vamp import but, like her colleague Emil Jannings, found herself unemployable after the advent of the sound film.

murder only gives Lubitsch the licence to stage a spectacular revue with many formal arabesques."[12]

Aware of the shortcomings of the period film, Lubitsch repeatedly makes fun of the genre's infatuation with material excess and human tragedy. His self-critical attitude is nowhere clearer than in the opening title of *The Eyes of the Mummy:* "This film had a big budget, that is, two palm trees, and was shot on locations in Egypt, that is, in the Rüdesdorf limestone mountains [near Berlin]." While complying with the "materialism" of the period film, Lubitsch disrupts the fatalistic atmosphere through comical subplots and ironic commentaries. His almost sarcastic portrayal of suicide attempts—a recurring motif in the early films—bears witness to the same kind of resistance in the melodrama. As if to preclude forever the specter of death, Lubitsch himself introduces the suicide motif in *The Pride of the Firm.* First he falls from a ladder; the inter-title reads: "It seems I am dead!" Having lost his job, he then tries to drown himself but, at the last moment, decides: "I'll have supper first!" For the same reason, the sympathetic pharmacist in *Romeo and Juliet in the Snow* sells the unhappy lovers a bottle of sugar water instead of the requested poison. In *The Doll,* Hilarius prevents his suicidal apprentice from swallowing expensive paints. Even the hunchback of *One Arabian Night* takes poison and survives. All these scenes attest to a strong, unshakable belief in life that, by demonstrating rather than arguing the joy of human existence, contradicts the period films and their conspicuous death scenes.[13] Not surprisingly, comedy remains the genre that is best suited for Lubitsch's cinematic explorations.

While perfecting his directorial skills, Lubitsch established contact with a number of actors who soon appeared regularly in his films. Ossi Oswalda, Pola Negri, and Emil Jannings provided the human material—the bodies, the faces, the gestures—around which he could construct his narratives and mise-en-scènes. These three popular actors also guaranteed the commercial success that was necessary for his further development as a filmmaker. Among the first directors to work in this manner, Lubitsch would later blame the German cinema for its lack of real star personalities, claiming: "The German film industry, most of all, must try to build women stars whose personalities can draw international attention. This is the weakest

[12] Ulrich Gregor and Enno Patalas, *Geschichte des Films*, vol. 1 (Reinbek: Rowohlt, 1980), 49.

[13] Death plays only a marginal role in the Lubitsch universe. All later "suicide" scenes take place either in the context of revengeful fantasies or in theatrical productions (*The Marriage Circle, The Love Parade, To Be or Not to Be*). The only dead protagonists in the American films are, aside from Henry Van Cleve in *Heaven Can Wait*, a German soldier (*The Man I Killed*) and a Nazi spy (*To Be or Not to Be*), evidence perhaps of a conscious distinction between humor and politics.

point of the German industry."[14] His first discovery was the comedienne Ossi Oswalda (née Oswalda Stäglich) who, after her debut in *Leutnant auf Befehl* (1916, "Lieutenant by Command"),was soon typecast as the assertive child-woman, a kind of modern ingenue. Known as the "Mary Pickford of Germany" because of her great popularity, Oswalda actually stood closer to the American flapper, as portrayed by actresses like Clara Bow or Colleen Moore. Perfecting her screen persona in a series of short film comedies that were specifically written for her (e.g., *Ossi's Tagebuch* [1917, "Ossi's Diary"]), she charmed audiences through an almost ferocious joy of life and, at times, a surprisingly uninhibited eroticism.

Lubitsch's stories of female liberation take place within the context of a playful, rather than serious, redefinition of sexual difference. Here the notion of androgyny comes into play as it contains the more threatening aspects of a liberated female sexuality within a sexually neutralized aesthetics. Not surprisingly, *Ich möchte kein Mann sein* (1918, "I Wouldn't Want to Be a Man!") remains the only film in which Lubitsch explores the comic potential of the cross-dressing plot. In this unjustly neglected film, Oswalda plays a young girl with a rather unfeminine passion for cigarettes, alcohol, and poker. No longer willing to endure the pedagogical terror regime of uncle and governess, she seeks refuge in male clothing. The girl acquires a most elegantly tailored evening wardrobe, complete with top hat, tails, white tie, and gloves. These male accoutrements allow Ossi to leave behind the traditional definitions of gender and, though only for a short time, to experiment with her new identity and enjoy its privileges. In so doing, Ossi behaves like the typical Lubitsch hero who relies largely on good taste in clothes and impeccable manners to prove his masculinity. As a smashing young man, Ossi attends a ball and, coincidentally, makes the acquaintance of her new legal guardian, Dr. Kersten (Curt Goetz). In the beginning, the two men compete for the ladies' attention. But under the influence of numerous drinks, they become increasingly critical of modern women and conclude the evening with a celebration of male companionship. Their good-bye scene culminates in a kiss whose homosexual overtones are promptly denied through Ossi's visible discomfort. Dr. Kersten's reassuring "But you are a man!" only underscores the issues at stake and elicits a meek response, "You say that so easily!" from the girl. After that, only the unmasking of the woman, and her subsequent domestication, can save a story of mistaken identity that works as long as the traditional gender roles are maintained. However, while *I Wouldn't Want to Be a Man* closes with

[14] Lubitsch, "Unsere Chancen in Amerika," *Lichtbild-Bühne* 56 (17 May 1924). The letter has been translated into French by Michel Sineux as "Nos chances en Amérique," *Positif* 292 (June 1985): 13–15.

a reassuring heterosexual embrace, Ossi's "You say that so easily!" continues to haunt the problem of a desire without boundaries.

Where Ossi Oswalda communicates innocence and cheerfulness, Pola
Negri (née Barbara Apolonia Chalupec) surrounds herself with images of
death and destruction. As the other woman in Lubitsch's erotic equations,
the temperamental Negri, with her piercing glances and the jet black curls
framing a pale face, plays the dangerous vamp, the destructive seductress,
the quintessential femme fatale. Beginning with *Gypsy Blood*, a story perfectly suited to show off her dubious accomplishments as a dancer, Negri
introduced a kind of exotic, almost oriental eroticism. The repressive atmosphere of Wilhelmine society had already prepared a fertile breeding
ground for such sexual phantasms. The unbroken popularity of the vamp
figure throughout the twenties, however, must be seen against the backdrop of women's emancipation and the feelings of disempowerment experienced by many men, especially in the lower middle class. While real
women entered the public sphere and gained power in many formerly all-
male professions, the vamp led her admirers into imaginary spaces where
the unproductive excesses of sensuality could still be celebrated and where
it was still possible to indulge in an unrestrained gender essentialism. Under these conditions, Negri came to embody woman as the ultimate Other.
This also explains the numerous aggressive impulses against her. Stabbed
by her former lover in *The Eyes of the Mummy* and *Gypsy Blood*, hanged by
the revolutionaries of *Passion*, and "personally" murdered by Lubitsch in
One Arabian Night, Negri met her final "destiny" in the role of the prosti-
tute Yvette of *Montmartre* who, significantly, takes her own life in a desperate act of suicide.[15] Sexuality as a profession and a calling—in the book
to the film, author Hans Müller lets Yvette explain: "Men don't know.
They easily throw the first stone. They take us in their arms . . . and in their
arms, when we . . . burn—then they are terrified by the flame."[16] Only *The
Mountain Cat* and *Forbidden Paradise* (1924), two films with strong comical
overtones, offer alternatives to the fatal association of sexuality and guilt,
as Negri wisely relinquishes her objects of desire. Consequently, she not
only escapes a violent death but is sufficiently compensated for her losses
through the arrival of new potential lovers.

Lubitsch's collaboration with Henny Porten, Germany's first real film
star, deserves at least a brief mention, for he took full advantage of her
comic and dramatic abilities. After the challenging double role of ugly and
pretty sister in *Kohlhiesel's Daughters*, Porten's work with Lubitsch was
crowned by her touching portrayal of Anna Boleyn in *Deception*. However,

[15] In the American version of *Montmarte*, Pola Negri and Alfred Abel are granted a happy
ending.
[16] Hans Müller, *Die Flamme* (Stuttgart: Cotta, 1920), 48.

as the embodiment of the asexual, maternal woman, Porten never played a central role in his erotic scenarios. Solidly built rather than slender, with two blond braids framing a rather plain face, Porten from early on worked with minimal makeup and concentrated more on her melodramatic acting style than her physical appearance. While this approach distinguished her favorably from the grand gestures, frozen poses, and suggestive stares cultivated by Negri and Jannings, it also made her less interesting to Lubitsch, for whom style always represented a quality in its own right.[17]

As Lubitsch's work with Oswalda and Negri shows, the links between specific genres (comedy, period film) and notions of femininity (Oswalda, Negri) point toward sexual difference as the central problem.[18] For that reason, the male characters required skillful casting as well. Again, two well-known actors came to personify the director's approach. As the romantic lead in countless popular comedies and melodramas, Harry Liedtke appealed especially to female audiences. His early films include Rudolf Biebrach's *Irrungen* (1919, "Mistakes"), with Henny Porten in the female lead, and Carl Boese's *Die Tänzerin Barberina* (1920, "The Dancer Barberina"), one of the many films about Frederick the Great. Lietdke's sympathetic appearance in the Lubitsch films inspires sexual as well as maternal impulses. Yet he essentially remains a supporting actor, an object of desire, rather than a worthy opponent, for his stronger female partners. The comedies, in spite of their stories of female domestication, are structured around the physical appeal of Ossi Oswalda who functions as the subject and the object of visual spectacle. By contrast, the period films are characterized by the overwhelming presence of Emil Jannings, who was one of the first actors to leave the stage for the screen. Jannings made his first screen appearance in *When Four Do the Same* and, a little later, played the part of Louis XV in *Passion*. After long negotiations, Lubitsch gave him the challenging role of Henry VIII in *Deception*, though it was originally written for the well-known character actor Eduard von Winterstein. In his work for Lubitsch, Jannings often expresses a vitality that is archetypal in its strength and intensity. Yet behind the subtle gestures that characterize his tyrants and madmen, more disturbing weaknesses of character—perversion, and even insanity—always lurk beneath the surface.

[17] On Lubitsch's work with Porten, see Helga Belach, *Henny Porten: Der erste deutsche Filmstar 1890–1960* (Berlin: Haude and Spener, 1986), esp. 65–69.

[18] The emphasis on sexual difference is also reflected in Lubitsch's choice of film titles. A survey would reveal the following categories: titles with women's names (*Madame Dubarry, Anna Boleyn, Lady Windermere's Fan, Ninotchka, Cluny Brown*), titles referring to women's social status or character traits (*Die Austernprinzessin, Die Puppe, Die Bergkatze, The Merry Widow, Angel, Bluebeard's Eighth Wife, That Lady in Ermine*), and titles that are more or less synonymous with sexual desire (*Rausch, Die Flamme, Forbidden Paradise, Trouble in Paradise, Desire, That Uncertain Feeling*).

Although Negri and Oswalda represent clearly defined female stereotypes, Lubitsch refrains from exploiting their typicality within the context
of the narrative. Since each actress dominates a particular genre, there is no
need for moralistic confrontations between the "good" and the "bad"
woman. Instead, both exist freely and independently in their respective
worlds. The melodramatic confrontations between Jannings and Negri are
doomed from the outset through the fatal association of death and desire.
By contrast, the counter-designs of modern love find a perfect expression
in the chance encounters between Oswalda and Liedtke. Obviously counting sexuality among the diversions rather than obsessions, the comedies
advocate an uncomplicated kind of eroticism that stands much closer to
the act of consumption than consummation. The problem of sexual difference is at once highlighted and denied through explicitly infantile scenarios; deliberate regression emerges as the new model for sexual and social
behavior. While regression is essential to the comic genre as a whole, Lubitsch carries its implications beyond the generic considerations and, in
memorable scenes of cinematic perfection, evokes the lost paradises of
childhood and the explosive force of utopian thought.

This subversive quality is most evident in his treatment of women characters. Behind the stereotypes and formulae probing the limits of their own
credibility, the female protagonists are allowed to be one signifier among
many and, in a few rare moments, to be many themselves. No longer the
primary objects of exchange, they join the world of images and objects and,
given the equalizing spectatorial regimes that prevail in the early Lubitsch
films, they become their own subjects in an economy of looks that is no
longer exclusively tied to sexual difference. In its place, a more undifferentiated eroticism develops. Without doubt, Lubitsch's use of women as
narrative agents conforms with the requirements of the respective genres.
But each film also grants the women an excess of representation that is
conceivable only in the context of a pronounced antihumanism. This systematic dismantling of humanist values like identity, authenticity, and self-
determination amounts to a radical questioning of the masculinist ideals
that govern the human equation. The beautiful women on the screen may
have to compete with the equally appealing world of consumer goods but,
as the quintessential consumers, they also have privileged access to these
objects.

Furthermore, it is through the conscious play with formal elements,
through what is frequently referred to as style, that the films' deceptively
smooth surfaces turn into treacherous mirages. This quality surfaces above
all in the preoccupation with eroticism and the great power attributed to
the look. However, it would be misleading simply to equate stylization
with eroticism; that would mean subordinating the stylistic interventions
to the mere exigencies of plot construction and character development. A

different approach is called for, an exploration of the critical—indeed, the theoretical—potential of eroticism. To begin with, eroticism and hermeneutics are ruled by a similar drive economy. Freud has pointed out that all curiosity is based on the investigation of sexual difference. The quest for the object of desire and for the more abstract object of knowledge are both set into motion by a perception of lack, a condition of need, that from then on influences all configurations between reality and its available interpretations. Sexual desire in this context simply provides the most powerful motivation for interpretive acts. It offers an appropriate means for tracing the daring convergences of desire and interpretation. Given its intellectual nature, eroticism in the early Lubitsch films functions as a demonstration object for the laws of interpretation as such. The resultant displacement of eroticism into cinematic space—or, to phrase it differently, the eroticizing of the material world rendered visible by the camera—establishes desire as the fulcrum of all narrative and visual strategies. Here eroticism reaches its full meaning, liberating the imagination but also reentering the endless chain of deferrals that constitute all signification processes. Stylization becomes the primary mode of expression.

Three elements constitute these erotic scenarios: the look, consumption, and dance. The look makes possible the beginning of seduction. It indicates the direction of desire, names its aim. It is usually a look that marks the story's beginning and, in a more disquieting way, also predetermines its ending. Rarely is there full closure; the last shots often suggest that a new and equally interesting story is about to begin once the screen turns dark. In a world ruled by looking, a world moreover where the medium, silent film, already bears witness to the look's omnipresence, meaning originates in the relationship between the moving image and the (physically) passive spectator. Indirectly referring to this condition, Pola Negri, at the end of *Forbidden Paradise*, inspects a new, prospective lover. Her pensive "Not bad—not good—but not bad" can be seen as mimicking the spectator's own position between skepticism and optimism, distrust and belief. However, as Lubitsch shows, such moments call for the presence of a third person in order to become meaningful. This explains the need for the voyeur, the camera, the spectator. While the third person usually participates in the scene through absence, it is precisely this experience of separation that draws attention to its parameters.

The image of someone peeking through a keyhole represents one of the primal scenes of cinema.[19] Doors, curtains, screens, closets, and corners, depending on the exigencies of set design, the variations seem unlimited.

[19] On its implications for female spectatorship, see Judith Mayne, "The Woman at the Keyhole: Women's Cinema and Feminist Criticism," *New German Critique* 24 (Spring 1982): 27–43.

However, all constellations inevitably force the onlooker to accept the loss of true presence. Here Lubitsch's obsession with closed doors, and with situations of exclusion in general, may very well be founded on personal experience. In this sense, the closed doors stand for a social problematic, namely the awareness of one's otherness in view of the social and cultural norms. Social marginalization creates a longing for participation and integration that finds expression in the pitiful or ridiculous figure of the voyeur, but it also extends to the disenfranchised groups in the motion-picture theater. Their voyeurism is motivated both by erotic and social desires. Even the problem of anti-Semitism returns to the surface in its scenarios of exclusion, as Grafe has astutely noted. With such implications, social experience provides the basis for the development of specific stylistic means. That is how doors and similar objects of exclusion become Lubitsch's favorite metaphors of cinematic representation. The ubiquitous props prevent direct access to the scene of action but, through the many open keyholes and faulty curtains, also enable the outsider to overcome the trauma of exclusion. Mirroring the experience of watching a film, he functions as a kind of stand-in for the spectator for whom the frame lines mark the boundary between the visible and the invisible. Victor Janson, Adolphe Menjou, and Edward Everett Horton, these quintessential Lubitsch voyeurs of the teens, twenties, and thirties, challenge time and again the parameters of this order but always fail to introduce another perspective. Like the spectators in the theaters, they never are and, in fact, never can be admitted into the center of the narrative. However, their presence at the margins helps to neutralize the disturbances produced by the play with presence and absence and makes the experience of exclusion a source of humorous self-recognition.[20]

Whenever the look of the third is obstructed, he or she seeks refuge elsewhere and finds a substitute in mediations, for instance in mirrors and photographs. The Egyptian ex-slave girl Ma (Pola Negri) of *The Eyes of the Mummy* experiences the dangers of reflection, literally as well as figuratively speaking, as she looks into a mirror and meets the piercing stare of Radu (Emil Jannings), her old master. Their mediated encounter foreshadows the film's dramatic climax when Radu stabs Ma in the same room (fig. 3). In *Passion*, Count DuBarry unknowingly interrupts a tête-à-tête between Don Diego and Jeanne (Pola Negri), the attractive young milliner and future Madame DuBarry. While the woman's body is still hidden from view through a fire screen, her head has appeared twice in the frame: peeking over the screen and as a reflection in the opposite mirror. Drawn into this world of mirror relations, DuBarry literally invades the exchange of blown

---

[20] On the door motif, compare Barthélemy Amengual, "Il faut qu'une porte soit ouverte et/ ou fermée," *Positif* 292 (June 1985): 4–12.

3. *The Eyes of the Mummy*: Pola Negri and Emil Jannings

kisses between Jeanne and her lover, and by taking over the mirror image—
he establishes eye contact—makes the whole woman his own (fig. 4).

As soon as these fleeting impressions are arrested by means of photography or painting, however, representation begins to develop its own dynamic. The portraits not only represent the desired object in its absence, as
seen by Rischka's reaction to the photograph of Alexis in *The Mountain
Cat*. They also compete with the absent referent, often replacing it in a
fetishistic manner. The implications of this process are spelled out in Radu's destruction of Ma's portrait in *The Eyes of the Mummy*.[21] At times, the
second-order images give rise to tensions, rivalries, and even reversals between what might be called the discourses of the original and the substitute. Other directors would have staged this opposition with tragic overtones, but Lubitsch decides to challenge, rather than affirm, its underlying
assumptions. By emphasizing the substitutions, he undermines the character's sentimental attachment to the original and questions its privileged
status as the sole manifestation of authenticity and truth. In the place of
the original, appearance emerges as a higher form of reality, a reality freed
of false hierarchies and therefore free to strive toward a more perfect form.
The liberating effect of these reversals can be studied in *Kohlhiesel's Daugh-*

4. *Passion*: Pola Negri, Magnus Stifter, Eduard von Winterstein

[21] Examples from Lubitsch's later films include the family portraits in *Three Women*, Lenin's
photograph in *Ninotchka* and, as a vicious attack on modernist art, Alexander Sebastian's
pseudo-surrealist painting in *That Uncertain Feeling*.

ters. The ugly daughter, Gretel, herself a rather dubious image of identity given Henny Porten's double role, wants to buy a pin. She asks the peddler whether the pin is made of real gold, whereupon he exclaims: "Are you crazy! This is genuine rolled gold." Gretel still believes in precious materials and their real value, whereas the peddler, as the representative of a profession based on persuasion and deception, praises the beauty of a good imitation. In that regard, this scene offers much more than a sly comment on modern marketing strategies. By undermining the traditional categories of value, the verbal exchange between seller and buyer gives rise to a more adequate definition of the real—namely as a function of desire. Later Gretel turns to her dowry chest, lifts the heavy top, opens box upon box only to finally retrieve her new fake pin from the much more valuable receptacle. The play with appearances and effects, the scene suggests, determines the libidinal relationship to consumer goods. An emotional investment has been made in the promise of beauty rather than in a specific value, in this case the value of gold. The resultant reassessment of what constitutes meaning affects not only the characters but also the films themselves.

The opposite could be said about the body, which never gives up the belief in truth. That is why the many dance sequences in the Lubitsch films tend to resolve the same conflict between appearance and reality very differently. "There is more danger in dancing than in dinner" reads an intertitle in *The Marriage Circle* (fig. 5). Dance introduces the possibility of erotic fulfillment as well as narrative suspension. Country fairs, elegant parties, and spectacular costume balls provide the settings, and fox-trots, Charlestons, polkas, waltzes, and polonaises provide the forms. Thus anchored in the narrative and the mise-en-scène, dancing provides a welcome opportunity for legitimate transgressions. A crucial scene from *The Eyes of the Mummy* may clarify this point. During her official introduction into London society, Ma suddenly hears a musical tune, quickly changes into an oriental costume, and begins to perform a lascivious belly dance. The members of high society react with consternation. Only a theater impresario responds adequately: "The girl is made for vaudeville," he exclaims, thus lending the voice of the expert both to Lubitsch and his audiences. Upon Ma's hesitant "What am I supposed to do there?" he replies, even more enthusiastically, with a threefold "Dance, dance, dance!" With Lubitsch, one is only alive when dancing. But instead of reserving the pleasures of dance for the romantic couple, his German films stage wild mass festivities, reminiscent of the Bacchanalia and Saturnalia, thereby also celebrating a corporeality that annihilates the boundaries of class and social decorum.

Ostensibly set against the pleasures of looking and dancing, consumer goods enter the scenes of seduction on their own behalf. Most importantly, they distract the gaze from the human object of desire. Culinary pleasures,

5. *The Marriage Circle*

they claim, can be just as satisfying. For instance, *Kohlhiesel's Daughters* introduces food as a signifier of abundance and a crucial asset in the trading of favors between characters. Even the unhappy marriage between the ugly Gretel and her husband, Peter, turns into romance once he has convinced himself of her excellent cooking skills. Such strong emphasis on bodily pleasures prepares the ground for more sarcastic comments. In *Romeo and Juliet in the Snow*, the village judge uses the scales of Justice to weigh two sausages against each other, the bribes offered to him by the two fighting parties, the Montekuglers and Capulethofers. Since the sausages are equally delicious, the judge orders a settlement and, with visible pleasure, devours both of them. Sometimes, the hierarchies between food and sexuality are completely reversed. Then the substitute takes hold of the systems of exchange, and the stomach triumphs over the claims of love. When Gretel's rejected suitor in *Kohlhiesel's Daughters* chews on a sausage and forgets the cause of his unhappiness, eating can no longer be reduced to its compensatory functions. It simply represents a more infantile form of bodily satisfaction. Not surprisingly, characters complain more than once "I am so sick to my stomach!" because they had too much to eat or drink. To satisfy all senses, literally to devour everything within reach—this wish may have been inspired, to a large degree, by the experience of lack that was part of everyday life in the late teens but, as a formal principle, it survived that particular historical juncture in order to uphold the promise of a more complete plenitude.

With its modern urban atmosphere, *Das fidele Gefängnis* (1917, "The Merry Jail") becomes the first Lubitsch comedy to explore the relationship between consumption and eroticism through more subtle means, thereby also initiating the transition from ethnic to sophisticated comedy. Based on the Johann Strauss operetta *Die Fledermaus*, the film's story anticipates the marital complications of the American comedies, especially of *So This Is Paris* (1926). Paris is still Berlin, and problems are still resolved with the down-to-earth pragmatism that characterizes the Prussian capital, but all the basic ingredients of the sophisticated comedy are already firmly in place. The film's upper-class setting virtually calls for characters like Alex von Reizenstein (Harry Liedtke), the philandering husband, and his flirtatious wife Alice (Kitty Dewall). Their sophistication, in turn, calls for a more restrained approach to the conflict between sexual desire and social convention. The emotional anarchy of the early comedies gradually makes room for psychological manipulation as well as a distinctly modern egotism. For instance, *The Merry Jail* and *So This Is Paris* both contain scenes in which the characters debate the advantages and disadvantages of adultery. In the 1917 version, the rendezvous between Alice and her secret admirer Egon Storch (Erich Schönfelder) is disrupted by the appearance of a police officer who has a warrant for her husband's arrest, charging him with being a public nuisance. In order not to compromise Alice, the man poses as her husband, thus accepting the undeserved imprisonment but also enjoying the sweet kisses of a fake marital farewell scene. In contrast to *So This Is Paris*, the earlier version still grants the rival a pleasant jail experience. Rather than having him join a chain gang, *The Merry Jail* allows him to play the role of a dangerous trickster admired by the other inmates and the good-hearted jailer (the famous part of Frosch, played here by Emil Jannings). In an ending that seems surprisingly indifferent to questions of morality, all protagonists are rewarded for their actions, though not necessarily with their first choice of persons, possessions, or circumstances.

Substitution may be regarded as the central principle that, across the boundaries of plots, themes, and characters, left a mark on all German Lubitsch films made after 1919. After the "primitive" anarchy of his earlier films, a more theoretical investigation of the system of equivalents and the conditions of exchange had to take place if the films were to maintain their subversive thrust. Consequently, Lubitsch turned to stylization and irony, from then on using them as means of resistance against the increasing standardization in the cinema. Indicative of these rules, *The Merry Jail* portrays a philandering husband who promises his wife a new hat in order to ease his bad conscience. His equation of guilt and appeasement collapses as soon as his wife enters the hat salon and makes the acquaintance of her new admirer. With her gains both material and emotional, Alice is overcome by joy—a reaction that the camera documents through alternating close-ups of the new hat, the new man, and, time and again, the woman's beaming face.

According to Lubitsch, the petty bourgeois, such plenitude can only be achieved in the private sphere, the world of love and desire. Here the outside world disappears before the arranged surplus of the beautiful interiors, here the stage is set for another economy of desire. Consequently, the bourgeois salon, the elegant store, the intimate club, and the festive ballroom become Lubitsch's favorite settings. Their sumptuousness finds an equivalent in the ultramodern fashions worn by the main protagonists. By contrast, the public sphere exists primarily to facilitate the passage from one rendezvous to the next, from one private amusement to another. The comic heroes only enter the street when they pursue unknown ladies or stagger home at dawn. Lubitsch's preference for upper-class settings and the marks of privilege, however, must not be interpreted as an apology of class difference. The rich and privileged merely provide him with the "working materials" for highly stylized scenarios of desire: the elegant rooms, the precious objects, the beautiful robes, but also the immaculate manners and the acute awareness of social conventions. In that regard, the salons show consumer capitalism at its most seductive—a capitalism that allows both for the ultimate fetishizing of its products and their simultaneous destruction in a potlatch of sensuality.

Comedies like *When Four Do the Same*, *The Merry Jail*, and *The Oyster Princess* marked an important phase in Lubitsch's rise as a filmmaker with international ambitions. Having reached the height of his German career and having developed a unique filmic style, Lubitsch was ready for a change, and the American film industry seemed to offer new, exciting opportunities. Because of the critical success of German art films in the United States, Famous Players Lasky had already expressed an interest in collaborating with German film studios. Since the Germans were interested in gaining access to the international market, first negotiations resulted in the 1921 EFA (Europäische Film-Allianz) agreement. During that time, Lubitsch considered several possibilities, including another extended contract with Paul Davidson. He also reassured audiences of his commitment to German film culture: "I shall always retain what I consider typically German: the careful composition and logical structure of the scenario and the special nature of our dramatic arts."[22] Looking for new contacts

[22] Lubitsch, "Der deutsche Film in 1921: Neue Aufgaben der Produktion," *Der Film* 2, no. 8 (January 1921): 25. As proof of his early interest in organizational issues, Lubitsch wrote

abroad, Lubitsch first traveled to New York in December of 1921 to attend the American premiere of *The Loves of Pharaoh*, an EFA production, but, unexpectedly, canceled all further plans and returned home to direct *Montmartre*. Once the EFA project had been abandoned, Famous Lasky Players decided to import new talent rather than renegotiate and, therefore, renewed their offer. Lubitsch left for America in mid-December 1922, initially for a short working stay and not, as it turned out, for good.

With his departure, the German cinema lost one of its most innovative and successful directors. The development of a specifically German tradition in film comedy was arrested, if not altogether prevented. Reinhold Schünzel, who is known best for *Viktor und Viktoria* (1933, "Victor and Victoria"), continued to explore the theme of sexual ambivalence throughout the twenties.[23] Ludwig Berger's Scribe adaptation *Ein Glas Wasser* (1923, "A Glass of Water"), as well as his silent version of the Oscar Straus operetta, *Ein Walzertraum* (1925, "A Waltz Dream"), stood out through an almost atypical lightness and gaiety. But like Lubitsch, Berger and Schünzel eventually left for Hollywood: the one following an invitation by Paramount, the other forced into exile by the Nazis. Only Carl Froelich, one of the most prolific Ufa directors and producers of the twenties, was opportunistic enough to experience no difficulties in moving back and forth between formulaic comedies and nationalist epics. The early Froelich is remembered primarily for his work with Henny Porten (e.g., *Kammermusik* [1925, "Chamber Music"], *Meine Tante, deine Tante* [1927, "My Aunt, Your Aunt"]); he continued to produce escapist entertainment throughout the thirties.

---

several articles on film production and distribution, including "Deutsche Filme und die Welt," *Film-Kurier* 155, 5 June 1921 and "Film-Internationalität," in *Das deutsche Lichtbildbuch: Filmprobleme von gestern und heute*, ed. Heinrich Pfeiffer (Berlin: Scherl, n.d.). For an interview given during his first American trip, see Herbert Hove, "The Film Wizard of Europe," *Photoplay Magazine* 23, no. 1 (December 1922): 28–29 and 98–99, reprinted in *Spellbound in Darkness: A History of the Silent Film*, ed. George C. Pratt (Greenwich, Ct.: New York Graphic Society, 1973), 310–14.

[23] On Schünzel and Lubitsch, see Thomas Brandlmeier, "Der Regisseur," in *Reinhold Schünzel: Schauspieler und Regisseur*, ed. Jörg Schöning (Munich: edition text + kritik, 1989), 25–26.

Three

Hollywood—The Silent Films,
1923–1929

WHEN Lubitsch arrived in Hollywood, his prospects for success could not have been better, given the enthusiastic reception of *Passion* and *Deception*. His own attitude was equally positive, as is evidenced by the many references to things American in his German comedies. Commenting on Lubitsch's willingness to adapt to the existing mode of production in Berlin and Hollywood, Jean Domarchi notes: "In his two last films Lubitsch directly addressed America. He offered his services." Highlighting the ideological implications of such market orientation, Domarchi concludes: "Lubitsch's American oeuvre is an illustration of the benefits of artistic Taylorization."[1] The Hollywood studios, on the other hand, were more than eager to attract European film talent and profit from the craftsmanship of German filmmakers, though they were also aware that foreignness could cause anxieties and, in the case of Germany, political resentment. In 1921, *The Golem* and *The Loves of Pharaoh* ran for more than eight weeks in New York's famous Criterion Theater. In the same year, Lubitsch made the Top Ten List of the National Board of Review with two films, *Deception* and *One Arabian Night*. "If you say this picture's no good I'll put on a beard and say it was made in Germany. Then you'll call it art"; this mocking inter-title from Will Rogers's *The Roping Fool* (1921) captured the general atmosphere. The underlying ambivalence is evident in Peter Milne's suggestion to sell an unknown American film under the German label and the name of Lubitsch and his subsequent conclusion that Lubitsch "is an artist, potentially very great without a doubt, but not as mature as many of his sponsors would have us believe."[2]

Officially, Lubitsch had followed an invitation by "America's sweetheart," Mary Pickford, who wanted to move away from the "Little Mary" and "Pollyanna" roles and explore more mature parts. After lengthy discussions, Lubitsch and Pickford settled on *Rosita* (1923), with its title figure of a beautiful Spanish singer modeled on Negri in *Gypsy Blood*. Though well directed, the film turned out to be a flop, since Pickford's portrayal of a femme fatale met with the disapproval of her many devoted fans. Despite

---

[1] Jean Domarchi, "L'homme de partout," *Cahiers du cinéma* 198 (February 1968): 17.

[2] Peter Milne, *Motion Picture Directing. The Facts and the Theories of the Newest Art* (New York: Falk, 1922), 204.

these problems, *Rosita* illustrates Lubitsch's new motto, "Good-bye slapstick, hello nonchalance." Taking various generic elements from the German films and introducing them into the American cinema, the film bears witness to the process of adjustment and transformation. The confrontation between the passions (Rosita-Don Diego) of the period film and the calculated marriage arrangements (queen-king) of the sophisticated comedy finds a most appropriate expression in the differences between the two couples. Uncontrolled passion is increasingly associated with the lower classes. The queen and king, as the modern couple, still stand at the margins of the dramatic complications. But with their refined appearance, their impeccable manners, and, above all, their perfectly reasonable behavior, they already attract much of the camera's attention. The queen (Irene Rich), in fact, becomes one of the first Lubitsch heroines to pursue her love interests with subtlety, discretion, and intelligence. Witnessing a secret rendezvous between Rosita and the king from an opposite window, she simply takes out her pocket mirror to spy on them more effectively. Such behavior in a way anticipates the strategies soon to be applied by the majority of characters and, figuratively speaking, by the director as well. Open resistance disappears and makes room for more cunning schemes of empowerment and control. Instead of making a scene, the queen tolerates her philandering husband as long as the rules of social intercourse are observed. Opposing a tragic ending, she puts to use the instruments of reason and prevents the execution of Don Diego. Later she thwarts the king's plan of giving Rosita a pearl necklace by tacitly accepting it as her own. Establishing the basic conditions from which irony can arise, the queen seems omnipresent but, like the filmmaker, is only able to play this role because of her emotional detachment. Practicing tolerance and patience, using her knowledge of human weakness and foibles, stating her demands with subtle emphasis, she always knows, she always is already there—knowing that, in the end, she will be rewarded. In so doing, the queen personifies the pleasures of an ironical detachment founded on love.

Forbidden Paradise (1924), a period film in contemporary costume, comments on the transition from one national cinema to another through its irreverent play with different temporalities. The result is an unusual piece of cinematic mockery. Praised by Jacobs as "a source picture for a circle of young directors,"[3] *Forbidden Paradise* brilliantly parodies the genre of the

[3] Lewis Jacobs, *The Rise of the American Film: A Critical History* (New York: Teachers College, 1968), 357. On sophisticated comedy during the twenties, see William K. Everson, *American Silent Film* (New York: Oxford University Press, 1978), 268–69. Everson mentions Lubitsch's "sophisticated *frou frou*" but, as such terminology already implies, dismisses his films as too insignificant for further critical attention. For a historical survey of Lubitsch's silent American films, see also George C. Pratt, ed., *Spellbound in Darkness* (Greenwich, Ct.: New York Graphic Society, 1973), esp. 307–24.

period film by mixing different historical periods. Vaguely alluding to
Catherine the Great, the film presents a czarina whose external appearance,
from her bobbed hair to her sleek twenties silk dresses, is clearly modeled
on the American flapper (fig. 6). The spectacular, pseudo-oriental sets by
Hans Dreier exist side by side with modern paraphernalia like wrist-
watches, checkbooks, fast convertibles, and, not surprisingly, a distinctly
Freudian symbolism.[4] The deliberate conflation of past and present even
affects the visual representation of revolutions, the hidden specter of the
old period film. The planning of a military overthrow is made visible

6. *Forbidden Paradise*: Pola Negri

[4] For a close reading of central scenes, see Hadeline Trinon, "Les structures narratives à
partir de l'oeuvre d'Ernst Lubitsch," *Les Cahiers de la Cinémathèque* 20 (Summer 1976): 66–
73. Many critics have found Freudian symbolism in *Forbidden Paradise*, especially in the love
scene between Alexis and the lady-in-waiting. Their kiss is shot through its reflection in a
pond, whose smooth surface is invaded by a fish, symbolizing the more disquieting forces of
sexuality. Also note the tie scene in *Three Women*, which has been analyzed by Freud disciple
Hanns Sachs as an example of displacement in "Film Psychology: *Drei Frauen*, by Lubitsch,"
Close Up (November 1928): 14–15.

through the close-up of a wine cooler, as it quickly fills up with the corks of empty champagne bottles. Approaching the historical process from the "lower" side of its remnants and leftovers, Lubitsch uses this particular shot to repeat old reservations about the rhetoric of political idealism, but he also introduces a more contemporary, perhaps even cynical, touch. This becomes evident in a later confrontation between the insurgent officers and the chancellor (Adolphe Menjou) who, in tail coat and top hat, is also a character inspired by twenties fashions. Again, the events are depicted through a series of revealing close-ups. The general draws his rapier, Menjou reaches into his vest pocket, the general's hand stops in mid-action. The next close-up shows why: instead of a gun, Menjou had fetched his checkbook. Preventing a military overthrow through the writing of a check, *Forbidden Paradise* demonstrates to what degree social interactions and filmic techniques have become calculated as well as calculable.

After the release of *Rosita*, Warner Brothers approached Lubitsch and, following long negotiations, offered a four-year contract that guaranteed him complete artistic control, including the selection of stories, scenarists, actors, and—very unusual for that time—supervision of the editing process. Having been given such enormous privileges, Lubitsch adapted quickly to the studio system and, within four years, emerged as one of Hollywood's leading directors. At the same time, Warner Brothers, though not among the leading studios, built a reputation on relatively inexpensive comedies, drawing most of their profits from that unlikely trio referred to as "Ernst, John, and Rin Tin Tin—Warner Brothers' Unholy Three" (i.e., Lubitsch, John Barrymore, and Rin Tin Tin). The studio's contract actors were known for their natural, restrained acting style and included Adolphe Menjou, Monte Blue, Irene Rich, Florence Vidor, and Marie Prevost. Working repeatedly with these actors, Lubitsch directed five sophisticated comedies in a relatively short time: *The Marriage Circle* (1924), *Three Women* (1924), the lost *Kiss Me Again* (1925), *Lady Windermere's Fan* (1925), and *So This Is Paris* (1926). The films deal almost exclusively with extramarital affairs and love triangles. Lubitsch used them to introduce the sophisticated comedy, European style, to American audiences. Until that time, only Chaplin's *A Woman of Paris* (1923), a film Lubitsch greatly admired, had represented sexual relations in an equally uninhibited fashion.

Many American films of the twenties still operated within the framework of a distinctly nineteenth-century sensibility. Sexuality continued to be associated with sin and evil; the work of D. W. Griffith virtually embodies this tradition. However, a number of directors responded to the changes in society and offered daring insights into modern marriage and the new fun mentality. In his domestic dramas, Cecil B. DeMille portrayed emancipated, sexually liberated women characters who demanded their right to independence as well as the satisfaction of their sexual needs. Films like

Don't Change Your Husband (1919), *Forbidden Fruit* (1921), or *Adam's Rib* (1923) told stories of infidelity and indiscretion but also suggested the possibility of finding satisfaction in marriage. Whereas DeMille associated sexuality with fun and, given his luxurious interiors, with conspicuous consumption, Erich von Stroheim presented a much bleaker picture. Films like *Blind Husbands* (1919), *Foolish Wives* (1922), or *The Merry Widow* (1925) portrayed sexuality—like the lust for money or power—as an egotistical and frequently destructive force, a threat to the narrative equilibrium. In this situation the films of Lubitsch introduced a fresh perspective. He only needed to satisfy the demand for sophisticated entertainment while not offending prevailing standards of morality. The result was a highly codified visual style that left it to the spectators to discover the actual meaning behind the subtle innuendos and suggestive hints.

The newly founded Motion Picture Producers and Distributors Association (MPPDA), an instrument of moral self-censorship, increased the need for such visual strategies but, until the introduction of the stricter Production Code of 1934, also made them still possible. This existence of external restraints inspired a directorial personality like Lubitsch to experiment with new filmic techniques, to find more indirect ways of conveying ideas, and to make the spectator's imagination an integral part of the narrative; hence also the sparse use of inter-titles.[5] His famous temporal and spatial ellipses reached such perfection that he rarely encountered censorship problems. Clearly, then, the Hollywood studio system provided a framework in which Lubitsch could flourish, at times even challenging or changing its rules of propriety. While the process of economic concentration led to an increasing standardization in all areas of filmmaking, the cinema was still young enough to support and even encourage experimentation. This explains why the twenties were Hollywood's most productive decade. Lubitsch mastered this balancing act between idiosyncrasy and profitability with surprising ease, especially compared to other European directors. As Gregor and Patalas note: "Lubitsch was the only European director who could successfully prove himself in Hollywood. He was also the only director from the generation of the twenties who, while pursuing his artistic ambitions, complied with the demands of the marketplace without being forced into compromises."[6]

The problem of interpretation, the story of its gains and failures, and the ongoing struggle for critical mastery—these elements constitute Lubitsch's

[5] Mordaunt Hall gives the following numbers: 54 inter-titles in *The Marriage Circle*, 45 inter-titles in *Three Women*, as opposed to the 150 to 250 inter-titles in the average film. In "Mr. Lubitsch's Direction Outshines His Narrative," *New York Times*, 12 October 1924, reprinted in Pratt, ed., *Spellbound in Darkness*, 316–17.

[6] Ulrick Gregor and Enno Patalas, *Geschichte des Films*, vol. 1 (Reinbek: Rowohlt, 1980), 121.

work in the sophisticated comedy. In the films he directed for the Warner studio, its parameters are worked out to perfection. The genre provided the mold into which Lubitsch could pour the raw materials of that other story, the story of interpretation. The tight economy of filmic means and meaning may have been necessitated by the "limitations" of the silent cinema in which the image and the look rule tantamount. Lubitsch, however, took advantage of these restraints and carried the investigation of spectatorial relations far beyond all external requirements, thereby virtually depleting the heterogeneity of the image through his omnipresent figures of speech. With such devious moves the sophisticated comedy foregrounds its own conditions of production. Hidden behind the beautiful fashions and the decorative interior designs, the filmic means engage in a highly intellectual play with conflicting perspectives and interpretative strategies. Lubitsch's play with recurrent patterns and the strong emphasis on film as a construction actually facilitate the investigation of the rules of interpretation in the cinema. However, this project succeeds only because of a distinct separation between the story and the underlying discourse about the story's construction. Through strict generic conventions, a limited number of characters, highly stylized interiors, and the precise mapping of boundaries (including those of public morality and social convention), the sophisticated comedy provides, quite literally, the mise-en-scène in which the basic rules of interpretation can be identified and redefined. Moreover, the static and mobile aspects of framing and the tension between conflicting point-of-view shots supply the most powerful tools for carrying out this project.[7] Through frequent close-ups, shot/reverse-shot patterns, and extensive point-of-view cutting, a field of inquiry is set up in which the alternating positions of anticipation and verification—the basis of all interpretation—can be inscribed.

The way Lubitsch organizes the relations between shots invites a comparison to Eisenstein's notion of montage as conflict, even though montage for the latter means above all a conflict of ideas, not of perceptions.[8]

[7] For a formalist reading, see David Bordwell, *Narration in the Fiction Film* (Madison: University of Wisconsin Press, 1985), 178–86. Bordwell sees *Lady Windermere's Fan* as an example of classical narration and describes the Lubitsch style as the "law-abiding ingenuity of a certain director and the flexibility of the classical paradigm" (186). For a similar discussion of point-of-view cutting, see also Edward Branigan, "Formal Permutations of the Point-of-View Shot," *Screen* 16, no. 3 (Autumn 1975): 57–58.

[8] Compare Eisenstein's discussion of montage: "The strength of montage resides in this, that it includes in the creative process the emotions and mind of the spectator. The spectator is compelled to proceed along that same creative road that the author traveled in creating the image." In Sergei M. Eisenstein, "Word and Image," in *Film Sense*, trans. and ed. Jay Leyda (San Diego: Harcourt Brace Jovanovich, 1975), 32. On Lubitsch and Eisenstein, see also H. H. Wollenberg, "Two Masters: Ernst Lubitsch and Sergei M. Eisenstein," *Sight and Sound* 17, no. 65 (Spring 1948): 46–48.

Montage, in Eisenstein's definition, originates in the shot. With its endless possibilities of combination, the shot represents the basic cell in the production of new meaning. Like Eisenstein, Lubitsch uses montage as a discursive means through which to invite the spectator's active participation and define his own position as enunciator. But unlike Eisenstein, he limits himself to the exploration of human perception and interaction. With the problem of sexuality functioning as a heuristic device, the relationship between men and women becomes the main vehicle for visualizing interpretative strategies; hence also Lubitsch's different politics of montage.

The growing interest in films about modern love, marriage, and sexual relations was the main reason for the popularity of the sophisticated comedy. The release of *The Marriage Circle*, for instance, was noted by *Variety* as being "the first time any director has had the nerve to put a farce comedy on the screen,"[9] but it also prompted *Motion Picture World* to warn exhibitors that films like these "will not appeal to the conventional minded."[10] Lubitsch was hailed as someone who had special insights into the American psyche, as a reviewer of *Forbidden Paradise* noted: "Lubitsch has demonstrated that he has grasped the American psychology of entertainment . . . in which sex is always uppermost."[11] Presenting the films as the work of a foreigner with different moral standards, *Motion Picture World* was able to assure its readers that "at the same time they [the new comedies] don't in the least destroy our taste for the home product."[12] The superimposition of different cultural traditions indeed played a crucial part in the reception of the Lubitsch comedies. Once transplanted to America and adapted to the screen, even the most conventional boulevard plays from Paris (*Divorçons* [1880, *Lets Get a Divorce*] by Victorien Sardou and Emile de Najac, *Réveillon* [1872, *Midnight Supper*] by Henri Meilhac and Ludovic Halévy), Berlin and Munich (*Nur ein Traum* [*Only a Dream*] by Lothar Goldschmidt, pseudonym Schmidt), and Budapest (*The Czarina* by Lajos Biró and Melchior Lengyel) acquired new qualities. The critical assessment of this oscillation between formula and its ironic transformation, however, is often very difficult.[13] Be that as it may, the foreignness of the literary

[9] *Variety*, 7 February 1924.

[10] *Motion Picture World*, 16 February 1924. Arguing along similar lines, the National Board of Review warned: "not primarily for the young girl." In *Exceptional Photoplays* 4, nos. 3 and 4 (December and January 1924): 1.

[11] *Forbidden Paradise, Motion Picture World*, 19 November 1924.

[12] *Motion Picture World*, 20 April 1924.

[13] This problem continues to haunt the critical writing on Lubitsch. In the case of *So This Is Paris*, film historians waver between enthusiastic praise (Mast: "another brilliant style piece"), benevolence (Robinson: "an unjustly neglected film"), and scathing criticism (McVay: "in the manner of sub-Feydeau boulevard frivolity"). The quotes are taken from Gerald Mast, *The Comic Mind: Comedy and the Movies* (Indianapolis: Bobbs-Merrill, 1973), 215; David Rob-

sources made possible the presentation of daring subject matter and, at the same time, guaranteed its acceptance by mainstream audiences, namely under the label "European sophistication." Lubitsch only had to take advantage of the distancing effects provided by the genre itself (e.g., the European locales) and make them part of the adaptation process to the screen. In this project, Lubitsch profited greatly by the favorable reception of Hungarian plays on the New York stage. Several comedies by Ernest Vajda, who wrote most of the screenplays for the Lubitsch musicals, were performed in New York during the twenties, including *Grounds for Divorce* (1924) and *The Crown Prince* (1927). The *Czarina* by Biro and Lengyel premiered in 1922. While these plays were often little more than second-rate Molnar imitations, they undoubtedly contributed to an atmosphere in which light farces and comedies were appreciated by a growing audience.

The precise calculation of time and space is everything in the sophisticated comedies. It establishes the framework for the choreography of relationships. As a rule, the comedies with a circular structure (*The Marriage Circle, So This Is Paris*) focus on two married couples who, through an initial act of transgression, are thrown into a vertigo of desire, jealousy, and revenge. They also invariably end with a reaffirmation of bourgeois marriage; hence their conservative outlook, hence their claustrophobic atmosphere. Highly conventional in the treatment of characters, the "marriage circles" are set into motion through stereotypical figures like the "virtuous wife" and the "femme fatale" and, as their respective partners and antagonists, the "romantic hero" and the "cuckolded husband." Though marriage is depicted as an institution based on convention rather than romance, the films never really question its social and emotional necessity. The characters, for instance, hardly ever change; they only learn to accept their weaknesses in a more graceful manner. Many critics have emphasized this conciliatory and, in the final analysis, restorative side in Lubitsch's work, among them Gerald Mast who interprets the "marital much ado about nothing" as part of a profound learning experience: "But though original relationships are restored, the characters' experiences have led them somewhere. They have a greater understanding of their own fallibility. . . . The process they live through in a Lubitsch film, though circular, is also educational."[14]

Given the interchangeability of stories, settings, and characters, there is really little room, and actually no need, for such learning experiences. Even the strong emphasis on communication, instead of action, and romantic love, instead of aggression, cannot hide the fact that the narratives follow

inson, *Hollywood in the Twenties* (London: Methuen, 1973), 61; and Douglas McVay, "Lubitsch, The American Silent Films," *Focus on Film* 32 (April 1979): 32.

[14] Mast, *The Comic Mind*, 211.

a highly normative direction, moving from the *status quo* to the *status quo ante*. In contrast to the German comedies, whose linear structure is libidinal rather than oppressive, the American comedies are modeled on the figure of the closed circle. They take up the story of desire where most German comedies end, that is, after the formation of the heterosexual couple. But even as they recognize the negotiation of commitment and desire as an integral part of marriage, the American comedies virtually domesticate the vestiges of their own ambivalence by introducing the notion of legitimacy and by organizing it along the lines of gender. The degree to which female sexuality has to be repressed or branded as a kind of social aberration is evidenced by the sharp distinction between the respectable wife and the seductive "other woman." Male sexuality, on the other hand, finds a provisional outlet in extramarital affairs and habitual flirting. Given the fate of all moral double standards, its domination comes at the expense of a truly liberating, all-encompassing eroticism. Thus desire in the sophisticated comedy is doomed to end up as mere lechery.

As a new anthropocentric and, ultimately, male perspective takes hold of the mise-en-scène, the objects lose their autonomous status; they become mere props. *The Marriage Circle* bears witness to this gradual change in the order of things, for instance, when the success of a marriage becomes synonymous with the kind of attention the characters devote to objects associated with the body. These include clothes, accessories, and cosmetics but also food and drink. Accordingly, the film approaches the unhappy marriage between Professor Josef Stock (Adolphe Menjou) and his capricious wife Mitzi (Marie Prevost) through a closer look at their morning rituals. The sequence opens with a close-up of the professor's foot as it emerges from under the covers, introducing the first disturbing image: a sock with a large hole in it. This is followed by a silent struggle for control in which Mitzi takes his clothes from a chair and throws them onto the bed. The professor gets up and opens a drawer only to be confronted with three forlorn-looking collars. These suggestive point-of-view shots brand the woman, for the rest of the film, as the typically uncaring and selfish wife.[15] Now Mitzi turns to the chest of drawers, closes the drawer with the collars, and opens another one, with "her" point-of-view shot showing rows of neatly arranged silk stockings. She sits down on the bed to put on her stockings, but not before throwing his clothes back onto the chair. Patiently, the husband walks to the window and, checking his movements in a small mirror, begins to lather up for shaving. Again, Mitzi invades the frame, takes the mirror, and uses it to complete her hairdo. Confronted

---

[15] Aside from turning the architects of the original play into psychiatrists, Lubitsch and Kräly also portray Mitzi in a much more negative fashion. For instance, they added a scene in which she invades Franz's medical office and stages a hysterical attack, complete with broken vases.

with such blatant egotism, the professor smiles—it is the smile of male supremacy—and returns to bed, hiding his head under a pillow to escape further accusations of laziness. As soon as she exits, he gets up and, with a sigh of relief, walks to an exercise machine to begin his morning calisthenics.

The morning sequence of *The Marriage Circle* is noteworthy for two reasons. It is structured around the assumed identity of camera position and (male) point-of-view and, because of that, serves to legitimate the woman's exclusion from the site of meaning production. As is demonstrated by Lubitsch's use of point-of view shots, the eyeline matches, and the shot/reverse-shot patterns, the techniques associated with the classical narrative cinema pave the way for an increasingly misogynist attitude. Menjou's amused behavior in *The Marriage Circle* can be seen as an invitation to the spectator, here clearly posited as male, to identify with his gentlemanly tolerance of woman's otherness. It reaffirms, from a position of male superiority, her primary function as the object of the look. The implications are spelled out in the almost didactic exercise on repetition and opposition: twice the drawers, twice the pile of clothes, twice the mirror. By moving back and forth between the "here" and the "there," the sequence plays with positions of lack and fullness that, in psychoanalytic terms, might even be thought of as a reenactment of the threat of castration; note the holey socks and the empty drawers. And just as the "castrating woman" is held responsible for the problems in this male-female relationship, she also comes to represent the ruptures and threats associated with the early, the spectacular, the experimental cinema—in short, with the "other" forms of cinematic representation.

A closer look at the "positive" sequence confirms this assertion. The handsome psychiatrist, Franz Braun (Monte Blue), and his gullible wife, Charlotte (Florence Vidor), perform their morning rituals with love and devotion. Portraying what Charlotte describes as a marriage of "perfect happiness," the camera quickly turns away from the objects of daily use to concentrate on the characters themselves. Close-ups of a breakfast egg and a cup of coffee are followed by close-ups of two hands. When the man's hand cracks open the egg and the woman's hand stirs the coffee, the traditional separation of labor between the sexes surfaces even in such seemingly innocent gestures as these. Suddenly his hand disappears, hers follows suit, the dishes are pushed aside, obviously making room for other, more satisfying activities. In both sequences, Lubitsch uses objects to comment on the two marriages presented in the film. However, only the unhappy marriage is characterized through an almost pathetic emphasis on possessions as a means of power and control. This traditional use of metaphor demonstrates more than anything to what degree the classical Hollywood cinema, including that of Lubitsch, subsumes all images under an anthropocentric order, thereby reducing them to mere reflections of the individual who stands at the center of the narrative. The result is an overall impoverishment of the visual field.

As the filmic metaphors relinquish their raison d'être—that is, the defense of eroticism against the onslaught of morality—they lose their liberating effect on the spectator. The introduction of moral double standards coincides with a growing stylistic ossification, a virtuoso display of formal means without inner motivation. Metaphors become an accessory to sentimental moods and clichés, as is the case in *The Student Prince* (1927). In this MGM film Lubitsch uses photographs and, above all, different kinds of hats to introduce the title figure Karl Heinrich (Ramon Novarro), the crown prince of a small German principality and to tell his story. The famous hat sequence at the beginning presents solemnly dressed men as they lift their hats and pay tribute to the present grand duke. The sequence opens with the close-up of a top hat and, with every dissolve, moves further and further away until the camera reaches an aerial position from which the hats look like an abstract ornament. The arrangement is repeated when Karl Heinrich returns from Heidelberg to assume the official duties of his ailing uncle. But now it is umbrellas, not hats, that are being lowered in identical gestures of respect—proof of the tragic circumstances of his return. Under these circumstances, Karl Heinrich's fraternity cap comes to represent the other world, the world of camaraderie, romance, and *Gemüt-lichkeit* associated with Heidelberg. The cap accompanies the prince on harmless pranks with other fraternity members, and it bears witness to his growing romantic involvement with Käthi (Norma Shearer), the innkeeper's niece. When Karl Heinrich is forced to leave this world behind, it is through the packing away of fraternity cap, fraternity sash, and Käthi's photograph that he accepts the responsibility. Back in the loneliness of the palace, Karl Heinrich hides the Heidelberg mementos in the royal desk, imagining, in a remarkable daydream sequence, his glorious yet impossible return to Heidelberg. As these examples indicate, the metaphors in *The Student Prince* fulfill affirmative functions within the narrative, as is evidenced by their participation in the staging of the love-versus-duty motif. In addition, they make the film seem old-fashioned. It may have been in awareness of this very crisis of metaphor that film historian Paul Rotha writes: "In reality, tearing aside the veil of glamour, Lubitsch's famous subtlety had degenerated into a lot of men taking off their hats at the same moment and the interplay of opening and shutting doors."[16]

Lubitsch's last silent films, just as the first American film, are somewhat uncharacteristic of his work in the twenties. In periods of transition he resorted to old formulas or chose ill-suited story material, as is evidenced

---

[16] Paul Rotha, *The Film Till Now*, rev. and enl. ed. (London: Vision, 1949), 180.

by *Eternal Love* (1929), a sentimental Swiss mountain drama without the usual innuendos. According to contemporary reviews, *The Patriot* (1928), based on Alfred Neumann's drama about the mad Czar Paul I, would fall into the category of unsuccessful repetitions, in this case of the German period film. Both films were shot as silent films but released with an added synchronized sound track. During this time, Lubitsch also returned to his native country for on-location shooting, first for *The Student Prince* and later for the antiwar film *The Man I Killed* (1931). He created nostalgic vignettes of a Germany that was as much a product of his imagination as the Paris of the sophisticated comedies. While it was clear that the United States had become his new home, other changes were imminent. Lubitsch decided to leave Warner Brothers before his contract expired, perhaps because of an overall feeling of artistic stagnation. Other changes were imminent, too. In 1928 he joined Paramount, the studio to which he had already been loaned out for *Forbidden Paradise*. Counting Stiller, von Stroheim, and von Sternberg among its leading directors, Paramount was then known as the most Continental among the Hollywood studios, emphasizing style and sophistication rather than the kind of monumentality typical of MGM. Beginning with *The Patriot* and spanning a period of eleven years, Lubitsch's work for Paramount comprises his most popular and most critically acclaimed films, including those commonly associated with the term "Lubitsch touch." The comedies of the early thirties, in particular, would influence filmmakers like George Cukor, as is evidenced by *Dinner at Eight* (1933) or *Holiday* (1938), and later generations of filmmakers. However, it did not bring the expected box-office returns. Lubitsch's short tenure as head of production between 1932 and 1936 even turned out to be a real financial loss for Paramount.[17] For the first time, stylistic perfection came to be associated with financial loss.

[17] In this function, Lubitsch supervised the production of Sternberg's *The Devil Is a Woman* (1935) and Borzage's *Desire* (1936), a film often falsely attributed to Lubitsch because of its similar style. In 1936, Lubitsch was replaced by William Le Baron but remained at Paramount as head of an independent production unit. He supervised, among others, the Claudette Colbert and Marlene Dietrich films. Economic and artistic considerations led to a termination of his contract in 1938.

Four

The American Sound Films,
1929–1932

LUBITSCH's interest in sound, and music in particular, reaches back to the German films and their spectacular dance sequences. What was then only suggested by the ecstatic movements of the dancers and the enthusiasm of musicians could now, in 1927, be expressed directly on the sound track. What then depended on the skills of piano accompanists or, for big productions like *The Oyster Princess* and *Passion*, the opening-nights orchestras could now become an integral part of every film. Therefore Lubitsch turned to the musical as that genre in which sound—including speech, music, and sound effects—could be treated with greatest freedom and imagination. By using the new medium as a way of exploring old interests in a new light, he encountered relatively few problems with the new technology. The same could be said about one of Lubitsch's contemporaries, the French director René Clair, who also used his experience in silent film for innovative sound experiments. Musical comedies like *Sous les toits de Paris* (1930, *Under the Roofs of Paris*) or *Le Million* (1932, *The Million*) bear witness to the unfailing sense of space and time with which Clair staged musical numbers and organized auditory space; his work might very well have had an influence on Lubitsch.[1] Over the following years, Lubitsch directed a number of musicals that were all relatively successful: *The Love Parade* (1929), *Monte Carlo* (1930), *The Smiling Lieutenant* (1931), *One Hour With You* (1932), and the classic *The Merry Widow* (1934). He also contributed three episodes to the all-star revue *Paramount on Parade* (1930). The Lubitsch musicals were often shot in a silent and a sound version. Later, different foreign-language versions were added, a common practice that made *The Merry Widow*, with its four versions, one of MGM's most expensive productions of all times. Given these favorable circumstances, it came as no surprise that Lubitsch was again included in *Film Daily*'s Fifth List of the Ten Best Directors of 1930, an honor that had already been granted to him in previous years.

The Lubitsch musicals stand closer to the European operetta than to the American film or Broadway musical. They could perhaps be characterized,

[1] On Lubitsch and Clair, see Mario Verdone, *Ernst Lubitsch* (Lyon: Serdoc, 1964), 23–27.

in the words of Rick Altman, as a sub-genre of the fairy-tale musical.[2] With the charm, coziness, and quiet melancholia of the Austro-Hungarian Empire as an omnipresent referent, the stories and themes are firmly rooted in turn-of-the-century culture. Not surprisingly, Lubitsch and Hungarian-born scenarist Ernest Vajda found most of their literary sources among works from the European boulevard theater and operetta: *The Love Parade* is a free adaptation of Léon Xanrof and Jules Chancel's play *Le prince consort* (1919, "The Prince Consort"); *Monte Carlo* a combination of the Hans Müller play *Die blaue Küste* (1914, "The Blue Coast") and the operetta *Monsieur Beaucaire* (1901); *The Smiling Lieutenant* is based on Müller's novel *Buch der Abenteuer* (1905, *Book of Adventures*); and *One Hour with You* inspired by the Lothar Schmidt comedy *Nur ein Traum* (1909, *Only a Dream*). Vajda's screenplays for Lubitsch contain such standard ingredients as spectacular palaces, impoverished nobility, scheming servants, smashing young officers in shining uniforms, grand ballrooms, champagne and waltzes, endless nights and sobering mornings, flirtatious maids, sentimental heroines, charming adulterers, and so forth. Again formula gives way to self-reflexivity. By turning to operetta at the point of its decline, Lubitsch—in the words of Roberto Paolella, the "director of a time gone-by"[3]—was able to use its generic elements in an almost ironical, parodistic fashion. Thus the stories of mistaken identity and love between the classes became vehicles for probing the old opposition of appearance and reality. And the theatrical settings provided the appropriate backdrop against which the calculated effects of cinema could be played out.

The influence of Viennese operetta is also present in the choice of songs, and the use of music in general. Characterized by a strong emphasis on simple, sentimental melodies, the Viennese operetta has its origins in the nineteenth-century boulevard theater. With comedians or bar singers rather than schooled operatic singers cast in the principal roles, it catered, from its inception, to popular tastes in music; hence the obligatory military march, the sentimental duets, and the many waltzes. In contrast to the classical Hollywood musical, dancing remains the privilege of individuals; there are few spectacular dance numbers in the operetta, except for the finales. As for the kind of musical influences, composers like Sigmund Romberg (1903, *The Student Prince*), Oscar Straus (1907, "A Waltz Dream"), and Franz Lehár (1905, *The Merry Widow*) proved very important; even the silent *The Oyster Princess* takes its inspiration from a popular operetta, Leo Fall's *Die Dollarprinzessin* (1907, *The Dollar Princess*). The

---

[2] For a close reading of *The Love Parade* and a very insightful definition of the Lubitsch musical, see Rick Altman, *The American Musical* (Bloomington: Indiana University Press, 1987), esp. 129–58.

[3] See Roberto Paolella, "Ernst Lubitsch, regista del tempo perduto," *Bianco e Nero* 19, no. 1 (January 1958): 1–19.

musicals with an original musical score, too, have a distinctly Viennese
flair, either because of their setting (*The Love Parade*) or their literary
sources. For instance, Hans Müller himself wrote several original librettos
for operettas, including Ralph Benatzky's *Casanova* (1928) and Erik Cha-
rell's *Im weißen Rössl* (1931, "At the White Horse").

Following in the tradition of the operetta, songs in the Lubitsch musical
function as an outlet for hidden or suppressed emotions. Solos and duets
predominate, and the songs contribute to, rather than disrupt, the flow of
the narrative. There is little need for the usual integrating devices (e.g., the
production of a show), a fact that, ironically, adds to the films' old-fashioned atmosphere. As a rule, singing in the American musical is as much
an expression of love for another character as a bearing of witness to the
protagonist's own desire for public recognition and self-fulfillment. The
many chorus numbers and the spectacular finales provide ample opportunity for staging these ambitions. By contrast, the Lubitsch musical uses the
public sphere as a backdrop for its exclusively private pursuits. The fulfillment of romantic love, it is implied, can only be achieved in the context of
social conformism. Where sexual difference is treated as such an absolute
category, sexist overtones are almost unavoidable. What needs to be taken
into account, however, is the distinction Lubitsch makes between the narrative and the process of narration. From their difference arises the possibility of other readings, including a more playful approach to sexual difference. Because of the rigid gender roles, the characters function almost like
ciphers. Their typicality provides the material for the daring innuendos and
risqué comments about love and desire, but it also makes possible the foregrounding of formal concerns. Thus in privileged moments the musicals
are able—as films—to overcome their generic limitations and focus on the
effects of cinema rather than on the problems of morality.

In terms of their spatial layout, the musicals move back and forth effortlessly between big cities like Paris or Vienna and imaginary Ruritanian
countries like Sylvania (*The Love Parade*), Flausenthurm (*The Smiling Lieutenant*), or Marshovia (*The Merry Widow*)—all of them countries that, as
The Merry Widow demonstrates, require a magnifying glass in order to be
found on ordinary maps. These escapes into an imaginary time and space
are facilitated, on the visual level, by the splendid interiors and extravagant
costumes. Taking advantage of the historical ambitions of the operetta and
the period film, Lubitsch uses the historical forms and styles to celebrate
the genre's inherent artificiality. His bon mot "But you know, I think, I
prefer Paris, Paramount, to Paris, France"[4] bears witness to a calculated
illusionism that, at worst, produces meaningless, artificial worlds but that,
at best, also turns them into a travesty of themselves. Under these condi-

---

[4] Roy Pickard, *The Hollywood Studios* (London: Tantivy, 1978), 444.

tions, the deceptive play with temporal and spatial dislocations actually helps to identify the emotions that constitute a disposition like nostalgia, including the nostalgia for rigid boundaries between the sexes and the classes.

The mixing of disparate elements—a crucial precondition for travesty—is most evident in Lubitsch's casting of singers, which reached perfection in his pairing of American soprano Jeanette MacDonald and French chansonnier Maurice Chevalier.[5] With sexual difference distributed along the lines of nationality, the leading ladies (Jeanette MacDonald, Miriam Hopkins) are modeled on the typical American woman who, at least from Lubitsch's European perspective, possesses traditional feminine virtues as well as a healthy pragmatism. Chevalier, on the other hand, embodies a specific brand of European masculinity that combines female traits (flirtatiousness, charm) with an almost didactical insistence on sexual difference. Their double existence as actors and performers, however, gives rise to two different kinds of opposition: between the operatic American singer and the popular European chansonnier, on the one side, and between the female aristocrat and the male commoner, on the other. Within these constellations, the woman, who is usually a member of the aristocracy, represents the sophistication, tradition, and sensuality of the Old World. The man, though often inferior in social status, personifies the freedom of choice associated with more democratic settings. Lubitsch uses these hackneyed clichés about male and female, American and European, in order to transform them in the most duplicitous ways. By combining different musical and literary traditions, by driving a wedge between the determinants of role-playing, acting, and singing, and by creating exotic settings for a distinctly modern audience, he draws an imaginary map of desire where gender roles, though firmly in place, still reveal the traces of their inherent artificiality.

Unlike the sophisticated comedies, the musicals focus on the increasingly complicated process of becoming a couple. And in contrast to the early German comedies, this process is no longer made difficult by class barriers, family strife, or tragicomical coincidences. The male-female relationship itself becomes a problem, with solutions inextricably tied to woman's domestication. Strong and independent women (Queen Louise in *The Love Parade*, Princess Anna in *The Smiling Lieutenant*, the rich Sonia in *The Merry Widow*) set the narrative into motion by rejecting the idea of marriage (*The Love Parade*, *Monte Carlo*), by escaping to Paris and Monte Carlo, or by exhibiting typically male behavior. Jeanette MacDonald, for

---

[5] Because of contractual problems and personal tensions between the leading stars, Chevalier was cast opposite Miriam Hopkins in *The Smiling Lieutenant* and MacDonald opposite Buchanan in *Monte Carlo*. In both films, the European/American opposition is maintained, with the men again representing Old World charm and suaveness.

instance, instructs her new prince consort in *The Love Parade*: "But don't forget your nap. You must keep your strength." Once they fall in love, however, the women give up their independence. This moment of submission is often accompanied by gestures such as Countess Helene's tearful pledges in *Monte Carlo*, Princess Anna' s "Dress up your lingerie" motto in *The Smiling Lieutenant*, or Queen Louise's public bowing to "her king" at the ending of *The Love Parade*: "I am going with you. Wherever you go, I'll follow. You can't get rid of me."

As the films become increasingly misogynist, they also acquire a certain blatancy in sexual matters. The bedroom makes its splendid entry into the Lubitsch universe. Part of elegant white-on-white sets, the bed becomes the stage where the heroine awakes from her sweet dreams to deliver sweet, romantic love songs. In contrast to the German films which acknowledge their openly voyeuristic glances into the bedroom, the musicals establish an identity between camera and spectator through which the woman is turned into a spectacle and eroticism reduced to male sexuality. As a result, the male-female relationship depends exclusively on the question of sexual consummation. In *The Smiling Lieutenant*, for instance, the bed of Anna (Miriam Hopkins) and Niki (Maurice Chevalier) becomes an unmistakable indicator of marital happiness. Inspecting the nuptial bed before the wedding night, busy court marshals first place the pillows closer to each other and, after intense moments of thought, put one on top of the other. The failure of such planning is made visible in the following scene in which the frustrated daughter and her concerned father play a game of checkers on the same bed. The problem of the bed is finally solved when Niki proposes a game of checkers, but only to throw the board onto the bed and, after the camera has already turned away, to push it aside for their belated sexual union. Lubitsch's growing reliance on visual clichés, it seems, also requires their fleshing out in more risqué scenes—a calculation, however, that is bound to fail. Replacing one thing with another only functions when critical analysis and formal innovation rule this exchange.

Consequently, even the world of objects—once so powerful—becomes part of the shot/reverse-shot patterns that privilege the human perspective. Still a potential rival in the silent films, the objects are now reduced to auxiliary functions. No longer independent from or at least equal to the characters, they become a prop on the film set, a background filler and, at best, a meaningful extension of their owners. A famous example from a later musical, *The Merry Widow*, may illuminate this gradual process of devaluation. The film opens with Sonia (Jeanette MacDonald) expressing her secret longings in a touching rendition of "Vilia." Her musical confession is heard by Danilo (Maurice Chevalier) who, in a brilliant mockery of operatic conventions, does not even respond in person but asks his orderly, a talented tenor, to take over the song. Nevertheless, their brief musical encounter leaves a strong impression on Sonia. Her lust for life returns as she frantically fills the empty pages of her diary (sole entry: "nothing!"). From resignation to desire, from silence to expression—in the end, with her ink-well empty, Sonia decides: "There is a limit to every widow." The symbolism of the writing scene carries over into a series of revealing close-ups of Sonia's closet that contains black hats, black dresses, black corsets, black shoes—and a matching black lapdog. As a comment on her changed mood, the following dissolves strip each object of its original color and shower them with pure white, again including the color-coordinated dog.

Even the old rivalry between food and desire disappears in light of this new anthropocentrism and, occasionally, inspires rather crude innuendos. In *The Smiling Lieutenant*, Niki and Franzi (Claudette Colbert), the pretty violinist, meet in his apartment to play music together. First, she coyly rejects his breakfast invitation with the words "First tea. Then dinner. Then, maybe, breakfast." The next shot, however, shows them already at the breakfast table. Musical expressions, casual remarks, culinary pleasures, everything now assumes a subordinate function in relation to the myth of romantic love—a notion of love, however, that barely conceals its origins in prudishness and, as its underside, lechery. Consequently, even the permissive Franzi of *The Smiling Lieutenant* steps back in favor of Niki's virtuous wife, a generous gesture that is accompanied by the remark "Girls who start with breakfast don't usually stay for dinner." The similarities between such dubious wisdom and Sonia and Danilo's final declaration of love, then, show one more time what happens if "style," that mimicry of subversion, turns into formula—but without the formal ambitions. In this regard, Sonia's "any man who could waltz through life with hundreds of women and is willing to walk through life with one" and Danilo's reply "should be married" marks the end of Lubitsch's challenging play with the representation of eroticism and the eroticism of representation.

Once the objects have renounced their power, the unifying male gaze takes control of all spectatorial relations, thereby also constituting woman as the film's central spectacle. The objects no longer return the look and, consequently, lose their power of rupturing the narrative. In fact, even the direct stare into the camera seems doomed. This is most evident in the sound remake of *The Marriage Circle*, *One Hour With You* (1932) when André Bertier (Maurice Chevalier) addresses the film's (male) audience directly, asking them: "What would you do?" In that particular scene, he seeks advice on how to respond to the amorous advances of an unknown woman who later turns out to be his wife's best friend. The spectator receives a clear answer in the closing scene as André Bertier and his naive wife Colette (Jeanette MacDonald), having withstood all assaults on their marriage, turn toward the camera for a second time. Now they ask in unison "What would you do?" and decide to kiss.

Sometimes, however, the musicals allow for brief glimpses of irony and parody. Here Lubitsch imitates and makes fun of modern consumer society and, in so doing, comments on precisely those practices of ruthless appropriation that characterize the musicals themselves. The frequent references to advertisement serve to highlight the artificiality of all industrial productions, and of cinema in particular. This recognition stands behind the hilarious Americanisms in *The Love Parade*: the royal radio program ("And don't forget, ladies and gentlemen, this program comes to you by courtesy of the Sylvania Hardware Cooperation, the company that gives you two pots for the price of one"); Queen Louise's Hollywood-style reception for Prince Consort Alfred; and, of course, the American tourists on their European culture trips ("See Sylvania!"). As an advertisement come true, Chevalier's famous smile in *The Smiling Lieutenant* first leads to a state affair and later to a royal marriage. Exploited by the business world in the slogan "Famous Lieutenant Uses Kalodont Toothpaste Exclusively," Chevalier's smile, however, suffers a fate that is not dissimilar to that of the musicals themselves. Arguing in this vein, Kracauer criticizes the musicals for their superficial, trivial stories but only unwittingly to identify their subversive qualities as well: "Nothing against Lubitsch; he superbly mixes, like a second Reinhardt, the degenerated elements and thereby accommodates the wishes of bourgeois audiences in all civilized countries."[6] And he concludes in a later review: "They [the films] consist only of abstractions and share this impoverishment of content with other generalizations. They turn love into a flirt, an ideal figure into a star and reality into a shadow. The Lubitsch film has already reached rock bottom."[7] But this irreverent mixing of feudalism and capitalism, America and Europe, and history and modernity also represents one of the greatest strengths of the musicals.

Jacobs's claim, "The dangerous year for Hollywood, as it turned out, was not 1929, but 1933,"[8] is especially true for Lubitsch. The early thirties have often been described as a turning point in Lubitsch's career. Beginning with the Depression and the New Deal, his preoccupation with eroticism was increasingly regarded as un-American. Jacobs wrote: "Specializing, however, in the sophistication and realism of promiscuous sex relationships, a theme in keeping with the old post-war days, his most recent films do not show that he is keeping abreast with the swiftly changing times."[9] While film historians tend to emphasize the growing distance between the filmmaker and his audience, some public figures saw more evil

---

[6] Siegfried Kracauer, review of *The Smiling Lieutenant* (1931), *Kino. Essays Studien Glossen zum Film*, ed. Karsten Witte (Frankfurt am Main: Suhrkamp, 1974), 191.

[7] Kracauer, review of *One Hour With You* (1932), *Kino* 192.

[8] Lewis Jacobs, *The Rise of the American Film: A Critical History* (New York: Teachers College Press, 1968), 422.

[9] Jacobs, 361.

forces at work. European sophistication, and Lubitsch's films in particular, had to be regarded as a dangerous threat to public morality according to Martin Quigley, a leading figure in the struggle for stricter film censorship. Quigley explains: "Even in its comparatively refined status it [*Design for Living*] is an evil influence because it presents conduct on the part of attractive and likeable people which indicates denial and contempt of traditional moral standards, presenting, charmingly, wrong conduct as it if were right conduct."[10]

Trouble in Paradise (1932), Lubitsch's first nonmusical sound comedy, marks the end of a highly productive period that spanned two decades, included two national cinemas, the silent and the sound film, and involved very different conditions of production. While the New Deal provided film comedy with new story material, even making films more socially conscious (e.g., Capra's populist comedies), Lubitsch continued to direct sophisticated comedies that had well-constructed but predictable plots, that sparkled with witty dialogues, and that featured slightly cynical, well-mannered upper-class characters. However, their luxurious environments and their liberated eroticism no longer represented a provocation, neither in the disguise of ironic detachment nor as the promise of a more primeval bliss. Since the films repeated the old formulas without refining their ironic subtexts and their devious styles, they no longer needed the kind of audience participation that had been the basis of their successful functioning. As a result, they lost their uniqueness and gave up the difficult balancing act between subversion and conformism—perhaps for more socially conscious and humanistic films, but also for a more conventional involvement with cinema.

Lubitsch's revealing investigation of the gaze as the dominant form of perception in modern society, his subversive celebration of commodity fetishism, and the use of ironical detachment as a form of empowerment all

---

[10] Martin Quigley, "Decency in Motion Pictures" (1937), in *The Movies in Our Midst: Documents in the Cultural History of Film in America*, ed. Gerald Mast (Chicago: University of Chicago Press, 1982), 342–43. As a result of these changes, Lubitsch's strengths were suddenly perceived as weaknesses. In 1937, a reviewer of *Angel* still spoke of a creative crisis: "Ernst Lubitsch seems to have lost his touch or, at the very least, mislaid it, and in consequence, *Angel* stands at Paramount with folded wings" (*New York Times*, 4 November 1937). But in 1938, a reviewer of *Bluebeard's Eighth Wife* already noted: "In these days it's bad enough to have to admire millionaires in any circumstances; but a millionaire with a harem complex [Gary Cooper] can't help starting the bristles on the back of a sensitive neck" (*New York Times*, 24 March 1938). And in 1942, a reviewer of *To Be or Not to Be* exclaimed: "As it is, one has the strange feeling, that Mr. Lubitsch is a Nero, fiddling while Rome burns" (*New York Times*, 7 March 1942). Without doubt, Lubitsch's films still attracted audiences and they still received critical praise. But reviewers increasingly used the changed social and economic conditions to criticize his frivolous attitudes—a rather surprising argument, one might add, given the overwhelming escapism of the Hollywood film.

reach a turning point with *Trouble in Paradise*. While Lubitsch continued to make films, even remarkable ones like *Design for Living*, he increasingly tried to accommodate mainstream concerns and perspectives, sometimes with astonishing success. By denying his background in the silent cinema, by reformulating his erotic scenarios in the context of morality, and by abandoning ironic detachment for quiet melancholia, Lubitsch lost sight of the potential inherent in his artistic limitations and, in so doing, sabotaged his own achievements. Something else emerged, something that, at best, continued the old perfection in a more empathic style (*Ninotchka*) or, at worst, recycled old material (*That Uncertain Feeling*). If one wanted to join those speaking in favor of Lubitsch, the humanist, one might want to mention the first appearance of a Nazi in *Ninotchka*, an incident that could be interpreted as evidence of a growing sense of responsibility and commitment.[11] But these later years also belong to an entirely different paradigm of cinema and cinematic pleasures.

[11] There are, in fact, a significant number of political remarks in Lubitsch's later films, beginning with the discussion of America's foreign policy in *Desire* (Madeleine to Tom: "Tell me, Tom, what would America's attitude be if it really came to a crisis?"). This leads, only one year later, to the mention of international summits in *Angel* (Graham to Barker: "Well, it looks as if Europe is going to have peace—at least for the next three weeks"); *Ninotchka*'s desperate plea for peace in 1939 (Ninotchka: "Comrades! People of the world! The revolution is on the march. I know, bombs will fall, civilization will crumble. But not yet, please. Wait. What's the hurry? Give us our moment. Let's be happy."); the comical defeat of the Nazis by a troupe of actors in *To Be or Not to Be* (1942); and *Cluny Brown*'s belated call for arms in 1946 (Andrew to his father: "Father, you're sitting on a volcano! And battleships and tanks won't help you. Believe me, England won't be safe until we produce our own Belinskis.").

Part II _____

FILM ANALYSES

Five

Wayward Women: *The Oyster Princess,* *The Doll,* and *The Mountain Cat*

MEASURED against the standards established by the classical narrative cinema, many Lubitsch films from the late teens seem primitive, unrefined, indeed "flawed." With their naive characters, fairy-tale–like stories, and cardboard sets, they stand closer to late-nineteenth-century popular diversions like the curio show or panorama than to the "masterpieces" of the silent German cinema. Affinities to the transgressive style of the cabaret and the commedia dell'arte and the presence of strong female characters further contribute to this impression. While the so-called Expressionist films, with their uncanny atmosphere and highly stylized settings, received much critical attention, Lubitsch's early film comedies were for the most part dismissed as remainders of the cinema's primitive origins. The tragic circumstances of the male identity crisis, it seems, endowed Expressionist films with an air of respectability and importance that was not just lacking in the Lubitsch comedies but in fact inspired the most irreverent attacks on social roles and institutions.[1] In this regard, films like *Die Austernprinzessin* (1919, *The Oyster Princess*), *Die Puppe* (1919, *The Doll*), and *Die Bergkatze* (1921, *The Mountain Cat*) present a challenge to widespread notions about early German cinema, and Expressionist film in particular. Part of an equally powerful, but suppressed tradition, these films are punctuated by moments of visual excess that disrupt the narrative and replace the concern for continuity with sheer specularity. Lubitsch's authorial interventions draw attention to the artificial nature of cinema and utilize that self-reflexivity to explore the artificiality of other conventions as well. Moreover, the casting of independent, high-spirited women in the title roles points to a growing need for new female identification figures. By offering cheerful solutions to the problem of sexual difference, the Lubitsch comedies thus convey a rare sense of joyful eroticism. By using set and costume design to create a fairy-tale–like atmosphere, they explore formal solutions outside of the artificial opposition of realism and fantasy. Finally, by opening up a space for other configurations among narrative, spectacle, and visual pleasure, they make possible the representation of female desire; hence their

[1] Examples include *The Student of Prague* (1913, 1926), *The Other* (1913), *Backstairs* (1921), *Sylvester* (1923), *The Street* (1923), and many others.

exceptional status both in the work of Lubitsch and the early German cinema.

Using Eisenstein's notion of attractions, Tom Gunning has described the early cinema—he refers to films made before 1906—as a "cinema of attractions." According to Gunning, this cinema is characterized by strong exhibitionist, rather than voyeuristic, tendencies, a distinctly antirealist orientation, and closer ties to the fairground than the theater. Vestiges of such "otherness" can be found in the artistically ambitious films of the late teens and the avant-garde films of the twenties. Gunning writes: "I believe that it was precisely the exhibitionist quality of turn-of-the-century popular art that made it attractive to the avant-garde—its freedom from the creation of a diegesis, its accent on direct stimulation."[2] Not only to the art film, one might add. While the basic rules of narrative continuity and psychological motivation had more or less been established by the late teens, genres like film comedy or the fantastic film continued to play with, rather than obliterate, these traces of difference. Because of their limited interest in questions of mimetic representation, these genres were free to combine the more "primitive" enjoyment of sensation and spectacle with a distinctly modern interest in the changing class and gender identities.

In addition to their closeness to an earlier "cinema of attractions," *The Oyster Princess*, *The Doll*, and *The Mountain Cat* are typical products of the "girl culture" that developed with the changing social and economic status of women in the twenties. The early cinema, more so than any other modern mass medium, contributed to the myth of the *New Woman*, satisfying the need for new role models while at the same time dispelling the anxieties caused by the problem of sexual difference. Given the cinema's ambivalent position between its lowly origins and its cultural ambitions, it provided a space where the problem of femininity could be addressed and where the implications of women's equally ambivalent position between private and public sphere, between emancipation and traditional femininity, could be spelled out without actual consequences. The focus on traditional female attributes—beauty, sexuality, and sociability—indicated very clearly the limitations of such emancipatory imagery. In this context, stars like Asta Nielsen, Pola Negri, and Lya de Putti came to embody a fashionable, highly ambiguous eroticism, often emphasized by cross-dressing roles (*Hosenrolle*). They had the kind of body consciousness that a growing number of women aspired to.[3] Everything from their roles to their star appeal,

[2] Tom Gunning, "The Cinema of Attraction: Early Film, Its Spectator and the Avant-garde," *Wide Angle* 8, nos. 3 and 4 (1986): 66.

[3] Discussing the popularity of androgynous female stars, Miriam Hansen has argued convincingly to what degree the articulation of sexual difference played a crucial role in the transition between the "archaic" and "classical" period of German cinema. However, she also warns film historians and theorists not to project their longing for a more authentic public

including the smallest details of makeup, hairdo, and dress, reflected this new spirit of liberation. By celebrating the aesthetic and erotic pleasures of androgyny, the Lubitsch comedies provided an imaginary space in which female desire could find expression and, at the same time, attach itself to the accoutrements of modern femininity. In so doing, they offered humorous insights into the changing definitions of gender but relied on parody and exaggeration to make these changes seem less threatening.[4]

Taking the configurations of women and early cinema as a point of departure, this chapter discusses three lesser-known comedies that bear witness to a crucial moment of transition between primitive and classical silent cinema. Directed by Lubitsch during a short but highly productive period, *The Oyster Princess*, *The Doll*, and *The Mountain Cat* take their inspiration from different literary traditions (grotesque, farce, fairy tale), modes of representation (narrative, spectacle), and cinematic styles (animation, realism). These provide the means for exploring alternative registers of visual pleasure—pleasures, to be sure, that still support the dominant order but also foreground its inherent problems. Based on Gunning's notion of a "cinema of attractions," the following chapter will explore this oscillation between affirmation and subversion from the perspective of sexual difference. Accordingly, the fate of femininity in *The Oyster Princess* will be related to the notion of cinematic spectacle. *The Doll* will be read as a case of female and cinematic masquerade, and *The Mountain Cat* analyzed as a challenge to definitions of the fantastic that are exclusively tied to a male problematic. Rather than providing a rigorous theoretical framework, these concepts represent crystallization points in the attempt to find correspondences between style and meaning in the early cinema. For all three films appropriate, though to different degrees and with different implications, the means of the spectacle, the masquerade, and the fantastic and

---

sphere onto these formative years and to romanticize the early silent cinema as the example of a more authentic proletarian sphere: "As a theoretical construct, this notion is useful only insofar as it acknowledges the contradictory dynamics of its historical reference point . . . Above all, the reclamation of early cinema for a theory/politics of the public sphere requires a revisionist attitude towards the rhetoric of cultural criticism and historiography; short of that, the theoretical project is bound to collapse into the reified mythologies that coopted the proletarian characteristics of early cinema in the name of uplift and integration." In Miriam Hansen, "Early Silent Cinema: Whose Public Sphere?" *New German Critique* 29 (Spring/Summer 1983): 159. On women audiences and the early cinema, see also Heide Schlüpmann, "Kinosucht," *Frauen und Film* 33 (October 1982): 45–52 and Patrice Petro, *Joyless Streets. Women and Melodramatic Representation in Weimar Germany* (Princeton, N.J.: Princeton University Press, 1989). The framework of this study does not allow for a more detailed analysis of the historical conditions of female spectatorship.

[4] For a very interesting contemporary account of "girl culture" see Fritz Giese, *Girlkultur. Vergleiche zwischen amerikanischem und europäischem Lebensgefühl* (Munich: Delphin-Verlag, 1920), especially the comments on modern dance and body culture, eroticism and industrial work patterns, women's emancipation, and Americanism.

turn them into points of resistance, both to the emergent classical narrative cinema and traditional images of femininity. Just as they use spectacle and the fantastic as weapons against the terror of mimetic representation, they test the possibilities of masquerade on protagonists as well as the mise-en-scène. To the same degree that the fantastic provides a generic framework in which the spectacle can survive, the masquerade reveals their common origins in popular traditions like the carnival, the circus, and the curio show. As will be argued, closer attention to these strategies of resistance is essential for a better understanding of Lubitsch's early work, especially as regards the problem of femininity.[5]

The Oyster Princess, Lubitsch's second feature-length comedy, was released in a situation of economic and political crisis. Its story about impoverished Europeans and nouveau-riche Americans made the film an instant success with contemporary audiences.[6] Skillfully combining old slapstick humor and new sophistication, the film satisfied the need for recognizable character types while at the same time responding to the growing interest in a psychologically motivated story line. The links to an earlier "cinema of attractions," however, are still strong enough to disrupt the simple love story and inspire an almost pre-Oedipal fantasy structured around images of oral, bodily, and visual pleasures. The traditional notions of morality and propriety dissolve before an endless stream of bodies and objects, overwhelming in their multitude and diversity. And in the place of romantic love, a notion of the erotic emerges that seems strangely unaffected by questions of propriety and hence is free to satisfy the most powerful desires in modern life: sex, money, power.

The almost obsessive display of material objects in *The Oyster Princess*

---

[5] The implications are manifold, especially in regard to the problem of femininity which is, after all, so fatally tied up with narrative and the Oedipal scenario. Proposing a feminist revision of narrative theories, Teresa de Lauretis, for instance, has claimed that "there is no image outside of narrative, and no filmic image outside of history." In Teresa de Lauretis, "Oedipus Interruptus," *Wide Angle* 7, nos. 1 and 2 (1985): 35. Speaking out against the nostalgic celebration of pre-Oedipal nondifferentiation, Lauretis call for "Oedipus with a vengeance." Gertrud Koch, on the other hand, has argued that the concept of identification needs critical revision and has pointed to the fact of spectatorial identification with objects, a characteristic of pre-Oedipal libidinal investments: "If film attaches itself to such early layers of experience, then questions of identifying with characters in fixed sexual roles have to be reconsidered. . . . We may, in fact, owe the invention of the camera not to the keyhole but the baby carriage." In Gertrud Koch, "Exchanging the Gaze: Revisioning Feminist Film Theory," *New German Critique* 34 (Winter 1985): 149.

[6] Note the amusing account given by actor Curt Bois who played the conductor: "I was eighteen. I still remember walking across the entire Johannisfeld carrying a box with my tail coat. During those years, an actor still had to provide his own costume. On location I put on the tail coat and started wriggling." In Curt Bois, *Sechs Schauspieler aus Deutschland: Exil* (Berlin: Deutsche Kinemathek, 1983), 9.

points, from the very beginning, to this other agenda, the celebration of consumption and consumerism. Establishing the mood, the film begins with a close-up of Mr. Quaker, the Oyster King (Victor Janson). The camera moves back, positioning him at the center of all activities. He is surrounded by servants who comb, wash, feed, and pamper him like a baby. A variation on the ornamental configuration of center and periphery, the next shot shows how the Oyster King dictates to a group of secretaries who all take the same notes; here they face him in a block formation (fig. 7). In this opening sequence, the film introduces not only one of the main protagonists but also some of its favorite rhetorical figures: multiplication, exaggeration, and hyperbole. Put to use with a mixture of envy and disgust, these figures must be seen as ironic comments on the process of commodification and reification. Behind their critical intentions, however, they also hold on to the old dream of paradisiacal abundance and bliss. Lines, circles, triangles, clusters, and spirals, all geometrical forms and configurations are called upon to negotiate the resultant tension between repression and eruption, between ceremony and chaos. But the excess of formal strategies, while upholding the promise of fulfillment, also leads to the aestheticization of its denial. The evocation of pleasures existing prior to the Oedipal mold remains irreversibly tied to consumer goods and the act of consumption.

While the film indulges in the most hackneyed clichés about rich Americans (e.g., the crude manners, the mania for titles), it uses the motif of enormous wealth to create an almost mythological backdrop for its feasts of pure quantity.[7] Moving from the father's attributes of power to the daughter's aggressive demands, the story introduces the other side of shameless consumption, namely that which is based not on accumulation but on instant and permanent gratification. Furious about the marriage of a millionaire's daughter to a count, the Oyster Princess (Ossi Oswalda) confronts her father and demands a prince. To prove her determination, she systematically destroys all objects within reach. Such signs of vitality (much in the style of robber-baron entrepreneurship) meet with the father's approval. Facing the camera, he politely hands her one last vase and comments: "Take it! Please!" But the following scene already has the consulted marriage broker handing them a most promising file card: "Prince Nucki, looks: first class, assets: none." As the impoverished European aristocrat whose assets have been reduced to refined manners and a melancholy eroticism, the man enters the story in a way traditionally reserved for women: as the object of desire. Representing the other side in this Euro-

---

[7] One of the literary sources for *The Oyster Princess* was the popular Leo Fall operetta *Die Dollarprinzessin* (1909) featuring the coal mogul Couder, his snobbish daughter Alice, and Fredy Wehrbuch as the impoverished beau.

7. *The Oyster Princess*: Victor Janson

pean-American encounter, Prince Nucki (Harry Liedtke) inspires most of the humorous comments on the loss of male power and the threat of feminization. Since he is still too class-conscious to break a date with his bohemian friends, Nucki sends a valet to investigate the actual wealth of the Oyster Princess. Having arrived at her spectacular palace, the false prince is asked to wait in the drawing room and soon begins to trace nervously the pattern of the star-shaped floor, turning and spinning with increasing speed until nausea clouds his senses. The drawing-room scene alternates with scenes from the dressing room where the Oyster Princess reigns supreme, surrounded, as her father before, by countless maids who scrub, comb, cream, perfume and, eventually, dress her (fig. 8). Here the allusions to new developments in industrial production are all too evident. With the woman's body representing the product, specialized groups of workers (maids)—distinguishable by their uniforms (aprons, frocks, caps)—enter the process of production (woman's beautification) at different stages and perform their respective tasks (cleaning, massaging, dressing), a process made even more visible through the repeated close-ups of hands at work. The staging of woman's transformation into a spectacle imitates early forms of the conveyor belt where the workers still follow the product through all the steps of a production assembly; at one point, for instance, the Oyster Princess is carried from the cleaning section to the massage section.

Eventually, the Oyster Princess enters the drawing room—very much like a luxury item on display. But contrary to the expectations raised by the previous sequence, it is the woman (i.e., the product) who does the "buying." After inspecting the prospective groom with a monocle, the determined girl follows through with her original plan and, without delay, drags him to a pastor who performs the wedding ceremony from the window of his private home. Such lack of etiquette is more than compensated for during the splendid wedding party, with its masterly choreographed scenes of eating and dancing. As the bride whispers saucily "Say something!" the false groom replies with a full mouth: "I haven't had such good food in ages!" Then consumption takes over and triumphs as the film's underlying principle, in the process annihilating the exigencies of narrative linearity and succumbing to a more "primitive" celebration of the spectacular. Grafe and Patalas write: "For the wedding party, Lubitsch hired three hundred real waiters. Behind each guest another waiter stands for each course. After each course the dish vanishes and so does the waiter. The next row steps up. The notion of consumption as real, devouring consumption is thus made obvious. Consumption has something literary in the Lubitsch films, something exhilarating."[8] Creating a feeling of vertigo in the film's

---

[8] Frieda Grafe and Enno Patalas, *Im Off. Filmartikel* (Munich: Hanser, 1981), 267.

8. *The Oyster Princess*: Ossi Oswalda and Julius Falkenstein

protagonists, as well as in the spectators, the wedding sequence culminates in a jubilant apotheosis of the body (fig. 9). What begins as a chorus line of waiters winding up and down the stairs with plates of food, of cooks preparing meals and guests chewing relentlessly, gradually turns into more abstract rituals. Through rapid editing, odd camera angles, lighting, and special effects, movement becomes dance and dance the celebration of life. While the false groom literally digests his rags-to-riches fate through gluttony—here the film cuts to Prince Nucki chewing on a tiny mackerel—a fox-trot epidemic breaks out. Through the device of a split-screen frame, several scenes are brought together in a triptych of dancing legs: with the kitchen personnel in the lower part (an indicator also of their social station), the frustrated bride with a waiter in the middle, and the ecstatic guests in the upper part of the frame. The visual spectacle of dance brings about the culmination of the narrative and, at the same time, makes possible its momentary suspension. It speaks of an explosive vitality, an intoxication with movement and rhythm. Yet through the controlled steps and turns, the art of dance safely guards that thin line between celebration and chaos. Its underlying dialectic of excess and control becomes evident in the repeated shots of the conductor's swinging hips, an image in which passion submits willingly to the mechanical regime of baton, drums, and dancing steps.

After regaining "consciousness," the film returns, almost unwillingly, to the mistaken-identity theme. The next morning Ossi attends a club meeting of "Millionaire Daughters Against Alcoholism" where she spots the intoxicated Prince Nucki among the drunkards awaiting treatment. Stating her claims in a wild boxing match with the other women, she secures him as her private patient. In the romantic bedroom scene that follows, Ossi and Nucki embrace passionately and, under showers of kisses, declare their love for each other. The entry of Nucki's valet, finally, eliminates all remaining problems: the new lovers are already husband and wife. Celebrating this happy ending, the film virtually rushes through a private dinner with Mr. Quaker and lets the happy couple retire to their sleeping quarters. *The Oyster Princess* closes with a repetition of the opening shot, that is, with the father's look aimed directly at the camera. Peeking through a keyhole to supervise his daughter's sexual performance, he comments: "That's impressive!"

In *The Oyster Princess*, the act of looking is not only presented as something highly pleasurable, but it actually provides the stimuli and impulses through which the narrative unfolds. The look does not necessarily have to fall on a man or woman. On the contrary, the passion with which the protagonists, and the filmmaker himself, celebrate the image as image suggests, rather immorally, that their desire is perhaps exclusively concerned with promise, and not actual fulfillment. What is doomed to fail in the

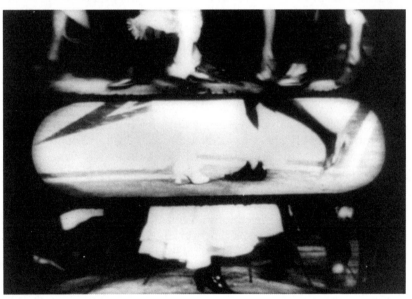

9. *The Oyster Princess*: The Wedding dinner and party

melodrama, namely imagination, now becomes the ultimate titillation. The mocking comments on sublimation—the false groom's craving for food, his spying on the dissatisfied bride—may very well be read as a questioning of the established order of primary and secondary drives. Looking, consuming, and dancing are shown to be equally gratifying and, because of that, become interchangeable. In that vein, the film not only sets up a provocative system of equivalences but also creates a world where appearances are valued more highly than the truth. Substitution no longer represents a second choice; it challenges the hegemony of the original. This daring reversal of the traditional hierarchies, this pleasurable play with slipping signifiers could very well be understood as a statement on the cinema's secret attraction. Then the longing glances of the protagonists become identical with those of the spectators, and Mr. Quaker's look into the camera completes their surrender to the power of visual pleasure.

In such rare moments of cinematic spectacle, the image and the look take hold of the most secret desires as well as the most public events; everything becomes representation. Earlier distinctions between characters and props dissolve under the equalizing force of cinematic spectacle. Consequently, vision takes over all acts of interpretation. That is the main reason why the spectacle defies narrative. It interrupts the flow of the narrative by means of a calculated, secondhand iconography, celebrating quantity as quality and plundering the archives of artistic forms, historical moments, and sociocultural stereotypes for the most unexpected combinations and effects. Through its affinities to commodity fetishism, the cinematic spectacle escapes the requirements of probability, verisimilitude, and psychology and continues to represent those pleasures that were sacrificed in the emergence of the classical narrative cinema.

Indeed, the notion of "spectacle" seems to capture most accurately the charm of *The Oyster Princess*. As a critical metaphor rather than a theoretical concept, the term invokes, on the one hand, the notion of the carnivalesque introduced by Mikhail Bakhtin in his influential study, *Rabelais and His World*. On the other hand, it points to the specter of universal commodification as described by Guy Debord in *Society of the Spectacle*. Between these two poles—the one reminiscent of the past, the other indicative of the future—the cinematic spectacle develops its critique of the anthropocentric order. It gives new life to older traditions that are based on ritual, spectacle, and festival, and, in the process, erodes the distinctions between high and low culture, the sacred and the profane. What Bakhtin describes as the carnivalesque finds its modern-day incarnation in the cinema and its rituals of passive participation. Relegated to the unofficial, plebeian side of the high/low culture distinction, the cinema becomes the medium of the urban masses and takes the place of cultural practices that require a more active involvement. Real participation ("Carnival is not a spectacle seen by the people; they live in it, and everybody participates because the very idea embraces all the people"[9]) is replaced by the unending play with shifting distances that is organized around the hegemony of the look. In his analysis of the function of spectacle in late-capitalist society, Debord has commented repeatedly on this transition from a culture based on participation to one based exclusively on consumption, including the consumption of images. The society of spectacle, according to Debord, organizes all social relations around images and institutes vision as the primary sense; hence its inherent tendency toward abstraction. This total commodification, however, comes with the possibility of its own self-destruction. Writes Debord: "The spectacle is the existing order's uninterrupted discourse about itself, its laudatory monologue."[10] The spectacle of *The Oyster Princess*, too, complies with the commodity fetishism of its times but also invites its quiet demolition in the spirit of irony. Such a utopian vision requires that the spectacle of the commodity be embraced with a vengeance. Bakhtin describes the process as follows: "Thus, in the grotesque concept of the body a new, concrete, and realistic historic awareness was born and took form: not abstract thoughts about the future but the living sense that each man belongs to the immortal people who create history."[11] As *The Oyster Princess* shows, only through the machinations of the grotesque female body—that is: only through her excesses—can transgressions in the realm of representation become possible. Only the contemporary potlatch of the American millionaire preserves the memory of more ancient traditions and gives expression to the undeniable demands of the body.

Yet the spectacle as an event, and a production, also needs a coherent narrative from which it receives its raison d'être and, closely related to that, a well-defined framework within which the woman is allowed to participate in these moments of disruption. The spectacle must be retained within

[9] Mikhail Bakhtin, *Rabelais and His World*, trans. Helene Iswolsky (Cambridge, Mass.: M.I.T. Press, 1968), 7. The notion of the carnivalesque and the subversive potential of laughter has been the source of much debate. Note, in this context, Umberto Eco's highly critical comments on the transgressional theory of carnival and its reversals. Referring to what he calls the *trompe-l'oeil* effect of the comic, Eco cautions that the comic text only presupposes liberation but never actually intends to attain it: "The hyper Bachtinian ideology of carnival as actual liberation may, however, be wrong." In "The Frames of Comic 'Freedom,' " *Carnival!* ed. Thomas A. Sebeok (Berlin, New York, Amsterdam: Mouton, 1984), 3. Also note, in the same collection, V. V. Ivanov's ethnological article, "The Semiotic Theory of Carnival as the Inversion of Bipolar Opposites," trans. R. Reeder and J. Rostinsky, 11–35, where the author uses Bakhtin's theory of carnival to discuss phenomena of inversion of male/female oppositions in transvestism and the cult of the androgynous. From the perspective of a feminist/feminine discourse, see also Hélène Cixous's remarks in "The Guilty One. Sorceress and Hysteric," in *The Newly Born Woman*, trans. Betsy Wing, forward Sandra M. Gilbert (Minneapolis: University of Minnesota Press, 1986).

[10] Guy Debord, *Society of the Spectacle* (Detroit: Black and Red, 1977), 24.

[11] Bakhtin, *Rabelais and His World*, 367.

certain sequences that are designated as different, as other; it must be associated with specific constellations between characters that give it an air
of legitimacy. The wedding party provides the perfect temporal and spatial
framework in which the spectacle, previously limited to the elaborate set
designs and the choreography of extras, takes over as the film's governing
principle. Other forms of containment are less innocent and point to the
gendered order of the narrative. The fulfillment of the woman's desire is
possible only through her close relationship with the father and, implicitly,
through a repression of everything that alludes to the mother or the maternal. This becomes very obvious when Ossi, during one of her lessons in
baby care, grabs the naked doll and begins to powder its face instead of its
behind. The father-daughter relationship brings into play oppositions like
passivity and hyperactivity, voyeurism and exhibitionism, status quo and
anarchy. The father is the one who constructs meaning, while the daughter
is the one who destroys it through her irreverent excesses. In this regard,
the film could even be interpreted as the return of the feminine in a patriarchal scenario gone berserk. However, an asymmetry in the relationship
does not necessarily imply an asymmetry in values. The assertion of difference in the interaction of father and daughter exists side by side with the
doubling effect produced by their similar characters. The name Oyster, after all, refers both to the father's magical wealth and the daughter's sex.
The Oyster Princess acts out what the father represents: the ruthless business methods, the greed and avarice, the total lack of concern for others.
Her erotic appeal and boyish behavior—in other words: her position inside and outside of traditional femininity—make possible the admission of
spectacular moments but, at the same time, prevent the complete dissolu-
tion of the narrative in the face of woman.

The tension between a liberated femininity associated with counternar-
rative tendencies and a more traditional positioning of woman within a
narrative of romance surfaces most strongly in the incongruities between
the art of performance—woman turning herself into spectacle—and the
requirements of story and character development. While Ossi Oswalda
holds together the fragmented narrative through her sheer physical presence, her performance and her role never quite reach complete identity,
thus opening up a space for the production of other meanings, including
those linked to spectacle. Appropriating elements from an overwhelmingly
male tradition in slapstick acting, Oswalda takes the possibilities of the
female body beyond the limitations of her role and aims at something beyond characterization. The bathing scene is a good example of this non-
identity between role and performance and reveals their different functions
within the narrative. The luxurious decor, the soft lighting, and, hidden in
steam vapors and satin robes, Oswalda's naked body recall an oriental-
bathhouse sensuality. Yet through the rapid editing and the calculated

movements, the scene mocks what it pretends to show. Oswalda's body at
rest is woman as spectacle; but her body in motion is efficiency gone crazy.
Her performance plays with images of sexual permissiveness while at the
same time mimicking the streamlined functionality demanded from
women in the new industrial professions; again mechanization, again the
assembly line. Thus the splendid set designs, the beautiful props, the hundreds of extras, in short, the film's sheer materiality functions simultaneously as an expression and a repression of the female body.

To conclude: *The Oyster Princess* moves back and forth between subversion and affirmation. Through the means of mise-en-scène and editing, the
film transgresses the boundaries that separate the human from the object
world. Through the means of narrative, it mocks traditional notions of
romance and eroticism and inspires short moments reminiscent of the carnivalesque. A space is created for pleasures outside of the fatal identification with characters and stories. However, this newly found freedom also
instills fear in modern audiences, namely of being controlled by the cinematic apparatus. Caught between the longing for older forms of popular
culture and complete surrender to the modern commodity, *The Oyster
Princess* reveals its own precarious conditions of production with unparalleled clarity.

RELEASED almost at the same time as *The Cabinet of Dr. Caligari*, *The Doll*
could very well be called a forgotten masterpiece. Whereas critics have
praised *Caligari*'s seductive male gloom, this film has been called primitive,
heavy-handed, mildly amusing at best. Pointing to the awkward mixture
of styles and the various levels of representation, critics saw only a faulty
verisimilitude. The illusion fails, as Kirk Bond maintains: "It [*The Doll*] is
heavy and labored and while it, too, had a parade of fantastic bits, the
fantasy does not come off."[12] However, *The Doll* and *Caligari* reveal striking similarities. Inspired by E. T. A. Hoffmann's tales, Meliès's cinematic
trickeries, and the attractions of the fairground, both films are set in imaginary worlds and use extreme stylization to create their peculiar dreamlike
effects. Both focus on the theme of creation and mastery (Caligari and the
somnambulist Caesare, Hilarius and his mechanical dolls). Both are characterized by the intervening presence of a narrator (the madman's framing
story in *Caligari*, Lubitsch's cameo appearance in *The Doll*). Yet in spite of
their shared origins in the genre of the fantastic, *Caligari* and *The Doll*
conjure up very different worlds and, indeed, promise almost diametrically
opposed pleasures. In contrast to the former's male universe of horror and
insanity, *The Doll*—therein almost *Caligari*'s alter ego—presents a happy
childhood paradise. And unlike the claustrophobic set design of *Caligari*,

---

[12] Kirk Bond, "Ernst Lubitsch," *Film Culture* 63/64 (1977): 144.

The Doll uses painted backdrops to convey a cheerful atmosphere full of play and possibilities. Its "four humorous reels out of a toy box" (according to the credits) escape the tyranny of mimetic representation and establish a dreamworld based on instant wish fulfillment where *Caligari* documents the failure of such attempts.

At first glance, however, the film's charming fairy-tale setting seems only to give rise to a pronounced chauvinism. The initial problem is, after all, fear of women, or, as the male hero programmatically proclaims: "I will not marry a woman!" Confronted with the marriage plans arranged for him by his rich uncle, the Baron of Chanterelle, young Lanzelot (Hermann Thimig) panics and, pursued by forty virgins, seeks refuge in a cloister.[13] There the greedy monks ("We give freely but little!") suggest his marriage to a doll, so that they can spend his inheritance on food and drink. Lanzelot agrees and visits the doll maker Hilarius (Victor Janson) who has just finished a beautiful, life-size mechanical doll modeled on his daughter Ossi (Ossi Oswalda). Critically inspecting the doll maker's collection, Lanzelot puts down the conditions of sale ("I want a doll with a respectable character!"). Meanwhile, in the workshop, Hilarius's rambunctious apprentice stages a wild pas-de-deux with the Ossi doll and accidentally breaks off its arm. Out of compassion for the desperate boy, Ossi agrees to take the doll's place. Lanzelot falls in love immediately, pays for the doll, and transports his new toy to the cloister where she entertains the monks with her mechanical dances. In the meantime, the old Baron of Chanterelle is dying of grief over his nephew's disappearance. The sight of greedy relatives fighting over his furniture, china, and valuables, however, revitalizes the ailing man, as does Lanzelot's sudden return with a beautiful bride. As in *The Oyster Princess*, a splendid wedding party follows. While the bridegroom tries successfully to conceal the bride's mechanical nature, she allows herself unobserved moments of gluttony and flirtation. Finally, the wedding night puts an end to these delicate complications. As Lanzelot lies down to dream of the kisses of a real woman, a mouse appears in the bedroom, bringing about the happy ending: Ossi suddenly jumps up, screaming, the best proof that she is a real woman after all. In the final scene, Hilarius, a victim of a severe case of somnambulism since his daughter's disappearance, returns to reality in a similar way. From the madness of his nightly

---

[13] Beginning with *Shoe Salon Pinkus*, harpylike groups of women seem to haunt the films' romantic leads. Notable examples include Lanzelot's flight from marriage-crazy girls (*The Doll*); Alexis's farewell to countless waving chambermaids and their "Papa!"-shouting children (*The Mountain Cat*); and, in an almost identical repetition of that scene, Danilo's first departure for Paris in *The Merry Widow* (1934). Such thematic continuity, however, does not necessarily suggest an identical meaning, for the purposeful quotation of such "primal" scenes can also serve to emphasize change. In other words, what looked contrite in 1934 may have been perceived as provocative in 1920.

balloon rides he falls back to the ground, only to be miraculously reunited with the happy couple. Again similar to *The Oyster Princess*, *The Doll* closes with a father's content nod toward the camera: "Now I'm rid of all problems."

For a better understanding of the tension between affirmation and subversion in *The Doll*, the notion of masquerade provides a useful framework in which questions of genre and gender can be addressed through, rather than in opposition to, each other. Applied to the fantastic set design, masquerade means the masquerading of reality as artifice; but applied to the problem of femininity, it also refers to the artificiality inherent in all gender categories. While *The Oyster Princess* still adheres to a more-or-less realistic mode of representation, *The Doll* takes the possibilities of spectacle one step further and makes it the basis of its very existence; hence the shift from comedy to fantasy, hence the need to move from a contemporary setting into the timeless spaces of the imagination. By organizing its disparate elements around the theme of masquerade—a masquerade performed by the title figure as well as by the fantastic sets—the film provides, quite literally, a mise-en-scène for multifarious transgressions.[14] All elements converge in the figure of the mechanical doll. Given her central position in the film's narrative and visual strategies, the doll provides much more than a convenient center in a humorous play on sexual identities. She exceeds that framework on her own terms and becomes a metaphor of femininity in the silent cinema. On the surface, the doll represents the most radical expression of a masquerade that has virtually become synonymous with the female body. Yet a similar kind of masquerade takes place on the level of representation, as is evidenced by the fantastic set design and the frequent use of animation techniques. By renouncing its ties to traditional notions of reality, *The Doll* unmasks as artificial what is considered natural. Moreover, by embracing the artificiality of human existence, the film makes possible the playful investigation of sexual difference and, ultimately, of representation itself. The subversive potential of masquerade originates precisely in this moment of inversion.[15]

[14] A frequent motif in Lubitsch films, the liberating effects of female masquerade (in the widest sense) are always taken back through their narrative inscription in scenarios of deceit (Pola Negri's male disguise in *Passion*, Marlene Dietrich's false identities in *Desire* and *Angel*), revenge (the disguised wives in *The Merry Jail* and *So This Is Paris*), or lack of femininity (*Kohlhiesel's Daughters*, *Ninotchka*).

[15] This explains the renewed interest in masquerade among feminist critics. Mary Ann Doane, for instance, writes: "The masquerade, in flaunting femininity, holds it at a distance. Womanliness is a mask which can be worn or removed. The masquerade's resistance to patriarchal positioning would therefore lie in its denial of the production of femininity as closeness, as presence-to-itself, as, precisely, imaginistic." In "Film and the Masquerade: Theorising the Female Spectator," *Screen* 23, nos. 3 and 4 (September/October 1982): 81–82. Compare the definition given by psychoanalyst Joan Riviere: "Womanliness therefore could be assumed

To begin with, the notion of masquerade is helpful in exploring the difference between the woman character in the story and her portrayal of the doll as a caricature of femininity. Within the narrative, both kinds of female existence refer back to the doll maker, Hilarius, who exerts double power as the woman's father and the doll's creator. The mother, though present in the film, plays a marginal role. The doll maker's control over the discourse of femininity is made evident in his sales presentation to Lanzelot. As soon as he sets the mechanical dolls into motion through the turning of a large wheel, they approach Lanzelot with aggressive dance steps. While this moment undeniably attests to the threatening side of female spectacle, the large wheel and the cranking movement also refer to the cinematic apparatus, with Hilarius now placed in the position of Lubitsch (fig. 10). The moment of greatest control becomes at the same time the moment of highest self-reflexivity. At the center of this double movement stands woman as the embodiment of the possibilities, and the dangers, inherent in masquerade. Again as in *The Oyster Princess* and *The Mountain Cat*, it is the daughter figure who facilitates the necessary compromise between male power and female liberation.[16] As the doll, she becomes, quite literally, the object of an exchange between two men, the father and the future husband. Yet precisely by acting out the implications of this paradigmatic scene, by drawing attention to its underlying patriarchal structures, the woman uses masquerade as an accessory in her continuous search for happiness and truth.

Profiting from a slapstick tradition that thrives on the equation of the human and the mechanical, *The Doll* derives most of its comic effects from the spectacle of female masquerade. Between the stereotypes of "emasculated son" and "devouring mother" ("What do you want from my baby?"), its sexual politics at times seem to suggest that the best wife is, indeed, a

---

and worn as a mask, both to hide the possession of masculinity and to avert the reprisals expected if she was found to possess it—much as a thief will turn out his pockets and ask to be searched to prove that he has not the stolen goods." Joan Riviere, "Womanliness as a Masquerade," in *Formations of Fantasy*, ed. Victor Burgin et al. (London and New York: Methuen, 1986), 38. Note, in this context, also Gaylyn Studlar, "Visual Pleasure and the Masochistic Aesthetic," *Journal of Film and Video* 37, no. 2 (1985): 5–27. Introducing the notion of a masochistic aesthetics, Studlar proposes to investigate the problem of bisexuality and visual pleasure from the perspective of the pre-Oedipal scenario that "allows the spectator to experience the pleasure of satisfying the 'drive to be both sexes' that is repressed in everyday life" (13). Though Doane and Studlar take the classical Hollywood cinema as their reference points (Doane the woman's film of the forties, Studlar the Sternberg/Dietrich cycle of the thirties), their findings also apply to the early German cinema, given its equally strong investment in mise-en-scène.

[16] Strong father-daughter relationships (or relations between women and older, powerful men) are the rule in Lubitsch's films. Examples include *The Eyes of the Mummy*, *The Oyster Princess*, *Kohlhiesel's Daughters*, *The Mountain Cat*, *Forbidden Paradise*, *The Smiling Lieutenant*, *Design for Living*, *Desire*, *Bluebeard's Eighth Wife*, *Cluny Brown*.

10. *The Doll*: Victor Janson

doll. The film choreographs in great detail the problems of mechanical
movement (repetition, stalling, malfunction) and documents with obvious
pleasure the inevitable conflicts that arise from the actual difference between the woman and her double. The exaggerated definitions of gender
roles that inform this didactical exercise lead to their critical exposure
through the means of parody. In this sense, the doll motif and, by implication, the theme of masquerade function at once as an expression of conformism and a means of resistance. The final triumph of the woman rather
than the doll, however, demonstrates the superiority of real desires, both
in regard to eroticism and consumption. The doll may have been introduced into the narrative in accordance with the generic conventions of the
fantastic but, in combination with other visual strategies, it becomes part
of a more dangerous play with imitation, suspension, and reversal. It is
within these parameters that *The Doll* carries out its investigation of the
freedom and the constraints of female masquerade. By pretending to be a
more perfect woman (i.e., a doll), the woman is able to enjoy the privileges
denied to her in a male-dominated society. Yet by playing herself, she gains
insights into the artificial nature of female identity and, as her own mirror
image, experiences a joy of life that refers back to the pleasures of primary

narcissism—and not, as one could argue, to her submission to the traditional female role.

The comparison to a related phenomenon, the male figure of the double (*Doppelgänger*), will further clarify the subversive qualities inherent in female masquerade. In the context of the Expressionist cinema, the double usually represents the dark and repressed side of the male psyche, an existence that is controlled by lust and greed, that shows destructive as well as self-destructive tendencies and has a fatalistic view of the world. Melodramatic and fantastic modes of representation have often provided the appropriate settings for these stories of male double identity, including an obsession with death as the only chance for narrative denouement. The female counterparts, however, seem to prefer comical variations on the double motif. Their stories focus on experiences of resistance (e.g., *Kohlhiesel's Daughters*) and use these as the source of a liberating humor—even though woman's double existence inevitably leads to her "unmasking," a moment of "second castration" sweetened by the obligatory marital kiss. As a result, the playful disruption of an oppressive sexual order and the subsequent affirmation of that same order need not be seen as mutually exclusive strategies. The parody of traditional male-female relations may still satisfy the spectator's desire for imaginary transgressions, even though its disruptive aspects are firmly kept in place through certain constraints within the narrative.

The liberating qualities of the fantastic are not limited to the characters and the narrative. On the contrary, *The Doll* demonstrates even more than *The Oyster Princess* to what degree the meanings of a film depend on the possibility of narrative and visual interventions. The prologue contains an exemplary token appearance of Lubitsch that draws attention to the film's artificiality and, therefore, to the presence of an author. Like a magician or puppeteer, the actor/director opens a toy box and sets up a miniature model with trees, a house, a bench, a pond, and two costume dolls (fig. 11). With the next dissolve on the entrance door, the transgression from model to reality is complete: now two identically dressed actors leave the house. The interpretation of film as a magic art, with Lubitsch as the magician, becomes evident in the prologue's ending. After having fallen into the pond, the man sends a shivering plea toward an overcast sky ("Dear sun, please shine, so that I won't catch a cold!") and gets an immediate response in the form of parting clouds and a smiling sun (fig. 12). As is programmatically stated in this unique opening sequence, *The Doll* takes place in a world of immediate gratification, a world characterized by simple desires and instant satisfaction. Its existence, however, requires innocence, trust, and belief; a kind of belief that may very well be aware of the conditions of its own artificiality but that remains unaffected by the calls for reason and modesty. The newly discovered power of imagination cannot be measured

11. *The Doll*: Ernst Lubitsch

better than through the speed with which the sunbeams in the prologue "steam-dry" the man's wet clothes.

Similarly, the doll maker's apprentice makes it possible to comment critically on aspects of story and character development. Reminiscent of the life narrator known from the flickers (*Kientopp*), the apprentice in a way takes over the functions that the director/magician gave up with the prologue's ending; he also brings to mind Lubitsch's own background as a comic actor. Throughout the film, the apprentice makes fun of the other characters by imitating their gestures and actions. In his various performances, one finds the self-indulgent moves of the grand charmer (kissing first the daughter, then the mother, he comments: "Nobody should feel set back") and the professionalism of the experienced businessman (e.g., when he receives customers). In a rare comment on slapstick acting, he involves Hilarius in a frantic chase through the kitchen that results in many broken dishes. And in a similar reference to the melodrama, he tries to commit suicide by first drinking paint (Hilarius: "Are you crazy to drink these expensive paints?") and then jumping out of the window of a ground-level room. Finally his desperate question, "What is a bad life's worth?" is answered by an attractively displayed apple that catches his attention. He grabs it and begins to chew, now smiling.

12. *The Doll*: The sun shines again

Another form of authorial intervention can be located in the film's shifting levels of representation. Instead of striving toward mimetic representation, *The Doll* moves toward abstraction, both in the sense of simplifica-
tion and caricature. Lubitsch himself once commented on the film's
fantastic set design: "It was pure fantasy, most of its sets were made of
cardboard, even some out of paper. Even to this day I still consider it one
of the most imaginative films I ever made."[17] The sets for *The Doll* were
designed by Kurt Richter, who also created the more sophisticated interiors in *The Oyster Princess*. Some designs, including the ornamental patterns
in Hilarius's showroom, reveal the influence of Expressionist and Futurist
film. But the majority take their inspiration from children's drawings and
folk art. Not surprisingly, the sets have been compared with "decorations
from a Christmas tale."[18] Trees are depicted through round and triangular
shapes; almost all surfaces are painted; a horse is played by two extras in a

[17] Lubitsch, "A Letter to the Author," in Herman G. Weinberg, *The Lubitsch Touch: A Critical Study*, 3d. rev. ed. (New York: Dover, 1977), 285.
[18] Uta Berg-Ganschow, review of *The Doll*, in *Lubitsch*, ed. Hans Helmut Prinzler and Enno
Patalas (Munich: C. J. Bucher, 1984), 136. Compare also Freddy Buache, "1918–1920: *La Pou-
pée* et le *Golem*," in *Le Cinéma Allemand 1918–1933*, intr. Michel Soutter (Hatier: 5 Continents,
1984), 19–29.

horse costume; and, surrounded by naively drawn clouds, the sun and the moon smirk repeatedly over the human follies taking place below. Even the characters, with their imaginative costumes and grotesque behavior, are fully integrated into this fantastic scenery.

While the fairy-tale atmosphere invites comparisons to folk art and children's tales, the frequent excursions into the realm of pure animation are responsible for the film's high degree of self-reflexivity. In addition to the visual manipulations, Lubitsch takes an almost childlike approach to language by trying to "visualize" a number of popular German sayings. When Lanzelot anxiously knocks at the door of the doll-maker's shop, something falls out of his trouser leg: a gingerbread heart which he quickly returns to his chest. The scene plays on the German saying "Ihm fällt das Herz in die Hose," which translates literally as "his heart falls into his pants," and means that he is nervous. After the inter-title "This is indeed hair-raising!" the hair of Hilarius actually rises and turns gray; with Ossi's happy return, his hair falls down again and returns to its natural color. Sometimes the play with the metaphorical qualities of language also inspires sharper criticism, for instance when the greed of the baron's relatives is exposed through a split-screen frame with twelve nagging mouths in close-up (fig. 13).

In real life and in the realm of metaphors, children and dreamers often represent a world closer to the primeval flow of desires. *The Doll* contains elements of such childhood happiness, for its visual and narrative strategies are founded on the willing suspension of disbelief and a radical openness to the products of the imagination. Through the film's naïveté and irreverent playfulness, spectators are invited to assume the position of children and dreamers. Yet through the shifting levels of representation and the numerous authorial interventions, they are also seduced into enjoying the experience of critical distance that takes them out of their childhood and their dreams. Masquerade—of the woman and of the visible world—makes this process possible and enjoyable. By testing the subversive potential of masquerade, the film reaches a complexity that emerges unexpectedly from behind its innocent surface. In fact, it is precisely the association with the fairy tale—and, as will be argued shortly, the marvelous—that facilitates the workable compromise between rationality and imagination. It is an association that even allows the female lead to use masquerade as a means of playful self-reflection. With these implications, *The Doll* tells the refreshing tale of a woman who, by being turned into an object of male desire, turns against that order. Not only does the woman-as-doll experience a sense of boundless freedom as she mirrors the male projections that constitute her new identity, and not only is this mirror effect carried beyond its own intentions: the happy ending of *The Doll* also shows why women may be preferable to dolls after all (fig. 14). This insight, however, comes

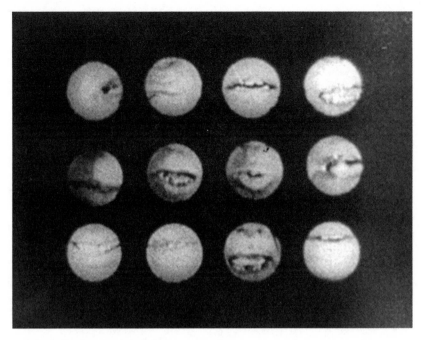

13. *The Doll*: The greedy relatives

only after the woman has deceived and disrupted the male order through the means of masquerade.

IN HIS letter to Weinberg, Lubitsch recalled that *The Mountain Cat*, at the time of its release, was considered "a complete failure, and yet this picture had more inventiveness and satirical pictorial wit than many of my other pictures. Released shortly after the war, I found the German audiences in no mood to accept a picture which satirized militarism and war."[19] Confronted with the sarcastic perspective on the events in a military fort, contemporary viewers may indeed have been irritated by the film's shocking antimilitarism. They must have been equally surprised about the sympathetic portrayal of a robberess, the "mountain cat," who prefers the wildness of the mountains to the trappings of civilization, including those of romantic love. As in *The Doll*, the love story virtually "disappears" amidst the abstract sets, behind the experimental devices, and before the almost exclusive preoccupation with filmic representation. But unlike *The Oyster Princess* and *The Doll*, love in *The Mountain Cat* fails to pacify the woman and ends in a proud affirmation of her otherness. With generic elements

[19] Lubitsch, letter to Weinberg (10 July 1947), *The Lubitsch Touch*, 285–86.

14. *The Doll*: Victor Janson, Hermann Thimig, Ossi Oswalda

from the comedy and the farce placed in a fantastic mise-en-scène, *The Mountain Cat* represents the culmination point in Lubitsch's "trilogy" of femininity. By refusing to offer the traditional happy ending, the film establishes a link between extreme stylization and social satire that makes possible the liberation, rather than the domestication, of the female title figure. On the following pages, these qualities will be used to analyze in greater detail the configuration of woman, spectacle, and masquerade and, from this vantage point, to challenge a few widespread notions about the Expressionist cinema, and its relation to sexual difference in particular.

The Mountain Cat begins on a wintery morning at Fort Tossenstein in the idyllic mountains of Pfiffkaneiro, one of those imaginary Balkan countries known from Lubitsch's later Hollywood musicals. Moving back and forth between the military fort and a robbers' camp, the film establishes a connection between both settings and, in so doing, explores their similarities as well as their differences. An atmosphere of irreverence prevails, beginning with the shot of the fort's trumpet player who tries to divide his attention between the trumpet and a sausage until he can no longer distinguish between chewing and trumpeting. Then the scene cuts to rows of sleeping soldiers who show no reaction to the trumpeter's signal. Suddenly a man's gigantic head invades the empty frame. With the statement "I guess, nothing works without me," the fort's commander (Victor Janson) throws the soldiers out of their beds. Despite their obvious disorientation, they eventually manage to assemble for the daily roll call but immediately return to bed once the commander has turned his back.

After this grotesque opening sequence, *Mountain Cat* introduces the romantic lead, Lieutenant Alexis (Paul Heidemann), who is about to leave a neighboring town for the fort and his new bride, the commander's daughter Lilli (Edith Meller). Living up to his reputation as a lady-killer, Alexis bids farewell to waving chambermaids and their illegitimate children (inter-title: "Papa! Papa!"). As a telling comment on men's irresistibility, this particular scene recurs frequently in Lubitsch's later films; in this early example, it also seems to anticipate the star cult of the twenties. Significantly, the hysterical female fans in *The Mountain Cat* can only be stopped by the "femininity test" already used in *The Doll*: two sacks of mice are opened and the women run away screaming. On their journey, Alexis and his group are attacked by the brigands who look very much like predecessors of the Marx Brothers; their fantastic names—Pepo, Tripo, Dafko, Zorfano, and Massilio—and their wild costumes add to the impression of humorous anarchy. Alexis arrives at the fort as a nobody, stripped of all military regalia, even his pants, and is only recognized by his adjutant after performing the customary kick in the buttocks. Immediately the adjutant stops the arrogant behavior and returns to his usual servility. Meanwhile, in the brigand camp, the chief's wild daughter, Rischka (Pola Negri), discovers a photograph of Alexis among the loot and instantly falls in love with him. Later Alexis is chosen as the leader of the punitive expedition into the brigands' territory. Amidst a naturalistic winter landscape, Rischka and Alexis meet in open combat, that is, through the throw of a snowball. Struggling with the adversities of snow and ice, they practically slide into each other and, making a similarly smooth transition emotionally, aggression turns into passion.

During the ensuing victory celebrations, the brigands secretly enter the fort. Mingling with the guests, they cause hilarious confusions and stage frantic chases through the fort's fantastic interiors. Rischka and Alexis meet again and celebrate their happy reunion with a kiss, while Lilli spies on them through a keyhole. Back in the camp, Rischka's father (Wilhelm Dingelmann) notices his daughter's lovesickness and, as a cure, orders her marriage to the dopey Pepo. On the day of their "double wedding" (Rischka-Pepo, Alexis-Lilli), the unhappy bride and groom wander off into the snow, miraculously run into each other, and arrange for one last rendezvous. Waiting for Alexis in his rooms, Rischka is suddenly approached by the weeping Lilli. Touched by her rival's despair, she promises to give up Alexis, but not without stealing Lilli's necklace during a sisterly embrace. As soon as the immaculately dressed Alexis enters the room, Rischka begins to mess up his fancy hairdo, spits champagne into his face, and aims at pieces of furniture with her pistol, now really living up to her reputation as an untamable mountain cat. With the film's ending, she returns to the mountains, her male companions, and her wild life-style.

Though Lubitsch already explored the relationship between femininity and antirealist tendencies in the comedies discussed above, *The Mountain Cat* remains his most powerful statement in this regard. With exaggeration and stylization as the dominant formal principles, the film repeatedly abandons its narrative in favor of overwhelming visual effects, including the fantastic set and costume designs, the grotesque acting styles, and the many cinematic trickeries. In order to achieve this feat, Ernst Stern took stylistic loans from the elegant floral ornaments of Art Nouveau, the stark contrasts of Expressionist painting, the bulbous forms of oriental architecture, and the clear lines and geometrical figures characteristic of modern graphic design. Every detail and every scene is subject to stylization. By quoting from very different periods and styles, the set design creates highly parodistic effects. It provides a backdrop for the narrative to unfold and defines the conditions under which the film's other story, its defiance of realism and verisimilitude, can be played out according to the rules of irony.

In *The Mountain Cat*, the human and the natural order suffer a similar fate, once they have been enlisted in the choreography of forms, ornaments, and visual effects. Even the presence of snow-capped mountains—location shooting for the film took place in the Bavarian Alps, near Garmisch—does not pose a challenge to the primitive cardboard decorations. In fact, the daring incorporation of nature into the world of art erodes the philosophical basis of such distinctions. That is why the snowy hills and icy hillsides look just as artificial as the confectioner's world of the fort (fig. 15). Its fantastic interiors, in particular, show how Stern's formal experimentation and Lubitsch's interest in antimilitarist satire come together to create an environment that is both appealing and disquieting in its formal beauty. With the paneled doors, wall decorations, and ornamental floors, each interior seems exclusively designed for one particular frame; hence the claustrophobic atmosphere. One room, for instance, contains rows of carefully arranged plaster cannons, each placed on a small pedestal. Another room is filled with miniature statues not dissimilar to toy tumblers known from the nursery. This series of beautiful tableaux ends with the victory celebrations and splendid fireworks (tinted, in some prints). With the advent of yet another spectacle, the cardboard world almost turns into an animated film.

The desire for stylization is indeed so strong that it inspires a number of scenes in which the defiance of reason—as epitomized by the ten ovens burning away in the open winter landscape—leads to actual film animation. Not only does a postcard virtually come to life, but the entire frame

15. *The Mountain Cat*: Fort Tossenstein

is taken over by countless variations on the art of masking. These masking devices appear in the form of circles, ovals, triangles, rhombuses, stars, rectangles, squares, zigzag lines, and cloverleafs—not to forget the keyhole and binocular masks and a particularly noteworthy mask in the form of kissing lips. There exist few frames that have not been altered, indeed imposed upon, through one of these variously shaped masks. Masks as a filmic technique, of course, refer back to the female masquerade in *The Doll*, namely as a kind of masquerading of filmic space. Masking on the level of technology accomplishes what the masquerade does through treachery and pretense: the transformation of reality. The resultant tension between narrative and spectacle, between mimesis and abstraction, gives *The Mountain Cat* its liberating qualities—qualities that, as the concluding remarks will show, allow for a more plausible conceptualization of sexual difference and the fantastic.

The Mountain Cat has been largely ignored by film histories that regard Expressionism, with its somber atmosphere and uncanny characters, as the predominant style of German silent cinema. With its animated sequences, its painted set designs, and its metaphorical investment of space, *The Mountain Cat* superficially resembles Expressionist films like *Caligari*, *Genuine* (1920, Wiene), or the later *Das Wachsfigurenkabinett* (1924, *Waxworks*) by Paul Leni. Aware of such affinities, Rudolf Kurtz, in his influential study *Expressionismus und Film* ("Expressionism and Film," 1926), even praised Lubitsch as the film artist who created "the first consequently executed art film (*Stilfilm*)." Characterizing Expressionism as a movement devoted exclusively to a higher spirituality, Kurtz goes on to define the Expressionist impulse as "the result of a unified creation that evenly seizes all components of film and transforms them accordingly."[20] Expresssionism's will to creation, however, inspired a very different definition by the poet Yvan Goll, who, appalled by the movement's political defeatism and lack

[20] Rudolf Kurtz, *Expressionismus und Film* (Berlin: Lichtbild-Bühne, 1926), 109. Beginning with Kurtz and Eisner, the term *Expressionist cinema* has had a slightly problematic reception history. From outright rejection of its significance as an influential artistic movement (e.g., Barry Salt, "From Caligari to Who?" *Sight and Sound* 48, no. 2 [Spring 1979]: 119–23) to halfhearted appraisal (e.g., John D. Barlow, *German Expressionist Film* [Boston: Twayne, 1982] and its misleading association with the horror film (e.g., S. Prawer, *Caligari's Children: The Film as Tale of Terror* [London: Oxford University Press, 1980]), the term has created more confusion than insight. For a tentative reassessment of its problematic status in literature and the other arts, see Anton Kaes, "The Expressionist Vision in Theater and Cinema," in *Expressionism Reconsidered: Affinities and Relationships*, ed. Gertrud Bauer Pickar and Karl Eugen Webb (Munich: Fink, 1979), 89–98 and Axel von Cossart, *Kino—Theater des Expressionismus* (Essen: Die blaue Eule, 1985). Evidence of a similarly problematic notion of the fantastic, the exhibition catalogue *Fantastique et realisme dans le cinéma allemand 1912–33* (Bruxelles: Musée du Cinéma, 1960), includes the Lubitsch films *The Doll*, *The Oyster Princess*, *The Eyes of the Mummy*, and *One Arabian Night*.

of formal restraint, described its products as "an amusement park of papier-mâché and stucco."[21] Goll's polemic remark about the primitive working materials of Expressionist film draws attention to its affinities with the circus and the fairground and reveals a similar investment in cheap thrills and great sensations.

To clarify this point, the excessive masking devices discussed above may at first glance illustrate perfectly Kurtz's definition of a "unified creation," but problems arise once their function within the film is examined more closely. For the most part, heavy masking has been perceived as an expression of anxiety or madness that transforms the external reality according to the inner vision of a protagonist. While the masks in *The Mountain Cat* speak to a similar desire for transformation, they escape the almost automatic pairing of Expressionism and (melo)drama and explore the comic potential of masking instead. In his reading of another heavily masked film, *The Golem* (1920), John S. Titford claims: "It is by no means an accident that German expressionist cinema, concerned as it was with the powers of darkness, with people trapped by their environment, and with the claustrophobia which pervades everyday life, would have made greater use of masking than the films of any other country or genre."[22] Interpreting the use of masks exclusively in the light of social pathology, however, makes it nearly impossible to include *The Mountain Cat* in the canon of Expressionist films, to which it (possibly) belongs because of its formal qualities.

Two alternatives offer themselves at this critical impasse. The concept of Expressionism in film needs to be reevaluated in regard to questions of gender; this would involve everything from Titford's assumption of a prevalent anthropomorphism "inherent in the German consciousness" to Eisner's well-known references to the "demoniac" and the strong influence of German Romanticism. Or *The Mountain Cat* must be placed within a larger framework that crosses the boundaries of film genres and film movements and establishes a "transsexual" place—again, a place for masquerades—by virtue of assimilating seemingly irreconcilable tendencies. Apart from the enormous difficulties involved in redefining an established concept like Expressionist film, several arguments speak in favor of the second alternative. To begin with, *The Mountain Cat* reveals equally strong affinities with the more dynamic, absurdist tradition of Surrealist and Futurist cinema. The influence of Surrealism is most evident in the radical investigation of filmic language, particularly the frequent use of visual metaphors, and the critical attitude toward public institutions like the military. Sharing

[21] Qtd. by Manfredo Tafuni, "U.S.S.R.—Berlin 1922: From Populism to 'Constructivist International,' " trans. Pellegrino d'Acierno, *Architecture Criticism Ideology* (Princeton, N.J.: Princeton Architectural Press, 1985, 143, n. 38).

[22] John S. Titford, "Object-Subject Relationships in German Expressionist Cinema," *Cinema Journal* 13, no. 1 (Fall 1973): 24.

these poetic qualities with French avant-garde films, *The Mountain Cat*
shows an awareness of politics (no matter how indirectly) that has been
suspiciously absent from the Expressionist cinema as a whole. Aware of
these qualities, film critics have tried to characterize films like *The Mountain
Cat* or *The Doll* through a combination of terms. Jean Domarchi, for instance, praises *The Doll* as a celebration of "comic expressionism,"[23] whereas
Sabath and Carringer call *The Mountain Cat* "a forgotten classic of surrealism."[24] Their laudable attempts reveal, more than anything, the difficulty
in finding a conceptual framework for films that challenge the standard
pairing of extreme stylization and male identity crisis.

In addition, the refreshing mixture of farce and fantasy in *The Mountain
Cat* makes the label "Expressionist" seem very inappropriate, almost
forced. The strong emphasis on motion and mobility further underscores
its distance from the frozen poses that characterize Expressionist acting
styles. *The Mountain Cat*, after all, does not resemble a nightmare but a
wish fulfillment. The film might take a similar approach to mise-en-scène
as classic Expressionist films—as is evidenced by the tightly constructed
frames, the famous chiaroscuro, the oblique angles, and distorted perspectives—but it does so to entirely different ends. The triumph of the fantastic
originates in a feeling of power, not disempowerment. Finally and most
importantly, *The Mountain Cat* stands in sharp opposition to the sexual
politics of the Expressionist cinema. It reverses almost all its basic tenets
and makes a mockery of its cherished problems. As soon as a female protagonist assumes center stage, the filmic devices take on different functions.
What changes take place, one could for instance ask, when a gullible brat
(*The Doll*) or a wild robberess (*The Mountain Cat*) take over the narrative,
or when the fantastic sets are invaded by the spirit of joyful anarchy?
Whose stories are told, whose class and gender position addressed, and
what desires satisfied? Is the uncanny, this unique experience captured in
the linguistic ambivalence of the German word *un-heimlich*, this wavering
between "what is familiar and agreeable and on the other, what is concealed and kept out of sight"[25] really the only libidinal source that fuels
these formal experiments? If the Expressionist cinema can indeed be interpreted as a cinema of castration anxiety, must the Lubitsch comedies not
be claimed for another tradition based on the claims of primary narcissism?
In the context of this study, these questions cannot be answered satisfac-
torily; they require a much more thorough discussion of narrative, style,
and sexual difference.

However, these questions can be rephrased within another critical

[23] J. D. [Jean Domarchi], *"Die Puppe," Cahiers du Cinéma* 198 (February 1968): 34.

[24] Robert Carringer and Barry Sabath, *Ernst Lubitsch: A Guide to References and Resources*
(Boston: G. K. Hall, n.d.), 20.

[25] Freud, "The 'Uncanny' " (1919), *The Standard Edition*, vol. 27, 225.

framework, that of the fantastic. Because of its independence from categories of genre, the fantastic might ultimately be more productive for describing the function of sexual difference in a film like *The Mountain Cat*.[26] This shift from an artistic movement to a critical concept with a much longer tradition leads to a similar shift from the fixation on characters, themes, and visual motifs to the recognition of spectatorship in the production of the fantastic as an aesthetic and emotional effect. Disengaging the fantastic and the uncanny, Tzvetan Todorov writes in his study *The Fantastic*: "It [the fantastic] seems to be located on the frontier of two genres, the marvelous and the uncanny, rather than to be an autonomous genre," and he concludes with a definition that seems much more useful with regard to films like *The Doll* or *The Mountain Cat*: "In the case of the marvelous, supernatural elements provoke no particular reaction in either the characters or in the implicit reader. It is not an attitude towards the events described which characterizes the marvelous, but the nature of these events."[27] *The Mountain Cat* contains many scenes that stand closer to the marvelous than the uncanny, including a remarkable dream sequence. Rischka lies asleep in her tent, dreaming of Alexis. Suddenly, her shadowy double rises from the primitive bedstead, ready to experience what she herself can only desire from a distance. The beloved Alexis enters the tent and, accompanied by the question "Do you hear my heart beat?" pulls a gingerbread heart from under his shirt. He throws it to Rischka who immediately begins to devour it with great pleasure, thus acting out the saying "You're good enough to eat" (i.e., "Ich habe dich zum Fressen gern").[28] Then they

[26] Thomas Elsaesser, for instance, has described the so-called fantastic films in relation to their audiences, arguing that "the films open up a perspective towards a class of spectators whose precarious *social* position . . . makes them members of the petit bourgeoisie, whose engagement with the class struggle takes the form of avoiding class struggle by imagining themselves above and outside." In "German Silent Cinema: Social Mobility and the Fantastic," *Wide Angle* 5, no. 2 (1982): 25. Elsewhere, Elsaesser also argues that "the 'defective' narratives of the Weimar cinema, their undecidability, their peculiar articulation of time and space, and their resulting problematic relation to visual pleasure and the look, all point to a form of perception that is neither altogether voyeuristic-fetishistic nor an imitation of 'normal' vision." See "Film History and Visual Pleasure: Weimar History," in *Cinema Histories, Cinema Practices*, ed. Patricia Mellencamp and Philip Rosen (Frederick, Md.: University Publishers of America, 1984), 78.

[27] See Tzvetan Todorov, *The Fantastic. A Structural Approach to a Literary Genre*, trans. Richard Howard, forward Roberts Scholes (Ithaca, N.Y.: Cornell University Press, 1987), 41 and 54. For a Bakhtinian approach to the interrelation between femininity and the grotesque, see Mary Russo, "Female Grotesques: Carnival and Theory," in *Feminist Studies, Critical Studies*, ed. Teresa de Lauretis (Bloomington: Indiana University Press, 1986), 213–29.

[28] Paul Willemen has discussed this scene as an example of cinema's use of metaphor (regarding consume/consuming passions) but fails to give a satisfactory reading of the underlying German, saying: "In fact, the eating of the heart most probably is only one of a series of lexies which associate Grishka [sic] with a lioness, thus again, but in a roundabout way,

dance to the inaudible tunes played by a snowman orchestra, until the imaginary movements of desire deteriorate into the involuntary spasms of sleep and Rischka awakes with a sudden, jerky movement.[29] The whole tent collapses; it was only a dream. In a way, the desiring woman in the film activates the same transgressive qualities that characterize the fantastic as a critical concept. As she moves back and forth between two social worlds and two different notions of reality, she virtually reproduces its fleeting qualities.[30]

To conclude: technological innovation and cultural ambition propelled cinema toward the ideal of a "seamless" appearance—a process that inevitably left traces in the films themselves. Punctuating and, at times, even disrupting the narratives, these traces document the losses and gains made in the name of "cinematic" progress. Spectacle, masquerade, and the fantastic are residues of earlier traditions of filmic representation and, therefore, crucial to any study of femininity and narrative in the early silent cinema. They are indicative of the differences in subject-object relationships that distinguish the early Lubitsch comedies, with their distinctly pre-Oedipal sensibility, from the sophisticated comedies of the twenties. And again it is women who provide the figure and the ground on which these processes take place. As characters and as images, they stand at the center of the negotiation process between affirmation and subversion that takes place in *The Oyster Princess, The Doll,* and *The Mountain Cat.*

---

imbuing the image with a metaphoric effect." In Paul Willemen, "Reflections on Eikhenbaum's Concept of Internal Speech in the Cinema," *Screen* 15, no. 4 (Winter 1974/75): 64.

[29] According to Barry Salt, the scene with the snowmen is taken from the 1916 Reinhardt production of Ferdinand Raimund's *Rappelkopf.* See "From German Stage to German Screen," in *Before Caligari. German Cinema, 1895–1920,* ed. Paolo Cherchi Usai and Lorenzo Codelli (Pordenone: Le Giornate del Cinema Muto, 1990), 414.

[30] By way of invoking one more time the power of names and naming, the reflections on the fantastic might also end with the moment that gave birth to the term *grotesque,* a term that links all three Lubitsch films to the problem of sexual difference and, more generally, differentiation. Its formulation was occasioned by the discovery of previously unknown Roman ornaments in the fifteenth century. "What is the character of these ornaments?" Bakhtin asks, only to give an answer that comments on the problems addressed above: "They impressed the connoisseur by the extremely fanciful, free, and playful treatment of plant, animal, and human forms. These forms seemed to be interwoven as if giving birth to each other. The borderlines that divide the kingdoms of nature in the usual picture of the world were boldly infringed. Neither was there the usual static presentation of reality. There was no longer the movement of finished forms, vegetable or animal, in a finished and stable world; instead the inner movement of being itself was expressed in the passing of one form into the other, in the ever uncompleted character of being" (32). In this suggestive description, the concepts of spectacle, masquerade, and the fantastic come together to attest to the power inherent in the process of demarcation, no matter whether between sexual identities, genres, film movements, or critical categories.

Filmography

Die Austernprinzessin (1919, *The Oyster Princess*). Director: Ernst Lubitsch, for Projections-AG Union. Scenario: Hanns Kräly. Camera: Theodor Sparkuhl. Sets: Kurt Richter. With Ossi Oswalda (Ossi, Mr. Quaker's daughter), Victor Janson (Mr. Quaker), Harry Liedtke (Prince Nucki), Julius Falkenstein (his valet), Curt Bois (conductor). Length: 3,753 ft. (1,144 m). Release: 25 June 1919.

Die Puppe, (1919, "The Doll"). Director: Ernst Lubitsch, for Union-AG. Scenario: Hanns Kräly. Camera: Theodor Sparkuhl. Sets: Kurt Richter. With Ossi Oswalda (Ossi, the doll-maker's daughter), Herman Thimig (Lanzelot), Victor Janson (Hilarius, the doll maker). Length: 4,511 ft. (1,375 m). Release: 5 Dec. 1919.

Die Bergkatze (1921, *The Mountain Cat*). Director: Ernst Lubitsch, for Projektions-AG Union. Scenario: Hanns Kräly, Ernst Lubitsch. Photography: Theodor Sparkuhl. Sets: Ernst Stern and Max Gronert. Costumes: Ernst Stern. With Pola Negri (Rischka, the mountain cat), Paul Heidemann (Lieutenant Alexis), Victor Janson (commander of Fort Tossenstein), Wilhelm Dingelmann (Claudius, the leader of the brigands), Hermann Thimig (Pepo), Edith Meller (Lilli) et al. Length: 5,965 ft. (1,818 m). Release: 14 April 1921.

Six

The Period Film as Palimpsest:
On *Passion* and *Deception*

"THE representative of the Republic paying tribute to a queen, even if only a historical one,"[1] this is how contemporaries described the unusual encounter between President Friedrich Ebert and actress Henny Porten on the set of *Deception* (fig. 16). Lubitsch himself, the master of effects, had invited the leaders of the Weimar Republic to attend the shooting of the spectacular coronation scene. With Ebert observing the masses from a safe distance and painter Lovis Corinth busily sketching Henny Porten for a planned portfolio,[2] four thousand extras in historical costumes pledged al-

16. *Deception*: Friedrich Ebert, Paul Davidson, Ernst Lubitsch, Henny Porten, Emil Jannings, Hanns Kräly

[1] L.K.F. [Lothar Knut Fredrik], "Der Reichspräsident bei *Anna Boleyn*," *Film-Kurier* 220, 1 October 1920.

[2] See Herbert Eulenberg, *Anna Boleyn. Originallithographien von Lovis Corinth* (Berlin, 1920). Note also Paul Eipper who, in *Ateliergespräche mit Liebermann und Corinth*, confirms the incident reported by Riess; reprinted in Helga Belach, *Henny Porten: Der erste deutsche Filmstar 1890–1960* (Berlin: Haude and Spener, 1986), 63–69.

legiance to English royalty in a grandiose setting that, down to the last details, brought Tudor London back to life. Merging in the imaginary the longing for a monarchy lost, its magical resurrection as cinematic spectacle, and the everyday reality of a republic unable to control its masses, Lubitsch's splendid settings conjured up a more perfect world in which individual desire and historical greatness were still one. However, this phantasmagoric effect could only be achieved in the context of other national historiographies.

The critics responded instantly to this incidental encounter of past and present and embellished its sparse details with the more lustful ingredients of public scandal. In his contribution to the historiography of German cinema Curt Riess fantasizes: "The unemployed have recognized the ministers. This seems to be the ideal opportunity for a political rally. Instead of forming for the coronation procession, they slowly approach the members of government with their spears. Instead of cheering Jannings and Porten, they boo the representatives of the republic. Then they shout in unison: 'We want jobs!' "[3] According to Riess's account, everybody anxiously left the studio. Only Henny Porten, the darling of the German people, stood like a fortress, tied down by the weight of her golden brocade train. Other, and probably more accurate, renditions of that day mention less dramatic details. They point to the bleak social conditions, the reminders of which jeopardize the visual perfection of the historical disguise: "Under those colorful, historical rags many shabby frocks become visible. The misery of the big city breaks through the picturesque exterior. A large contingent of extras seems to have been recruited from the army of the unemployed, and it was probably not easy to keep everything together."[4]

Whereas the visitors on the set of *Deception* still recognized the extras as human beings who lived in a miserable but at least discernible present, a later Lubitsch film, the oriental tale *The Loves of Pharaoh*, allowed the critics to abandon politics entirely for the aesthetics of a mass direction that could be accomplished only on the film set. Having witnessed the shooting of the masterly choreographed battle scenes, Hans Wollenberg could not help alluding to the glory of Prussian militarism, one of the period film's hidden sources of inspiration: "Issuing of orders: Lubitsch instructs the squadron leaders. Then a signal, a fanfare . . . the battle can begin. From the hills, men pour down in streams, from all valleys resistance rises, the rattling of vehicles, cavalrymen at full speed, brandished weapons, centuries erased: a veritable mirage."[5] As one might expect, the conditions of production left

[3] Curt Riess, *Das gab's nur einmal*, vol. 1 (Munich: Hanser, 1977), 89.

[4] L. B. [Ludwig Brauner], *"Anna Boleyn*. Ein neuer Großfilm der 'Union,' " *Der Kinematograph* 717, 10 October 1920.

[5] H. W. [Hans Wollenberg], "Pharao an der Oberspree," *Lichtbild-Bühne* 32, 6 August 1921. Compare another eyewitness: "These masses, colorful, fateful, a truly impressive sight, mas-

their mark on the finished product. The militaristic spirit returned to the surface in the spectators' patriotic reactions—evidence of the reciprocity of cinematic production and reception. One of *Passion*'s elated viewers felt compelled to make the following statement: "Ladies and gentlemen! We have just witnessed what revolution really means, what kind of atrocities it is capable of. (At the movies! The editors.) Therefore: Down with the revolution! The Emperor must come back!"[6] But the specter of a new militarism also prompted liberal critics like Kurt Pinthus to ask polemically: "Do you, Master Lubitsch, have ambitions to become the Ludendorff of the film, because your name also begins with the two letters Lu ? Keep in mind what damage Ludendorff did because he believed too much in the direction of the masses."[7]

Beleaguered by such associations, Lubitsch's period films entered the stage of film history. As the first German films to take advantage of historical subject matter, *Passion* (1919) and *Deception* (1920) successfully combined profitability with social respectability and artistic innovation. Nonetheless Lubitsch's work in the genre has failed to inspire the kind of debates that would do justice to its importance and that could illuminate its deceptive play with history, narrative, and spectacle. The strong emphasis on narrative that, until very recently, characterized German film criticism has prevented such investigations.[8] Focusing on specific themes and motifs, film critics and historians either have ignored questions of historical reception or they have interpreted the genre's dramatic constellations as the direct expression of a fatalistic world view. The period film could then be dismissed as escapist entertainment: sentimental and nostalgic at best, po-

terly directed, and probably irresistibly fantastic on the screen." In "Die Schlacht in den Gosener Bergen," *Der Film* 32, 7 August 1921: 50.

[6] "Sieg der Monarchie im Kino," *Vorwärts* 37, 21 January 1920. On the question of national identity, see also Tom J. Saunders, "History in the Making: Weimar Cinema and National Identity," in *Framing the Past*, ed. Bruce Murray and Christopher Wickham (Carbondale: University of Southern Illinois Press, 1992), forthcoming.

[7] Kurt Pinthus, "Lubitsch in Ägypten" (1922), reprinted in *Lubitsch*, ed. Hans Helmut Prinzler and Enno Patalas (Munich: C. J. Bucher, 1984), 101. For a brief historical assessment of Lubitsch's mass direction, see Lorenzo Codelli, "Lubitsch der massenregisseur," *Positif* 292 (June 1985): 23. For an account by Lubitsch himself, see also "Wie mein erster Grossfilm entstand," *Lichtbild-Bühne*, Luxusnummer "30 Jahre Film" (1924).

[8] Siegfried Kracauer's *From Caligari to Hitler. A Psychological Study of the German Cinema* (Princeton, N.J.: Princeton University Press, 1977) set the standard for this kind of film criticism. Examples include film histories like Ulrich Gregor and Enno Patalas, *Geschichte des Films* (Reinbek: Rowohlt, 1976) as well as close textual readings of particular films, such as Helmut Korte, "Der Einsatz der nationalen Propaganda—Beispiel *Madame Dubarry* (1919)," in *Film und Realität in der Weimarer Republik* (Munich: Hanser, 1978), 70–83. More recent studies have taken mass psychology (Le Bon, Durkheim, McDougall, Freud) as a point of departure for analyzing the function of masses in the period film. For example, see Markus Amann, "Massenpsychologie und Massendarstellung in Film," diss., University of Munich, 1983.

litically reactionary at worst. For the same reasons, the underlying assumption of a hierarchical relationship between form and content has prevented important insights into the genre's visual strategies. Thus the central question concerning the period film—that is, the blurring of the boundaries between past, present, and future—has been subordinated to the perspective of each theoretical framework instead of being taken as the vantage point for all further inquiries.

One of the aims of this chapter is to place Lubitsch's work in the cultural network of early Weimar culture and to link the reception of the period films more closely to questions of economic and national politics; here *Passion* serves as the main example. In the second part, set design and mass choreography are highlighted as the two filmic means that provided a projection screen for Lubitsch's own obsession with eroticism and the contemporary audience's longing for larger-than-life heroes and historical spectacles. Again the problem of femininity is central to this configuration. As in the comedies discussed in the previous chapter, the narratives are structured around the notion of sexual difference, and the problem of female desire in particular. Similarly, the specter of a liberated female sexuality manifests itself in the close attention to set and costume design—with one important distinction. While *The Oyster Princess* links the orgies of consumerism directly to the woman, the period films displace the relationship between sexuality and fetishism into the material ingredients of history itself. Whereas Lubitsch uses *The Doll* and *The Mountain Cat* to play with traditional notions of the fantastic, he uses the period film to recreate historical periods as realistically as possible. The crucial difference between the comedies and the period films lies in their different relationship to, and implication in, the politics of institutional and national power. As the more prestigious genre of the two, the period film obviously could not afford to question the order of representation. Thus *Passion* and *Deception* dealt with conflict in a more indirect way. Not dissimilar to a palimpsest, they allowed for the expression of such highly contradictory feelings as mourning, self-love, and revenge. Both films satisfied the need for sensationalism, chauvinism, and megalomania and gave meaning to the most diverse personal and national scenarios. Taking advantage of the multitude of voices that surrounded these films at the time of their release and paying special attention to the exaggerated rhetoric, then, may actually lead to the site where their truth is unwittingly spoken.

Passion and *Deception* were part of the process of economic concentration that had begun with the foundation of the Ufa film studio in 1917. Unlike studios such as Pathé, Fox, or Goldwyn, Ufa was not only controlled by economic and political interest groups (with the Reich and, later, the Deutsche Bank as major shareholders) but also participated actively in political decisions. During the postwar years, Ufa built a reputation with films that stood out through their sheer scale and volume. Technological innovations and the unparalleled availability of cheap labor contributed further to this development. Films with high production values proved instrumental in the studio's attempt to regain access to the international market and, in particular, to challenge the growing influence of the American film industry.

Riess reports that "the mark of the Ufa film was the authenticity of style, the precision with which decor, props, and costumes were designed and executed, in short: that everything was right."[9] Dimitri Buchowetzki (*Danton*, 1920), Richard Oswald (*Lucrezia Borgia*, 1922), and Richard Eichberg (*Monna Vanna*, 1922) were other leading Ufa directors who worked in the genre of the period film. But whereas they relied heavily on mass scenes, Lubitsch brought together elements from the history play, the mass spectacle, and the drawing-room comedy. Because of his background in slapstick and farce, he was able to add a touch of irony to an otherwise humorless genre and to compensate for the grand scale of history with his famed visual puns and innuendos. Of course, Lubitsch was also very fortunate to work with a team of experienced collaborators, consisting of actors Emil Jannings, Pola Negri, and Henny Porten, scenarists Norbert Falk and Hanns Kräly, cinematographer Theodor Sparkuhl, set designer Kurt Richter, and costume designer Ali Hubert. All contributed significantly to the popular success of *Passion* and *Deception*.

Ufa's struggle for international recognition found an adequate expression in the spectacular settings in which the new films were shown. The excesses of production continued in the conditions of reception, thus making the experience of cinema a social experience and an aesthetic pleasure. On September 19, 1919, the Ufa Palast am Zoo, soon to become Berlin's leading moving-picture theater, opened with the premiere of *Passion*. Following a musical potpourri and a dramatic prologue, the screening was accompanied by a full orchestra playing a musical score especially composed for the occasion. As was expected, *Passion*, because of what critics referred to as its "conscious use of all cinematic means,"[10] met with almost ecstatic reactions, from then on bringing forth a steady flow of dividends as well as critical acclaim. The film did so by creating excess in a situation of need, desire in the presence of want, and it provided the much-needed feeling of self-assurance that alone could end the nation's narcissistic crisis in the aftermath of World War I. Its potlatch of commodities and emotions was in fact so convincing that critics time and again set out to praise the osmotic relationship between the screen's imaginary world and the auditorium's architecture, as if to exorcize completely the realities of political

---

[9] Riess, *Das gab's nur einmal*, 102.
[10] Review of *Madame Dubarry*, *Vossische Zeitung* 481, 21 September 1919.

instability, mass unemployment, food rationing, and inadequate housing through the exuberant celebration of this other site: "The spacious auditorium of the former Palasttheater is perfect as a movie theater, with its discreet color schemes (the broad balconies in pale violet and gold, the circles in green and gold) contributing to a very tasteful interior design. Constructed like an amphitheater, this new Ufa theater, the Ufa-Palast am Zoo, provides excellent vision from every seat."[11] Kracauer would later disparage this synaesthetic collaboration between films and their framework of presentation as "elegant surface splendor" and "the total artwork of effects (*Gesamtkunstwerk*)."[12]

Brought into being through Ufa's expansionist politics and nourished by the cinema's cultural ambitions, Lubitsch's period films provided a context in which fears could be articulated, anger be expressed, and desires be fulfilled—even if only in the imagination. At the center of these processes stood the question of national identity. The films functioned, and were meant to function, like a living proof of the professionalism that distinguished the rising German film industry from its European competitors, especially those in France and Italy. Two kinds of arguments were involved: one centered on the international appeal of the period films, the other concerned their contribution to the redefinition of a German national identity. The inherent tension between these two arguments, however, must be seen as a function, rather than a shortcoming, of the dream of national empowerment through international recognition. The period films foregrounded and erased the contradictions in society in one sweeping gesture toward history. On the one hand, they attested to the atmosphere of (relative) political and economical stability that made such large-scale projects possible in the first place. The German film industry, according to this perspective, was a force to be reckoned with. By introducing new cinematographic techniques and by perfecting the creative possibilities of frame composition, dramatic lighting, and mass choreography, Lubitsch's contribution to the genre set new standards that were soon emulated everywhere. On the other hand, his films gave new meaning to the nationalist dreams of the old empire. This less obvious agenda manifested itself primarily on the level of film reception and involved a complicated negotiation between textual and contextual elements. The genre's formal characteristics provided the structure to which different interpretations could attach themselves. Combining historical spectacle and gripping melodrama, films like *Passion* and *Deception* satisfied people's longing for

[11] L. B., "*Madame Dubarry*," *Kinematograph* 664, 24 September 1919.

[12] Kracauer, "Kult der Zerstreuung: Über die Berliner Lichtspielhäuser"(1926), reprinted in *Das Ornament der Masse*, ed. Karsten Witte (Frankfurt am Main, 1977), 311 and 312. In English as "The Cult of Distraction," trans. Thomas Y. Levin, *New German Critique* 40 (Winter 1987): 91–96.

escapist entertainment. The beautiful historical settings displaced the country's monarchist heritage into aesthetic categories. Thus audiences could enjoy its blessings without really coming to terms with its failures. Finally, the historical narratives confirmed the value of authoritarianism, as they afforded audiences the opportunity to experience strong leader figures without suffering under their actions; hence the genre's conservative outlook.

At the same time that the historical impulse revealed an intense involvement with the past, it also gave expression to social experiences—the forced transition from a monarchy to a republic, the decline of bourgeois culture under the onslaught of mass culture—that were commonly equated with modernity and its deliberate rejection of history. Even the struggle for self-realization associated with the individual in modern society resurfaced in the settings of the past, though in more hidden ways. In the fixation on great personalities, Lubitsch's period films glorified the kind of individualism that was promoted by modern society but that could no longer be experienced without the aid of consumer goods, including films. Thus the protagonists came to represent emotional dispositions rather than historical characters. Their transgressions were perceived in direct relation to the restrictions and taboos in Weimar society. Similarly, through the strong emphasis on eroticism, very contemporary concerns—the changing attitudes toward sexuality, the emancipation of women—could be projected onto history's other times and places. Here it was the spectacle of a seemingly unrestrained, aggressive sexuality that compensated for the instability of sexual identities in reality. As a result, the historical material produced, through the mere impression of historicity, a wide spectrum of emotional and intellectual reactions that made the genre very appealing to contemporary audiences, no matter in which century or country the stories were set or which historical personages were involved. By confirming the individual's central position in narrative, indeed by highlighting his or her role in the hostile confrontation between individual and masses, *Passion* and *Deception* reconciled totalitarian and individualist tendencies, forcing them into a unified whole. Through their epic thrust and monumental scope, the films again made history and, through the preference for other national histories, this attempt again involved daring acts of transgression and appropriation. This process was made possible through the promotional campaigns and critical reviews that placed the films within the larger context of cultural politics and that ultimately determined their meanings.

Not surprisingly, the domestic and international reception of the period films focused on very different questions. The language of film criticism, with its many metaphors of warfare and conquest, is revealing here. The reception of *Passion* in German newspapers and cultural journals often sounded like an imaginary continuation of the First World War, with film now assuming the role of the avenging angel. In a way, the vision of German films invading the motion-picture theaters of Paris, London, and New York compensated for the traumatic war experience, the collapse of the Reich, and the humiliating conditions of the Versailles peace treaty. Reviews with headings like "The Monarchy—Victorious at the Movies," "The Entente in Tempelhof," "Paris in Berlin," or "The Fear of the German Film" bear witness to these fantasies of revenge. The German trade press, in particular, used the international success of *Passion* to indulge in a renewed sense of national pride. Aggressive self-confidence accompanied the marketing strategies for the film, as is evidenced by the eloquent writings of film journalists and promotion specialists who followed its triumphant itinerary through the major international moving-picture theaters. The New York correspondent of the *Lichtbild-Bühne*, for instance, informed his readers: "This moral victory makes it perfectly clear what kind of a splendid weapon film could become in Germany's struggle for international recognition. It also demonstrates how the film industry could be used in improving our trade deficit."[13] It was with unambiguous malice that some film critics even urged the French film industry to accept the fact "that a defeated, impoverished, exploited, and insulted Germany has passionately thrown herself into film production, thereby creating a means through which to conquer the world market."[14] Another critic had visions of a cinematic *Endsieg* (final victory): "Then we can shout with confidence: America, you are defeated!"[15] According to these polemics, *Passion* not only confirmed the technological superiority associated with the label "made in Germany" but also assured its audiences at home that the authoritarian foundations of Wilhelmine society had survived the onslaught of all disintegrating modernist tendencies. Evidence thereof was to be found in the film's mass scenes which, supposedly, proved the incompatibility of the terms *German* and *revolution*. For some critics *Passion* even offered an alternative image of the masses—or mass society, as it were—that emphasized integration instead of conflict, order instead of chaos, while at the same time celebrating the virtues of individualism rather than the threat of de-individualization. The spectacle of Lubitsch's film masses, they claimed, satisfied precisely those private and collective fantasies of heroism that had no place in modern mass society but were nonetheless necessary to its func-

[13] "*Madame Dubarry* in Amerika," *Lichtbild-Bühne* 46, 13 November 1920: 20.

[14] K. K., "*Madame Dubarry*—ein deutscher Sieg," *Lichtbild-Bühne* 15, 10 April 1920: 27.

[15] Artur Liebert, "*Madame Dubarry.* Der Aufschwung des deutschen Films," *Der Film* 38, 20 September 1919: 46. Years later, in a book published by the union of German motion-picture–theater owners, this rhetoric was forcefully repeated by another critic who praised the period film as an effective weapon of national propaganda. See Alexander von Gleichen-Rußwurm, "Kino und Weltgeschichte," in *Das deutsche Lichtspieltheater in Vergangenheit, Gegenwart und Zukunft,* ed. Rudolf Pabst (Berlin: Prismen-Verlag, 1926).

tioning—as individual fantasies. Caught between the logic of privation and compensation, the imaginary masses of *Passion* were called upon to participate in the nation's quest for a new/old identity.

While German critics emphasized the nationalist aspects, the international reception of *Passion* began with denial. Because of the still-prevalent anti-German sentiments that stood behind references to the "boches" and "huns" of the film industry, Ufa had planned to market *Passion* as an Italian film but then decided to advertise it in Paris as the work of a director from Vienna, in London that of a Swiss, and in New York that of a Parisian; these avoidance strategies also explain *Variety*'s reference to its Polish director, Emile Subitch.[16] And indeed, Lubitsch's films belonged to the first wave of foreign films that entered the American market, a process often referred to by critics as the "foreign invasion."[17] *Passion* became the first German film to be shown after the war, and it played for months at the Capitol, New York's largest motion-picture theater. The prospect of great profits even made it to the headlines of the American trade journals: "German-Made DuBarry Picture, Sold Here for $40,000, Worth $500,000, U.S. Rights Went Begging, 106,000 Saw Photoplay in First Week, $10,000 Estimated Daily Receipts."[18] Given this favorable reception, the promotional campaign for *Deception* already focused on Lubitsch as a major asset. The trade journal *Motion Picture World*, for instance, advised its exhibitors: "Make a heavy campaign on this and make the title the smallest part of the appeal. Drive on the fact that this is a story of Henry VIII made by the same masterhand which drew the story of DuBarry in *Passion*. That's the big selling point: not another *Passion* but another play by the same master of stagecraft."[19] Inspired by the film's innovative style, some American critics went so far as to call Lubitsch "the German Griffith" and "the great humanizer of history on the screen."[20] While such enthusiastic comments prepared the ground for Lubitsch's later negotiations with American film

[16] The title *Passion* was chosen to avoid confusion with a recent Fox release of *Madame Dubarry*. The English title for *Anna Boleyn*, *Deception*, then only continued in that tradition of catchy one-word titles, while at the same time referring to the film's melodramatic mood. In reviews of *Passion* (*Exceptional Photoplays* 1 [1920]: 3) and *Deception* (*Exceptional Photoplays* 5 [1921]: 3–7), critics frequently spoke out against these sensationalist titles.

[17] Alfred Kuttner, "The Foreign 'Invasion,'" *Exceptional Photoplays* 10 (1921): 1–2. See also Walter P. Eaton, "The German 'Invasion,'" *Freemen* 3 (1921): 208–9. On the American reception of *Passion*, see David B. Pratt, "'O, Lubitsch, Where Wert Thou?' *Passion*, the German Invasion and the Emergence of the Name 'Lubitsch,'" *Wide Angle* 13, no. 1 (1991): 34–70.

[18] *New York Times*, 23 December 1920: 28.

[19] "*Passion*," *Motion Picture World*, 30 April 1921. Also see the reviews of *Passion* in the *New York Times* 13 December, 1920: 19 ("one of the pre-eminent pictures of the day").

[20] Qtd. by Lewis Jacobs, *The Rise of the American Film: A Critical Theory* (New York: Teachers College, 1968), 305. Also note Lubitsch's public letter praising Griffith's *Orphans of the Storm*, "Lubitsch Praises Griffith," *Film Daily*, 5 January 1922: 1.

studios, they also prove that his choice of a particular period or setting was considered secondary in light of the mastery with which he integrated the historical subject matter into a coherent, psychologically motivated narrative.

Without doubt, the representatives of the German film industry were as interested in expanding their export business as their American counterparts were afraid of the foreign competition. Like the majority of American critics, they saw Lubitsch's period films as popular entertainment, not as examples of historical revisionism—a fact, however, that did not preclude the films' enlistment in the heated debates on national identity. Here the notion of the period film as an explicitly German genre deserves further scrutiny. Its implications were spelled out with great clarity in a controversy over *Deception* involving film critic Hans Wollenberg, film scenarist Hanns Heinz Ewers, and Lubitsch himself. The debate began with Ewers who, in response to Wollenberg's favorable review of *Deception*, had publicly accused Lubitsch of catering to foreign tastes. In his view, *Deception* had to be regarded as an artistic failure and a political scandal, for it revealed the film industry's total disregard for Germany's national myths. The increasing preference for alien story material, Ewers held, created an unhealthy mixture of racial and national characteristics that would eventually bring about the elimination of all differences. Demanding "We have to grow our own cabbage and must leave the neighbor's field alone,"[21] Ewers probably had in mind films like his own *The Student of Prague*. The full thrust of Ewers's argument becomes evident in his concluding remarks on what he defines as the true German spirit: "The only thing that can keep the German industry in competition is the idea as such: the idea that gives to film what belongs to it, that explores film's natural domains and brings out its possibilities!"[22] This unifying idea, of course, was the idea of nationalism which here remains hidden under the rhetoric of eternal values and pure beauty. In a public response to Ewers, Lubitsch rejected such arguments. He reaffirmed his commitment to an international cinema and, under the motto "The history of all nations belongs to the world!" called for the creative, responsible use of national imagery in films: "I see the world success of the German film in that it stands on its own feet artistically and thus offers an alternative to foreign productions."[23]

Given these different perspectives, Ufa's decision to take a well-known episode from French history for the story of *Passion*—and English history, in the case of *Deception*—may have been influenced by Madame DuBarry's reputation as one of history's quintessential seductresses—and, accord-

[21] Hanns Heinz Ewers, "*Anna Boleyn*," *Lichtbild-Bühne* 51, 18 December 1920: 24.
[22] Ibid., 24.
[23] Lubitsch, "Lubitsch contra Ewers . . . ," *Lichtbild-Bühne* 52, 25 December 1920: 29.

ingly, of Henry VIII as the ultimate philanderer—but in the final analysis, the producer was less interested in historical accuracy than market domination.[24] With economic expansion the key factor, it remains unclear to what degree and in what ways the period films, as films, served explicitly political purposes. As noted above, the reviewers in the German trade press frequently used the international success stories in order to discuss the films' nationalist tendencies. A strong German film industry, they claimed, was essential to Germany's new rise to power. This argument, while nationalist in its fantasies of economic expansion, was based on the premise of total marketability and, hence, cultural internationalism. It stood in sharp opposition to the chauvinistic attitudes that some ideologues expected from the period film. These ideas remained limited to the cultural sphere where they developed a life of their own, thus almost becoming the genre's evil double. Heated discussions took place between those who wanted to use the films as anti-French or anti-British propaganda, those who opposed the connection between film and politics on principle and, finally, those who questioned the relevance of the entire controversy. The oppositional categories of self and other introduced by the rhetoric of nationalism produced such an interpretative fervor that the distinctions between text and context almost disappeared. Seen in this light, *Passion* and *Deception* could indeed be read along the lines of national histories, whether such approaches were intended or not. The films assumed political significance because of the political discussions inspired by them. Though Lubitsch's interest lay primarily in showing the eroticism of power, his films could indeed be seen as highly charged political scenarios, thus almost becoming what they were not. Only in this context do *Passion* and *Deception* ransack the histories of the former enemy nations for sensational story material. Only from this perspective do the films appropriate specific emotional constellations for their own narratives of national identity. Then the extreme accessibility to ideological inscriptions makes their blatant misrepresentation of historical facts not a shortcoming but a great advantage in the unscrupulous attack on the historical imagination.

In the early twenties, this process took place in three intersecting spheres: cultural tastes, political attitudes, and psychological dispositions. To begin with, films with a historical setting were promoted by Ufa and other studios as a way of attracting middle-class audiences who were eager to combine entertainment with education. History provided the film industry with an almost inexhaustible supply of stories and allowed set and costume designers to demonstrate their latest accomplishments. Therein

[24] On films about the French Revolution, see Marc Silberman, "Imagining History: Weimar Images of the French Revolution," *Concepts of History in German Cinema*, forthcoming. By the same author, see also "Sex, Class and Revolution—Ernst Lubitsch's 'Passion,' " in "Imagining the Past: History and the German Cinema," unpublished manuscript, 9–43.

lay the genre's innovative power, therein lay its hidden modernity. As a way of turning the cinema into a showcase for German craftsmanship and technical know-how, the period film confirmed the audience's belief in technological progress, in spite of its apparent quaintness. The growing interest in historical narratives also made possible a compromise between the elements of spectacle that reminded audiences of an earlier, more primitive cinema and the demand for psychological motivation and narrative coherence that accompanied the cinema's elevation to middle-class culture. Bowing to the tight economy of filmic representation later brought to perfection in the classical Hollywood cinema, the period film provided cinematic spectacle but did so within a psychologically motivated narrative. The result was a product that looked convincingly high-class but that still accommodated the petty-bourgeois longing for lurid stories and spectacular settings. While the old flickers were rapidly disappearing, their spectacular elements found a new home in the period film, which allowed audiences to surrender to the pleasures of looking—but according to the new rules.

Moreover, the period film lured audiences into another world that was at once a counter-design and a reflection of the present one. *Passion* and *Deception* displayed the kind of material surplus—the extras, the settings, the props and costumes—that was lacking in reality. While a hidden fear of the masses inspired the glorification of ruthless individualism, the fascination with their secret power found an outlet in the many mass scenes. In the process, the political nature of these dispositions disappeared under psychological truisms. With politics subordinated to eroticism, nobody in the audience would link the revolutionary backdrop of *Passion* to the daily demonstrations that took place in Berlin, as some Ufa trustees had originally feared, asking: "Don't we encourage people's revolutionary tendencies?"[25] Rather, the film encouraged a turning away from daily politics and reinforced existing regressive tendencies. The spectators could withdraw from reality, flee into imaginary worlds, and see their grandiose fantasies acted out on the projection screens of the motion-picture theaters. Not surprisingly, many critics praised the period film as the ideal medium through which to forget the present and escape into the grand passions of distant times, heroic men, and seductive women. That this desire for forgetting was utilized in political debates seems only logical, given its origins in politics.

Finally, the period film enabled audiences not only to avoid confrontation with the present but also to displace its historical significance, and with it the entire question of history, into the imaginary worlds of cinema. This strategy of denial must be seen as a direct response to Germany's most

[25] Riess, *Das gab's nur einmal*, 77.

recent past and its legacies. In fact, the experience of the war and the technological advances in military cinematography were frequently mentioned in discussions about the genre's formal qualities. Eugen Tannenbaum, for instance, detected close affinities between the First World War and the process of genre formation. The war, he argued, was the true father of cinema, and its influence lived on in the period film's strong affinities with political spectacles: "Only the war, which has once again aroused and intensified our desire for the adventurous, the unrestrained, and the passionate, has given back to the cinema what belonged to it in the first place: sensations, crimes, attacks, chases."[26] Similar thoughts, though from a critical perspective, have been expressed by Kracauer who, in *From Caligari to Hitler*, relates the preference for skewed camera angles, bizarre close-ups, and rapid editing to the war years.[27] In his opinion, audiences had become accustomed to the sight of lacerated body parts on the battlefields; this experience found an expression in film's new aesthetics of fragmentation. As is evidenced by these remarks, which deal as much with film in general as with a particular genre, the period film stood at the forefront of a process that would ultimately lead to the fictionalization of politics and the politicization of fiction. National histories became individual stories, and collective memory was gradually replaced by industrially produced fantasies. Foreign national histories in particular fell prey to the film industry's almost cannibalistic search for appropriate story material. The main protagonists and periods of German history, on the other hand, were more often than not saved from such mutilation. Because of its absence from the thematic register of the period film, German history could be imagined as purer, stronger, and superior. Its domain was the historical film which, at least theoretically, aimed at historical accuracy and which often abstained from erotic subplots.

As I have argued so far, Lubitsch's period films inspired a wide range of conflicting interpretations and stood at the center of an intense debate on national identity. Caught between the call for a strong nationalist film culture and the need for films with clear international appeal, film critics used *Passion* and *Deception* to address issues that had more to do with economical and political questions than with their inherently aesthetic qualities. Evidence of this instrumental approach can be found in the trade press, the daily newspapers, and the cultural journals, all of which tended to portray

[26] Eugen Tannenbaum, "Der Großfilm," in *Der Film von morgen*, ed. Hugo Zehder (Dresden/Berlin: Rudolf Kaemmerer, 1923), 61. For more theoretical reflections on this relationship, see Paul Virilio, *War and Cinema. The Logistics of Perception*, trans. Patrick Camiller (London: Verso, 1989).

[27] For a highly polemical, but very interesting, discussion of narrative and spectacle in the period film, see Erich Benzinger's review of *One Arabian Night*, "Schaufilm oder Spielfilm?" *Das Tage-Buch* 44 (13 November 1920): 1332–36.

the domestic and international reception of the films in terms of empower-ment. However, the genre of the period film is far from being indeter-minate; its generic characteristics only invite such multiple inscriptions. *Passion* and *Deception* accommodated the desire for power in the widest sense through the appealing mixture of historical narrative and visual spec-tacle, while at the same time satisfying the emotional need for drama and eroticism. This correspondence between textual and contextual elements requires a closer look at the films themselves. For the remaining part of the chapter, the discussion will therefore concentrate on the function of set design and mass choreography in *Passion* and *Deception*; special attention will be given to the way these films negotiate the inherent tension between historical narrative and visual spectacle.

"World history from the keyhole perspective"[28] or "backstairs view[s] of history"[29]—statements like these summarize the prevailing view of Lu-bitsch's period films and attest to the continuing low regard for the genre as a whole. As has been demonstrated, opinions were less unified at the time of their first appearance on the stages of film history. In the case of *Deception*, most critics either praised the film as a colorful historical tab-leau—"a part of Old English history condensed into powerful images"[30]—or dismissed it as a dressed-up tale of power and sexual desire: "joy and pain of beautiful Queen Anna . . . [the first wife] goes into exile, Anna to the scaffold. The laughing Priapeian king lies in the arms of a third."[31] These differences in opinion could be dismissed as typical of a film criticism based on taste. However, when one recalls the extreme complexity of early post–World War I German culture—the context within which Lubitsch's period films were first received—it becomes clear that the conflicting opin-ions about the films only reveal their primary function as texts to which individuals from various perspectives could ascribe different meanings. This accessibility to interpretation was a direct result of the conflation of story and history, and closely related to that, the function of architecture and mass choreography in the Lubitsch period film.

In *Passion* and *Deception*, the narrative is set into motion through a series of transitions between the world of individual desire (Jeanne Vaubernier's beauty, Henry VIII's philandering) and national politics (the French Rev-olution, England's breaking away from the Church of Rome). By focusing on the tensions between the two spheres, Lubitsch pursues old and new interests. With their strong women protagonists and their complicated love triangles (Armand-Jeanne-Louis XV; Norris-Anna-Henry VIII),

[28] Gregor and Patalas, *Geschichte des Films*, vol. 1, 48.
[29] Edward Wagenknecht, *The Movies in the Age of Innocence* (Norman, Okla.: University of Oklahoma Press, 1962), 202.
[30] W. P., "Filmschau *Anna Boleyn*," *Vorwärts* 64, 16 December 1920.
[31] My., *Anna Boleyn*, *Vossische Zeitung* 612, 16 December 1920.

both films develop further the intricacies of the early comedies, most obviously by adding a touch of playfulness and frivolity. But in light of their
suggestive equations among power, desire, and death, they also capitalize
on the tragic grandeur that the bourgeois settings of the comedies fail to
provide. The combination of comic and tragic elements, as well as the constant moving back and forth between the public and the private spheres,
requires the introduction of a unifying force that holds together these disparate elements: this element is provided by the women characters (fig. 17).
Accordingly, *Passion* focuses on a young, attractive milliner, Jeanne Vaubernier (Pola Negri), who has affairs with a number of influential men (the
young Armand, the Spanish ambassador, the senile Count DuBarry) and
eventually becomes the mistress of Louis XV (Emil Jannings). Thrown
into the center of insidious political schemes rather than actively participating in them, Madame DuBarry acquires great power but is eventually
punished for her social climbing by the revolutionary tribunals. In the end,
she dies on the guillotine. Similarly, *Deception* tells the story of a lady-in-
waiting at the English court, the shy Anna Boleyn (Henny Porten), who
attracts the attention of Henry VIII (Emil Jannings) and is chosen to replace his old wife, Catherine of Aragon. Yet she, too, fails to bear him the
desired heir to the throne and Henry turns to a new favorite, Jane Seymour. Convicted of adultery, Anna also dies on the scaffold.

Both films tell stories of male desire and female victimization that are
played out against the backdrop of great historical events. "Because of
woman" ("Um des Weibes willen")—this programmatic inter-title from
The Loves of Pharaoh describes accurately the fixation on the erotic and on
woman as the primary object of desire that runs through all Lubitsch films.
Because desire has such an equalizing effect, the individual traits of femme
fatale Pola Negri (in the role of the sensuous Parisienne) and plain Henny
Porten (as the shy English maiden) are little more than a function of the
particular eroticism attributed to their specific historical periods: refined
perversion in *Passion*, healthy lust in *Deception*. With death shown as the
last moment of truth, the differences manifest themselves most strongly in
the respective death scenes. Pola Negri struggles with her hangmen to the
last minute, while Henny Porten walks toward the scaffold with great dig-
nity. Consequently, the spectator is spared her death through a discreet
fade-out.

In her critique of *Passion*, Lotte Eisner seems to leave no questions un-
answered: "But a king manicuring his mistress or artlessly pinching a
pretty wench is hardly Unadorned Reality, and even less History As It Was
lived."[32] Arguing along similar lines, Kracauer claims: "Instead of tracing

---

[32] Lotte Eisner, *The Haunted Screen*, trans. Roger Greaves (Berkeley: University of California Press, 1973), 82.

17. *Passion*: Emil Jannings, Pola Negri

all revolutionary events to their economic and ideal causes, it [*Passion*] persistently presents them as the outcome of psychological conflicts. . . . *Passion* does not exploit the passions inherent in the Revolution, but reduces the revolution to a derivative of private passions."[33] Consequently, Lubitsch's spurned lover-turned-revolutionary becomes a revolutionary out of unrequited love. The correspondences between story and history, however, are not that straightforward. They require, above all, a closer look at the individual's position in the staging of historical fiction, including a greater attention to his or her participation in the effects of cinematic spectacle.

As has been argued above, history provided Lubitsch with the necessary visual styles, moods, and settings. This interest in the historical effect—on historicity, in other words—accounts for the ease with which he moves back and forth between episodes from Western history (*Passion, Deception*) and more mythological periods such as Ancient Egypt in *The Loves of Pharaoh* or Persia in *One Arabian Night*. Though the choice of a particular historical setting appears to have played no decisive role, except for reasons irrelevant to plot construction, narrative films need a center, a point of convergence, around which to organize their stories/histories. This position is most frequently occupied by an individual who must be at once unique—distinguished by his or her power, beauty, or character—and fully interchangeable.[34] *Passion*, for instance, is held together by the figure of an attractive woman; but her presence at the center of the narrative does not necessarily imply her centrality to the historical process. Jeanne Vaubernier, though an inhabitant of prerevolutionary Paris, looks and behaves

[33] Kracauer, *From Caligari to Hitler*, 49. Kracauer's remarks in *From Caligari to Hitler* offer a useful point of departure for further inquiry, despite their blindness to the various levels of representation. He sets out by revealing the economic, social, and psychological conditions that stood behind the genre's success and were responsible for its nihilistic philosophy of history. In so doing, Kracauer provides supporting evidence for the existence of proto-fascist sociopsychological tendencies. The period film, according to his argument, anticipates the coming submission of the masses under the tyranny of the autocratic leader. Compare his very different analysis in "Die Photographie" (1927), in *Das Ornament der Masse*, ed. Karsten Witte (Frankfurt am Main: Suhrkamp, 1977), 24–25. Compare also his comments on the inherent limitations of the historical film in "Der historische Film" (1940), in *Kino: Essays Studien Glossen zum Film*, ed. Karsten Witte (Frankfurt am Main: Suhrkamp, 1974), 43–45 and in *Theory of Film. The Redemption of Physical Reality* (New York: Oxford University Press, 1960), 77–78.

[34] David Hull, for instance, has argued that every narrative needs such a center in order not to fall apart: "The notion of central subjects is crucial to the logical structure of historical narrative. Assuming for the moment that history could be analyzed completely into a single set of atomistic elements, there are indefinitely many ways in which these elements can be organized into historical sequence. The role of the central subject is to form the main strand around which the historical narrative is woven." In "Central Subjects and Historical Narratives," *History and Theory* 14, no. 3 (1975): 255.

like a typical twenties flapper in historical disguise. The character's control of the narrative stands in sharp contrast to the actress's distance from history. Through the means of visual spectacle, Lubitsch conceals the non-identity of history and narrative and creates a false authenticity based on set and costume design. The remaining discrepancies between the woman's narrative position and the historical setting, however, prove more than anything that the historical effects in Lubitsch's period films take place outside of narrative. They are linked to visual representation and must be examined accordingly.

The undeniably strong investment in history that gives the period film cultural respectability manifests itself primarily in visual—that is, architectonic, painterly, and choreographic—terms. This is no coincidence. According to critic Hans Siemsen, films—and, one might add, the period films in particular—were essential in the transformation of history into spectacle, as they "belatedly raced through Germany's development from 1870 to 1913. Now everything looks like those ostentatious representational buildings of the Wilhelmine golden age (*Glanzepoche*): with fake and real columns, marble, capitals, domes, towers, staircases, mosaics. Like the Emperor Wilhelm Memorial Church: showy and expensive, yet boring and shallow."[35] Speculating on the new possibilities opened up by photography and film, most critics welcomed such developments. In their opinion, the period film was a modern version of the nineteenth-century historical novel; therein lay its social and cultural relevance. Given the increasingly visual orientation in mass society, some even claimed that "in communicating the spirit of an epoch, film is probably the more convincing medium."[36]

Indirectly, critics also responded to modernist writers and critics who were calling into question the very notion of historical representation and who had begun to introduce more fragmented narratives, as well as more disturbing perspectives on the question of subjectivity. Relegated to the margins of high culture, historical narratives found a new home in the cinema: in the form of new genres, through set and costume design, as motion-picture theater architecture. At the forefront of this process stood the period film which supplied the unified vision through which the onslaught of modernism, as articulated by the literary and artistic avant-gardes, could be annulled, as in a magic trick. This convergence of narrative and history, however, was only possible through the means of cinematic spectacle.

Lubitsch, who always took great pride in the authenticity of his sets, the well-researched historical costumes, and the large numbers of extras, excelled in holding together present and past, story and history with his use

[35] Hans Siemsen, "Die Filmerei," *Die Weltbühne* 17, no. 1 (1921): 103.
[36] Pinthus, "Aus dem Tage-Buch, *Anna Boleyn*," *Das Tage-Buch* 51, 31 December 1920.

of set design. As early as 1916, he expressed interest in the ways set design contributed to a film's visual appeal. Yet he also was well aware of the dangers involved when quantity was sacrificed for quality. As Julius Urgiss reports in a portrait of the director: "He, too, is of the opinion that the decor has to be first rate, meaning: beautiful and authentic. But considerations of design should not predominate; they should not, as is often the case, become the major concern."[37] Trained in the intimate scale of ethnic comedy, Lubitsch knew how to avoid the pitfalls of historical spectacle. His goal was to develop an alternative to the Italian monumental film: "I tried to break with the operatic style of the fashionable Italian school. I wanted to invest my historical protagonists with humanistic features. I put as much emphasis on the intimate personal nuances as on the mass scenes. I combined both strands by finding a logical connection between them."[38] As a result, Lubitsch demanded detailed attention to all aspects of film production, including the latest trends in modern stage design and acting styles: "The more prominent the decor, the more we must pay attention to detail."[39] But with his family background in clothing manufacture, even he at times submitted to the sensuous appeal of silk, velvet, damask, ermine, lace, and brocade and fell prey to the splendid effects created by the interplay of light, movement, and precious materials; Porten's sixteen and Jannings's ten magnificent costumes for *Deception* offer sufficient proof of his infatuation with textures. And isolated moments like the opera ball sequence in *Passion*—with its ebb and flow of soloists and chorus—demonstrate that, sometimes, there was even room for the tableaulike spectacles characteristic of the earliest examples of the genre.[40]

Lubitsch's strong emphasis on set design and, hence, on mise-en-scène can also be found in other films of the early twenties. The silent German cinema depended, more than other national cinemas, on the innovative work of its set and costume designers. Technical and artistic developments in set design contributed significantly to the success of the Expressionist cinema but also influenced the period film, the Prussian film, and, in treating landscape as architecture, the mountain drama. The end result was a "metaphysics of decor" that, while meant to support story and characters,

[37] Julius Urgiss, "Ernst Lubitsch: Künstlerprofile VI," *Der Kinematograph*, 30 August 1916.

[38] Jerzy Toeplitz, *Geschichte des Films*, vol. 1, trans. Lilli Kaufmann (Munich: Rogner and Bernhard, 1977), 214. Contemporaries, on the other hand, often noted the influence of the Italian and American monumental films, for instance Léon Moussinac in his *Naissance du cinéma* (Paris: J. Povolozky, 1925), 129.

[39] "Ernst Lubitsch über Film, Filmkunst und sich. Ein Interview," *Film-Kurier* 194, 1 September 1920.

[40] The DuBarry novel, published in conjunction with *Passion*'s release, contains a lengthy sequence in which Jeanne and her lover, Jean DuBarry, meet, for one last time, in the middle of a devastating fire in the Paris opera. See Hanns Steiner, *Madame Dubarry* (Berlin: Buch-Film Verlag, 1919).

often dominated all other cinematic elements. Kurt Richter, the set designer for *Passion* and *Deception*, frequently sacrificed historical accuracy for
the kind of "higher truth" found in a specific atmosphere. For *Passion*, he
chose the Rococo charm of the palace at Potsdam rather than the monumental splendor of Versailles. On the set of *Deception*, he employed up to
fourteen foremen, two hundred carpenters, and four hundred sculptors
and plasterers, thus treating set construction with a perfectionism usually
reserved for more permanent structures (fig. 18). Anybody visiting the Ufa
lot at Tempelhof during shooting would have been enthralled by a fasci-
nating assemblage of fictional spaces: "The temples for *One Arabian Night*
are still up, standing side by side with the contorted houses of Old Prague.
A bewildering mixture of the most diverse styles, a peaceful community of
palaces, churches, and clay huts . . ."[41] In the middle of this pell-mell of
historical periods, Richter recreated entire sections of London, with Westminster Abbey alone standing ninety feet high.

Passion and *Deception* also show the expertise with which Lubitsch and
Richter approached different stylistic periods. Their prerevolutionary
Paris, for instance, conveys a distinctly urban atmosphere, with its pictur-

18. *Deception*

[41] "*Anna Boleyn* in Tempelhof," *Film-Kurier* 163, 27 July 1920.

esque quarters, narrow streets, and quaint marketplaces. The film's spatial organization—a reflection of the narrative—follows a woman's rise from the plain milliner's shop of her humble origins to the light-flooded salons and luxurious bedrooms of the royal palaces that are filled with deceptive mirrors, silk screens, embroidered brocade curtains, and satin sheets, and surrounded by geometrical pleasure gardens, rose cottages, and long alleys. After the uprising of the urban masses, Jeanne DuBarry is forced to return to the places of her past, as is suggested by the bleakness of her prison cell and, finally, the crowded marketplace that becomes the site of her execution. The spatial dramatics of *Deception*, too, are set into motion by a woman's beauty, her entrance ticket into the privileged world of male power. The film opens with the isolated figure of Anna, as she glances onto the open sea during her passage to England, but is invaded by the claustrophobia associated with spatial confinement and male domination. The king, portrayed masterfully by Jannings with his enormous proportions, controls every setting and every moment, just as the somber Tudor palaces and churches add a distinct touch of tragedy that is only momentarily relieved during a few scenes set in the bucolic English countryside. While the light-flooded interiors in *Passion* set the stage for a more playful kind of eroticism, the dark corners, closed doors, and revealing windows of *Deception* denote entrapment and death. This tyranny of space finds a most appropriate form of expression in a number of unusual masking devices, including the Gothic archlike mask that frames the Archbishop of Canterbury.

Set design, in combination with lighting and props, provides the stage on which the historical narratives come into their own. The architectural structures predetermine the social interactions that take place in and between them. Comparable perhaps to the phenomenon of petrifaction, space functions as the memory trace of past events and the inescapable mold for future ones.[42] The calculated spatial designs, the graphic interplay of light and shadow, the geometric patterns created by different forms and materials, and, finally, the painterly compositions of individuals and spaces attribute a kind of significance to the visible world that, in contrast to the transitoriness of desire, ultimately confirms the hegemony of structures, both architecturally and socially. It is therefore not through variations on

[42] Commenting on the role of architecture in Lubitsch's period films, Dieter Bartetzko has argued that the passionate debates about trends in modern public architecture during the twenties were, in fact, debates about new spaces for a new society. With Lubitsch and Lang as important forces behind this development, Bartetzko claims that their use of set design and choreography set the mood for the monumental architecture of the Third Reich. See Dieter Bartetzko, *Illusionen in Stein. Stimmungsarchitektur im deutschen Faschismus. Ihre Vorgeschichte in Theater- und Filmbauten* (Reinbek: Rowohlt, 1985). On architecture, silent German cinema, and the "Ausstattungsfilm," see also Helmut Weihsmann, *Gebaute Illusionen. Architektur im Film* (Vienna: Promedia, 1988), esp. the chapter "Raumplastiken," 60–99.

the "cherchez la femme" theme but only through the metaphorical invest-ment of mise-en-scène that Lubitsch's period films can be fully understood.

The portrayal of the masses, who represent both a continuation of and a challenge to the power of set design, underscores the importance of mise-en-scène. As the subject of similarly fleeting relationships, they must be seen as its natural extension—an architecture in process—and its counter-point. Appearing in changing states of ossification and liquefaction, the masses simultaneously threaten and protect the status quo of society, and of narrative as well. To be sure, many extras possess individual character-istics that distinguish them in the crowd and give them a personal story. Helma Sanders-Brahms has pointed to this quality: "And these mass scenes reveal once again how much more humanly than most of his colleagues this director thinks and works. . . . It is his love of mankind that makes him both overly critical of and highly sympathetic toward the individual."[43] The masses in Lubitsch's period films, then, are the sum of individuals acting in solidarity and a mere reflection of the main protagonists. They are too formless to acquire real significance within the narrative but also too dif-ferentiated as to function merely as an ornament. Here Reinhardt's theater productions with their spectacular mass scenes, the confrontation between individual and masses, and the dramatic lighting effects exerted a strong influence that can be traced to such details as the gesture of the raised arm borrowed from the 1910 production of *Oedipus Rex*.[44] Also similar to Rein-

[43] Helma Sanders-Brahms, review of *Madame Dubarry*, in *Lubitsch*, ed. Prinzler and Patalas, 135. A comparison to the distinct strategies of quantification and ornamentation that charac-terize the representation of the masses in the work of Joe May and Fritz Lang may serve to illuminate their ambivalent status in the early work of Lubitsch. With such highly successful monumental films as *Veritas Vincit* (1918) or *Das indische Grabmal* (1921, *The Indian Tomb*), May shamelessly indulged in the conspicuous consumption of men, animals, and materials, as Riess has rightly pointed out: "Joe May has brought more extras onto the screen. But they remained extras under his direction. They play around in the background, they walk across the screen making noises that nobody hears" (102). Without even a rudimentary story line, May's big productions lacked the technical perfection as well as the operatic pathos that at least distinguished the Italian monumental film as high spectacle. Lang's mass choreography, on the other hand, submitted the human body to the rules of a geometry that rendered insig-nificant all distinctions between individuals and objects and that obliterated all differences in favor of pure form. Clearly, the architectural and social formations in Lang's *Die Nibelungen* (1924, *The Nibelungs*) and *Metropolis* (1927) owe much to the exploration of mise-en-scène begun by *Passion* and *Deception*. But for him, man existed only as a part of geometrical config-urations, as a cog in the wheel of anonymous political machineries. Compared with the films of May and Lang, Lubitsch's period films, then, offer a third possibility. In contradistinction to May, Lubitsch always returns to the individual gesture. His extras are not a mere backdrop but, as individuals, create an atmosphere of diversity and heterogeneity—perhaps a hidden comment on the historical process as such. At the same time, Lubitsch's ironic approach to the historical material is also sharply set against Lang who also uses stylization but under the influence of a very different notion of history.

[44] Eisner was the first to discern connections: "In *Madame Dubarry* the revolutionary

hardt's stage productions, the films frequently situate the main protagonists within empty spaces that highlight their singularity but at the same
time anticipate their downfall. Precisely this empty space is claimed by the
revolutionary masses of *Passion*, first during the verbal confrontation between the incensed mob and the frivolous court society and, later, through
the chaos brought about by the revolutionary tribunals and public execu-
tions. *Deception* contains a sequence in which this empty space is literally
invaded only to be restored to its original state in the last scene. Shot from
a high angle, the camera shows the forecourt of Westminster Abbey as it
slowly fills with people gathering for the infamous coronation scene. Once
Henry VIII and Anna Boleyn leave the cathedral, the masses move toward
the royal couple, angrily demanding the return of the old queen, Catherine, and her daughter. Suddenly the king's pike staff enters the frame and,
through the ordering devices of their halberds, reconstitutes the old spatial
order.[45]

In the Lubitsch universe, the masses' triumph in *Passion* and their defeat
in *Deception* have the same political implications, since the dramatic and
visual function of the masses must be sharply distinguished from each
other. Only the sensation of movement counts, not its origin or direction.
While the masses fail to contribute to the advancement of the story, they
safeguard the existence of narratives centered on the individual precisely
by renouncing all claims to dramatic representation. Mediating between
history and desire, they protect the dominant order but are also able, at
every given moment, to reverse this order and introduce another state of
representation, namely that of spectacle. In other words, the masses in *Passion* and *Deception* function as a mirror for the elaborate spatial designs and
the main characters. Yet in performing that role, they also pose a threat to
these solidified spaces, a threat that is signified by their changing appearance as unified body and heterogeneous crowd. Such instability on the
level of representation may ultimately undermine their significance alto-

---

masses clamouring around the guillotine for the death of the former favorite raise their right
arms, a formalized movement frequently seen in German films whenever a crowd of extras
has to express fury or exultation. Reinhardt gave these gestures to the classical chorus in his
production of *Oedipus Rex*, performed in a Berlin circus in 1910. They lose all value in the
majority of German films in which inspiration has deteriorated into mere technique" (86).

[45] In *The Seven Lively Arts* (New York/London: Harper, 1924), 336, Gilbert Seldes praises
that scene for masterly involving "every correct principle of the aesthetics of the moving picture." In more general terms, the reciprocal relation between structure and structuration in
Lubitsch's mass scenes has also been commented upon by British critic Claire Lejeune: "but
Lubitsch had a way of manipulating his puppets that gave multitude, and in contrast, loneliness, a new face. No one before had so filled and drained his spaces with the wheeling mass,
rushing in the figures from every corner to cover the screen, disposing of them again like a
whirlwind with one single figure staunch in the middle of the empty square." In *Cinema*
(London: Alexander Maclehose, 1931), 64.

gether and replace revolutionary thrust with a glorified individualism. This has been the most frequent charge leveled at Lubitsch's period films. However, the stubborn insistence on individual desire that links the period films to the film comedies could also be seen as the point of departure for forms of historical representation that take such desires seriously.

History or myth, narrative or spectacle, mass ritual or drawing-room eroticism—Lubitsch's period films elude easy definition. But perhaps that elusiveness is also part of the affinities between history and cinema. As this analysis has shown, Ufa's interest in big, profitable productions, the many discussions that accompanied the reception of *Passion* and *Deception*, and, last but not least, Lubitsch's own preoccupation with eroticism all provided points of resistance to the genre's exploitation by the much less ambiguous scenarios of mass deception. Rather than being a means of manipulation, the period films participated in and granted access to conflicting inscriptions and meanings and, therefore, must be thought of as a site of production rather than a mere product of dominant culture or conservative ideology.[46] Thus it may actually even be more useful to conceive of the genre as a form of coming to terms with the past (*Vergangenheitsbewälti-gung*), that is, to theorize it in post-Wilhelmine rather than prefascist terms, as Kracauer has proposed. The critical discourses that accompany films like *Passion* and *Deception* make them part of an ongoing debate on national identity and reveal the continuities, rather than the teleological moments, in the history of cinema. Similarly, the stories and settings bear too many traces of the immediate past and present to be reduced to their anticipatory potential. With this in mind, a reassessment of the period film in terms of its mediation of past and future would not only open up the debate about the historical nature of cinema but also contribute to a better understanding of narrative, spectacle, and visual pleasure as its constituting elements.

To return to the image invoked at the beginning: The momentous encounter of Ebert and Porten on the set of *Deception* undoubtedly belongs to the much-maligned literary form of the anecdote. Nonetheless, precisely the triteness of the situation brings to the fore the powers that hold together such disparate temporalities. As the anecdote reveals, the genre's underlying operating principle, the encounter of real-life and fictional rulers, can be thought of as a metaphorical representation of its libidinal investments. Reality is invaded by a strong desire for fictionalization; repre-

---

[46] Thus Jean-Louis Comolli has argued: "It is my hypothesis that the filmic representation of History defies Fiction although it holds only through it. In such a paradoxical situation, both required and prevented, irresistible and imprisoned, historical fiction becomes a kind of analyser which pushes to their most revealing limit the conditions of exercise and stakes at play in all cinematic fiction." In "Historical Fiction: A Body Too Much," *Screen* 19, no. 2 (1978): 42.

sentation turns away from the exigencies of the present and, instead, raids the archives of history in order to satisfy an insatiable need—not for remembering but for forgetting. Such speculations find unexpected support in a photograph taken during the coronation scene. This remarkable group portrait casts together actors for yet another drama of public relations as they conscientiously smile into the camera: German president Ebert, Ufa director Davidson, scenarist Kräly with some officials in dark suits, actors Porten and Jannings in historical costumes, and, towering above everybody, the inattentive Lubitsch in casual attire. Given the complex strategies of meaning production that intersect with the genre's formulaic structure, Kurt Pinthus's half-serious campaign, "Henny Porten for President!"[47] points to the overwhelming success of that other scene, the scene captured in this particular photograph.

Filmography

Madame Dubarry (1919, *Passion*). Director: Ernst Lubitsch, for Projektions-AG Union. Script: Norbert Falk, Hanns Kräly. Camera: Theodor Sparkuhl. Sets: Kurt Richter. Costumes: Ali Hubert. With Pola Negri (Jeanne Vaubernier, later Mme. DuBarry), Emil Jannings (Louis XV), Reinhold Schünzel (Duke of Choiseul), Harry Liedtke (Armand de Foix) et al. Length: 7,480 ft. (2,280 m Prinzler, 1,375 m Sabath and Carringer). Release: 18 Sept. 1919.

Anna Boleyn (1920, *Deception*). Director: Ernst Lubitsch, for Projektions-AG Union. Script: Norbert Falk, Hanns Kräly. Camera: Theodor Sparkuhl. Sets: Kurt Richter. Costumes: Ali Hubert. With Emil Jannings (Henry VIII), Henny Porten (Anna Boleyn), Aud Egede Nissen (Jane Seymour) et al. Length: 9,163 ft. (2,793 m). Release: 14 Dec. 1920.

[47] Pinthus, "Henny Porten als Reichspräsident," *Das Tagebuch* 41 (1921) reprinted in Belach, *Henny Porten*, 82–85.

Seven

The Tyranny of Vision: *So This Is Paris* and Others

WOLFGANG ISER'S *The Act of Reading* (1976) opens with the following statement: "As a literary text can only produce a response when it is read, it is virtually impossible to describe this response without also analyzing the reading process. Reading therefore . . . sets into motion a whole chain of activities that depend both on the text and on the exercise of certain basic human faculties. Effects and responses are properties neither of the text nor of the reader; the text represents a potential effect that is realized in the reading process."[1] In film studies, theorists have become quite comfortable with using the term *reading* (i.e., interpreting) when referring to the close analysis of a film. Yet they have shied away from extending the concept of reading to the "average" spectator in the cinema who supposedly is under the sway of a more passive state of mind. The term *reading* in film studies, then, is what separates the lowbrow film fan from the highbrow film critic. Such distinctions crumble under close scrutiny. For in watching a film, both the "average" film viewer and the sophisticated film critic engage in an ongoing process of interpretation that only differs in the degree of critical detachment.

Playing with these different kinds of reading, this chapter on *So This Is Paris* (1926) examines some of the intellectual and emotional performances required in the "reading of a film" and tries to shed new light on the pleasures gained from such (dis)passionate involvements.[2] As will be argued,

[1] Wolfgang Iser, *The Act of Reading: A Theory of Aesthetic Response* (Baltimore: Johns Hopkins University Press, 1978), ix. The implications of such an approach are manifold but, within the context of this chapter, cannot be addressed in great detail. It may well be possible that only a small number of films qualifies for such an undertaking, perhaps only certain "anthropocentric" genres (e.g., sophisticated comedy, melodrama), perhaps only silent films (because of their different use of montage), perhaps only Lubitsch's sophisticated comedies. Be that as it may, it is with such interests and reservations that this chapter uses Iser's *The Act of Reading*, taking his concepts as catalysts rather than a coherent theoretical framework.

[2] Within this framework, many of the ideas developed by reader-response critics could be applied to film, even though they grew out of an engagement with literature and have been primarily concerned with the relationship between texts and their readers. For instance, the external affinities between the reading and viewing processes have inspired many metaphors. Stanley Fish evokes the image of the slow-motion camera to describe his method of slowing down the reading experience for critical analysis: "It is as if a slow-motion camera with an

"readership" in the cinema is as much tied up with sexual difference as is spectatorship. At the same time, their critical paradigms differ considerably. The notion of looking, especially as it has been theorized in the intersection of film theory and psychoanalysis, foregrounds the unconscious aspects of the viewing experience and, given the absolute primacy attributed to the Oedipal scenario, leads often into a "prison-house of vision." Conversely, the notion of reading, when used in the context of film theory, privileges the element of play and playfulness. It even opens up the possibility of reclaiming films like *So This Is Paris*—and some of the other sophisticated comedies discussed in this chapter—for a distinctly feminist perspective. The gendered refraction of interpretation can be seen as a narrative device in the story and a kind of meta-discourse made visible through the interventions of the camera/narrator. Identifying these processes, however, requires some preliminary remarks on how the turn to reading might introduce a new perspective on what look like rather conventional films.

Reduced to its basic form, interpretation in the sophisticated comedy takes place by means of an elaborate point-of-view structure. A scene opens from the perspective of a character who establishes, through his or her desiring gaze, a relationship with a looked-at object, most frequently a person or a precious article. However, the next shot introduces a different perspective and reveals the first impression as false, an illusion produced by desires and fantasies. This opposition marks the beginning of an exercise in self-reflexivity. All attempts at interpreting reality, the omniscient narrator seems to suggest here, are governed by specific preconceptions and thus doomed in their longing for the truth. This condition remains present through all stages of the narrative and affects all forms of looking, including the gaze clouded by desire, the look driven by suspicion, the glance of indifference, and the stare of close scrutiny. Therefore the bearer of the look must accept the subjective nature of perception and learn to treat it as an integral part both of the cinema and the human condition. Only then can he or she respond creatively to the uncertainties or, in Iser's words, the indeterminacies of the text; only then can the pitfalls of perception become a source of visual pleasure. Lubitsch's sophisticated comedies virtually re-

---

automatic stop action effect were recording our linguistic experiences and presenting them to us for viewing." See "Literature in the Reader: Affective Stylistics," in *Reader-Response Criticism. From Formalism to Post-Structuralism*, ed. Jane P. Tompkins (Baltimore: Johns Hopkins University Press, 1980), 74. In the same vein, Iser compares the activity of reading to "a sort of kaleidoscope of perspectives, preintentions, recollections. Every sentence contains a preview of the text and forms a kind of viewfinder for what is to come; and this in turn changes the 'preview' and so becomes a 'viewfinder' for what has been read." See "The Reading Process: A Phenomenological Approach," trans. Catherine Macksey and Richard Macksey, in *Reader-Response Criticism*, 54. Throughout *The Act of Reading* Iser frequently comments on the viewing experience in the cinema and quotes the writings of film theorists such as Béla Balázs, Rudolf Arnheim, Siegfried Kracauer, and Stanley Cavell to support his argument.

quire such preconditions. The films are structured around a spectator position that alternates between involvement and detachment and brings forth that other story—the underlying complicity among protagonist, camera, and spectator. Aiming beyond the marital quarrels and extramarital affairs, Lubitsch initiates a sustained reflection on the problem of hermeneutics. And at its center stands the problem of sexual difference.

In accordance with the prevailing fate of femininity in the cinema, an experience of lack, and hence of dissatisfaction, marks the beginning of the story. While the experience of sensory deprivation has found a perfect visual equivalent in the many empty frames, it enters the narrative through the figure of woman. To that end, the problem of femininity is broken down into the stereotypical characters of ingenue and femme fatale, both stock characters borrowed from the late-nineteenth-century comedy of manners. These stereotypes establish, through their differences, the field of contention against which the limits of perception and the pitfalls of interpretation are playfully tested. The film's story usually focuses on a happy bourgeois marriage that is temporarily threatened by the "good" woman's frustration, and it documents the complications that result from her growing inability to distinguish between imagination and reality. As a rule, the "good" woman initiates the chain of misreadings through her immoderate fantasies or unfounded suspicions (*Kiss Me Again, So This Is Paris, Lady Windermere's Fan*). She disrupts the initial equilibrium, but only for the sake of its reaffirmation (*The Marriage Circle, Three Women*). Her moral integrity, after all, makes impossible any serious involvement with a man other than her husband. Fulfilling her "natural" role, she acts as the protector of the marriage vow. Conversely, the "bad" woman, in spite of her physical attractiveness, self-confidence, and determination, is punished for having challenged male privileges. In the end, she stands alone. With the old husband gone and a new one not yet in sight, she embodies the risks involved when women give up the world of fantasy for actual participation in the adventures of life. Thus the "good" woman, precisely because she remains in her place, comes to represent the socially acceptable modes of reading, that is, those limited to compensatory functions. As the sophisticated comedy demonstrates, however, the risk of "reading too much" continues to lurk beneath the surface, always ready to unsettle the precarious balance between fantasy and reality.

Two "reading" scenes, one from *Lady Windermere's Fan* (1925), the other from *Three Women* (1924), might clarify this point. As an example of Lubitsch's reading Wilde, *Lady Windermere's Fan* draws attention to the reading process that stands at the beginning of every literary adaptation. The dynamics of such textual encounters have often been ignored because of the prevalent attitude that a literary source is superior to its filmed version. Repeatedly critics have pointed to the difficulties that arise when the witty dialogues of Wilde's *Lady Windermere's Fan* are to be translated into a medium as ill suited as silent film. Nevertheless, filled with admiration, they have noted how Lubitsch captured the spirit of the original, including the witty dialogues and the memorable bon mots delivered by the Wildean characters. This is also true for inter-titles like "Lady Windermere was facing a grave problem: of seating her dinner guests," which stand up rather well to Wilde's ironic touches. Not surprisingly, Sadoul calls *Lady Windermere's Fan* "Lubitsch's best silent film."[3]

For the purpose of this investigation such comparisons are less useful. They deny films like *Lady Windermere's Fan* their own perspective and reduce their significance to having successfully mastered the adaptation process from one medium to another. By adhering to the logic of substitution, the literary approaches to film tend to forget that every literary adaptation originates in a very specific reading experience. Seen in this light, *Lady Windermere's Fan*, the film, is as much about Wilde's play as it is a reflection of Lubitsch's reading of the text. The film establishes a link among Lubitsch as reader, the readers of the Wilde text, and the viewers of the film. The emphasis on the reading process, rather than on the originality of the work, poses a challenge to traditional approaches to literary adaptation—for it affords spectators and critics the opportunity to overcome the fixation on primary and secondary texts and to pay more attention to other registers of difference, differences that operate both on the level of narrative and representation.

As a result of these processes, *Lady Windermere's Fan* contains a number of tightly composed images that take up Wilde's fascination with the rituals of social intercourse and use them to criticize the hypocrisy that lies behind such obsession with form. Rather than trying to preserve the authenticity of the play, the film explores the metaphorical powers of language, and of poetic language in particular. This becomes evident after the arrival of Mrs. Erlynne (Irene Rich) and her hostile reception by London's high society. Lubitsch added a sequence that takes place during the famous horse races at Ascot in order to show the confrontation in all its details. Through the highly formal setting, the Ascot sequence serves two functions. It reveals the true intentions of a class whose obsession with appearances comes at the cost of honesty and whose rigid conventions almost cause a tragic ending. Yet the sequence also foregrounds the film's own interest in the experience of looking and being looked at. With Mrs. Erlynne and the members

[3] Sadoul, qtd. by Herman G. Weinberg, in *The Lubitsch Touch: A Critical Study*, 3d. rev. ed. (New York: Dover, 1977), 88. See also David Davidson, "The Importance of Being Ernst: Lubitsch and *Lady Windermere's Fan*," *Film/Literature Quarterly* 11, no. 2 (1983): 120–31. Comparing original play and screen adaptation, the author praises Lubitsch's film as the result of a remarkable metamorphosis made possible through the director's masterly exploitation of silent-screen techniques.

of high society seated in the stands, the shots alternate between Mrs. Erlynne and a group of society ladies who scrutinize her with the help of
various optical devices (binoculars, rolled program notes). The use of a
circular mask emphasizes the spatial and social distance between the curious onlookers and the recipient of the look. At the same time, it underscores the lack of social grace revealed by this public display of curiosity.
While the women's behavior is motivated by jealousy, Lord Augustus (Edward Martindel) introduces a distinctly male viewpoint, for his equally
scrutinizing glances are motivated primarily by erotic interests. The entire
sequence begins with a medium shot of three gossiping women and from
there cuts to two close-ups of Mrs. Erlynne, first of her expensive ring and
then of her graying hair. These are followed by a medium shot of Lord
Augustus whose interest in horse racing merely serves as a pretense for
other voyeuristic acts, as is evidenced by the next close-up of Mrs. Erlynne's uncovered knee. Only Lord Windermere (Bert Lytell) refrains from
such revealing activities. Because of his secret arrangement with Mrs. Erlynne, he must do everything to distract attention from her person. He
scolds Lord Augustus, who defiantly withdraws into the program notes.
Social interaction in high society, the Ascot sequence seems to suggest, is
structured around relationships of looking and, consequently, privileges
two kinds of feelings: sexual desire and sexual rivalry.

Lady Windermere's birthday party provides the occasion for another series of cinematic effects that is sparked by the sudden entrance of Mrs.
Erlynne. In the Wilde text, the scene reads as follows:

LADY PLYDALE: *That* woman!

DUMBY: Yes, that is what everyone calls her.

LADY PLYDALE: How very interesting! How intensely interesting! I really must
  have a good stare at her. (Goes to door of ballroom and looks in.) I have
  heard the most shocking things about her. They say she is ruining the poor
  Windermere. And Lady Windermere, who goes in for being so proper, invites her! How extremely amusing! It takes a thoroughly good woman to
  do a thoroughly stupid thing. You are to lunch there on Friday![4]

Lubitsch only needs one single shot, a medium shot of one of the salon's
walls, to visualize the strange mixture of outrage, excitement, and curiosity
of the Wildean dialogue. The empty wall becomes the stage where the individual reactions to Mrs. Erlynne's entrance are played out. First, nothing
happens; the frame remains empty for an unusually long time—evidence
of a concerted effort by the other guests to make the intruder disappear as
well. Suddenly a woman's head enters the frame from below, nervously

[4] Oscar Wilde, "Lady Windermere's Fan," in *Comedies* (New York: The Book League of
America, 1932), 105.

turns around, and withdraws again. After a brief pause, a second woman's head appears and disappears, then a third one. Through repetition and, more importantly, through the imbalance between what is present and what is absent, the frame captures perfectly the tense atmosphere in the room. The different heads that enter the frame represent the stages of denial (the empty frame), curiosity (the reaction of one individual), and intense interest (the reaction of society). Simulating the play with the absence and presence that underlies the Wildean epigrams, Lubitsch sets up a corresponding structure through the filmic devices of framing, editing, and point-of-view shots. But he also utilizes his appreciation of Wilde's snobbishness to introduce a more pungent critique of society and, last but not least, to draw attention to the process of interpretation.

As *Lady Windermere's Fan* shows, Lubitsch's sophisticated comedies—and, to a lesser degree, most of his silent films—use framing to develop a visual equivalent to specific figures of speech. In comparison to more "filmic" means of representation, framing has not received the critical attention it deserves. Eager to distinguish the cinema from the theater, film critics have rejected excessive framing as a residue of theatrical conventions. In so doing, they have failed to explore the very different function of framing within the film's shifting distances and settings.[5] This is most obvious in the case of the close-up, which becomes a critical tool of the highest order. Scrutinizing objects and characters with equal attention, the close-up transcends the anthropocentric perspective of the theater and brings forth a distinctly cinematic interaction among author, film, and spectator. Seen in this light, Lubitsch's confining interiors and calculated frame compositions provide the necessary conditions for his deceptive play with the laws of perception and interpretation.

Interpretation in the sophisticated comedy is inextricably tied to experiences of perception and deception. This is nowhere clearer than in *Three Women* (1924), the story of an older woman's quest for love and youth. The narrative is constructed around (photographic) images and their significance as a means of self-exploration and deceit. Photographs, paintings, and mirror images have always played an important role in Lubitsch's films, beginning with *The Eyes of the Mummy* and *The Mountain Cat*. These second-order images are introduced to probe the metaphorical strength of the image from within. The image-within-the-image produces a doubling effect and thus allows for a position of critical distance within the film's

---

[5] Gerald Mast has proposed a definition that cuts across the historically developed opposition of montage and mise-en-scène. He argues "(1) that the film frame is analogous to an *operation*, a process, almost all of which requires a present participle (that is wandering, roaming, masking, sighting, covering, focusing, shooting); (2) that the operation is analogous to *vision* itself in both possible senses of the term (as physical sight and as mental insight)." In "On Framing," *Critical Inquiry* 11, no. 1 (September 1984): 85.

diegesis. However, because of the truth value attributed to mimetic representation in the story, the image-within-the-image also reinstates photography (and, implicitly, cinematography) as a medium vastly superior to less
referential forms like speech and writing.

Three Women, Lubitsch's only sophisticated comedy set in America, uses
photographs to negotiate the public and private relationships among its
three main characters. The film introduces a complicated triangle of "misreadings" that includes an older society woman, Mabel Wilton (Pauline
Frederick), her college-age daughter Jeanne (May McAvoy), and an adven-
turess, Harriet (Marie Prevost). The three women compete for the love of
one man, the charming good-for-nothing Edmund Lamont (Lew Cody).[6]
The focus on the relationships among women is rather unusual for Lubitsch, who tends to present love triangles from the perspective of the man
or the primary couple. Moreover, it is the mother-daughter relationship
that becomes central in assessing the function of images in the struggle for
personal identity and narrative authority. In order to take possession of the
man, and of the narrative as well, each woman must gain control of the
images of femininity that are in circulation. The camera's close attention to
the spectacular evening gowns, the glittering pieces of jewelry, and the
extravagant hat fashions attests to this preoccupation with role-playing and
public images.

The narrative of *Three Women* unfolds through two different ways of
relating to images—the one concerned with truth, the other with fraud and
deception. It is through this opposition that modern society's obsession

---

[6] Lubitsch depicts such a situation in two of his Warner films, *Lady Windermere's Fan* and
Three Women. This is rather surprising given the suspicious absence of the maternal element
(i.e., of mothers or mother figures) in his films, as well as of meaningful relationships between
women in general. With the exception of a few unpleasant women figures (Marlene Dietrich's
dubious women friends in *Desire* and *Angel*; perhaps Swana in *Ninotchka*), the female leads
are usually separated from their own sex and take little interest in the traditional options
available to women (e.g., motherhood, family life). Lacking a meaningful occupation, strong
personal interests, or even close women friends, they are usually encircled by the desire of the
leading men, the propositions of elderly suitors, and the selfish advice of domineering fathers
or father figures. That is why the constellations in *Lady Windermere's Fan* and, even more so,
in *Three Women* must be regarded as exceptional and can only be explained with regard to
external influences. The desire to please his American audiences, and the studio bosses, was
probably the main reason for such atypical signs of "family life." Not surprisingly, *Three
Women* was Lubitsch's most "American" film of the twenties and, with the exception of two
later films, *That Uncertain Feeling* (1941) and *Heaven Can Wait* (1942), the only one set in
America. Mother-son relationships (*The Doll*, *Montmartre*), and the pertinent problems of
overprotection/dependency, also remain marginal to Lubitsch's work. The same holds true
for the authority conflicts that are usually associated with father-son relationships (*The Student Prince*, *The Man I Killed*). For the most part, then, the family as the place of social interaction was of little interest to Lubitsch, a fact that is rather extraordinary, given the overwhelming family orientation in other American sophisticated comedies of the twenties and
thirties.

with appearances, with what is called a person's image, can be addressed as well. At one point, Mabel Wilton, preparing for a rendezvous with Lamont, examines her looks in a full-length mirror in the privacy of her dressing room. Evidence of the woman's desperate longing for beauty and youth, the mirror almost takes over the entire frame, thereby replacing the film's diegetic world with that of her desire for another, more flattering, image of herself. And precisely because this desire must remain unfulfilled, because the mirror only gives back the reflection of a forty-year-old woman, Mrs. Wilton decides to conceal the discrepancies between the image and the self. She sets the stage for her imaginary double, the young, beautiful, and desirable Mabel Wilton. In order to achieve this effect, she lowers the lights in her oriental-style salon, thus resorting to the tricks of the theatrical stage. But Lubitsch, as the more powerful "director" of the two, rejects the soft-focus lenses and orders cinematographer Charles Van Enger to use strong lights and a particularly harsh lighting style.

The most crucial moment of "reading the image" occurs after Jeanne's marriage to Lamont when mother and daughter silently negotiate their new relationship by experimenting with different positions for the family portraits, on display in the living room. First the mother places the daughter's portrait at the center and arranges the portraits of Lamont and herself accordingly. In this scenario, the daughter's forward glance seems to aim at a point outside of the group, whereas mother and husband face each other in profile. Reacting to what she perceives as magnanimity, the daughter changes the arrangement and reinstates the mother at the center. Yet Jeanne's confirmation of the mother's central position, her expression of daughterly love, also threatens to reveal another scenario, the secret love affair between mother and husband. With the mother's portrait placed in the middle, Mabel Wilton and Lamont look as if they are exchanging intimate glances while Jeanne stands outside, seemingly begging for explanation. The mother immediately recognizes the compromising nature of this constellation, removes her portrait from the sideboard, and puts a flower arrangement in its place. Later, when Jeanne realizes that she, too, has been betrayed by Lamont, she returns to this test site of representation, obviously placing more trust in images than in words. She removes her portrait, tears it apart, and puts her mother's portrait back in place. Confronted with the intimate double portrait of mother and husband as they face each other lovingly, Jeanne realizes that they must have been lovers as well.

Photographs in *Three Women* not only function as a means of self-reflection. They also enable the spectator to look behind the social conventions, familial compromises, and individual secrets and recognize the pervasive nature of role-playing in society. In so doing, the photographs grant access to what the characters try to conceal from themselves and others. While firsthand experience is relegated to the margins, images become central to the experience of reality, hiding the real but also presenting a more accurate rendition thereof. *Three Women* explores both sides of the image, its function as an instrument of deceit and as a repository of truth. Precisely this tension between appearance and truth stands at the center of Lubitsch's continuous interest in "reading" the image. As a rule, the play with appearances inspires amusing misunderstandings and funny mistakes. Only in *Three Women*, perhaps because of the American setting, does it become the source of real emotional suffering. Accordingly, the comedy almost ends as a melodrama: Mabel Wilton shoots Lamont but is subsequently acquitted by a sympathetic jury. The older woman, after all, had only been the victim of images—of her longing for youth, her desire for a perfect family; in other words, a victim of the cinema and its allures.

So This Is Paris looks as if it were designed on the drawing board. Architectural forms and spaces dominate the film's visual design, and they impose their frozen structures on the limited number of settings and, figuratively speaking, the different points-of-view available to the protagonists. Architecture, in a way, becomes the enabling condition for the story to unfold and for interpretation to take place. Beginning with *When Four Do the Same*, the metaphorical investment of space in the Lubitsch comedy is closely connected to bourgeois interiors and, more specifically, to a strong emphasis on windows, doors, and similar means of admission and exclusion. This is especially true for *So This Is Paris*, where the story moves back and forth between two opposite apartment buildings in a quiet residential street in Paris. With the narrative structure thus modeled on a spatial order, the two couples in the film, the Girauds and the Lallés, come to occupy equally fixed positions in relation to each other and the problem of modern marriage. The street facilitates, quite literally, all significant acts of transgression. It offers a compelling spatial image through which the insurmountable difference between perception and experience can be made available to representation. The opposition of interior and exterior provides the basic structure for articulating this difference. As an alternative to the empty activism of the public sphere, *So This Is Paris* celebrates the sensuous world of the private sphere, which is controlled by women and their imagination. Comfortable and secure, these interiors provide a place not unlike the motion-picture theaters from which the spectators in the film's diegesis and in the theaters are called upon to scrutinize their impressions.

However, the imaginary space mapped out by window and street does not merely prefigure the film's narrative structure. It also creates a doubling effect. Wavering between the discourses of window (imagination) and street (action), the cinematic space—again, the mise-en-scène of the film and the motion-picture theater—produces a distancing effect and thus makes possible the critical analysis of all movements taking place within. This process relies to a large degree on the principle of repetition. As the narrative becomes part of the ongoing process of spatialization, its symmetrical configurations bring forth a suggestive metaphor of spectatorship and visual pleasure. The windows of both apartments, the viewfinder of the camera, and the projection screen: these framing devices are all based on, and achieve their best effects through, the tension between inside/outside and absence/presence. At first glance, such a proliferation of frames seems to partake in the aesthetics of the painterly still life, or the self-contained tableau. However, it only takes a slight pan, a sudden cut to another scene in order to prove that the stability of the frame is a deception. The cinema, Lubitsch seems to argue, is neither a window onto the world nor a mirror of the self; it is always both. Consequently, he shows how these two aspects of cinema are negotiated in an unending process of reading and rereading, a process made possible through the means of framing and editing.

Rejecting the customary establishing shot, *So This Is Paris* opens onto a scene of turmoil, of confusion. The spectator is confronted with the dramatic encounter between a young sheikh and a sparsely dressed lady of the harem who cling to each other with looks and gestures of burning passion (fig. 19). He pulls out a dagger, she collapses; no doubt, the spectator is more than justified in anticipating an oriental tale of beauty, love, and adventure. But the next frame disappoints such expectations and introduces a radically different perspective. The camera, seemingly without motivation, starts to pan to the side, only to reveal a piano accompanist looking on with obvious amusement. This act of reframing exposes the "oriental" characters as performance artists during practice hours. The spectator's expectations have been betrayed. Not surprisingly, visual representation never regains the status of truth too easily attributed to the cinema.

With this programmatic beginning, the film establishes a framework through and against which the following scenes will have to be measured. First, as a self-referential remark on the cinematic apparatus, the opening comments on the popular sheikh films of the twenties (e.g., Valentino's *The Sheik* [1922]) and Lubitsch's own preference for oriental scenarios (*One Arabian Night*, *The Loves of Pharaoh*). Second, it introduces, in a manner not dissimilar to the *roman à these*, the film's underlying project of initiating a story of (mis)readings and, at the same time, analyzing the act of reading. Instead of gliding smoothly from image to image, the opening sequence announces disruption and disillusionment. From the outset, then, the promise of visual bliss seems betrayed and the images forever contaminated by those critical operations traditionally attributed to reading. As a kind of compensation, however, the spectator is invited to participate actively in the making of meaning. Last but not least, the opening sequence defines the position to be occupied by Suzanne Giraud (Patsy Ruth Miller), the woman at the window and the film's model spectator/

19. *So This Is Paris*: Lilyan Tashman, André Beranger

reader. The first shot anticipates the perspective from which she will soon re-create, very much like the film's spectator, the scene's false reality for a second time. This "femininization" of perception has positive as well as negative implications. Setting the stage for her beauty, her lack of control, and her privileged relation to imagination, the "woman at the window" sequence undoubtedly conforms with the gendered order of representation, as is evidenced by the loving devotion with which the camera lingers on the spectacle of woman. However, the woman may also be seen as merely complying with her role in modern consumer society, that is, of producing "images" (e.g., through fashion, furniture, social etiquette). As the typical consumer, Suzanne Giraud gains access to the narrative through, literally and metaphorically speaking, window-shopping. Given the similarity between the fictional identities provided by fantasy novels and consumer goods, her active passivity leaves open the possibility of other readings. It is precisely because the woman withdraws into a surrogate satisfaction that she does have the power to set the narrative into motion. Through her daydreaming, which is the prerequisite of all creative imagination according to Freud, she takes the first step in this direction. She transforms her repressed sexual desires into more socially acceptable forms and, therefore, behaves like the imaginative writer who, in Freud's words, is only "a dreamer in broad daylight."[7] Because of such affinities between daydream and *ars poetica*, the woman is much more than the demonstration object in a moralistic tale. She becomes the enunciator in the film, perhaps even a stand-in for Lubitsch himself.

To return to the beginning: Suzanne Giraud, the bored and frustrated wife of a successful physician, sits at the window of her living room, completely immersed in a trashy novel.[8] Lascivious sighs and feline movements accompany the novel's ending. Closing the book, she raises her eyes toward the window. Perhaps intended as way of "facing reality," the movement only leads to the opposite effect. Looking at the window across the street, Suzanne catches sight of the sheikh, the incarnation of her most secret dreams. With the camera's return to the other side of this axis of misreadings (a precise 180-degree move), the spectator—but not the woman—traverses the imaginary screen for the third time, now investigating the bare-chested sheikh from the perspective of his living room. Here Maurice Lallé (André Beranger), dressed in turban and harem pants, is about to finish the cereal that his wife, Georgette (Lilyan Tashman), had handed him as a scornful comment on his frail masculinity. The same kind of disillusionment is repeated at the Girauds when Suzanne, still under the influence of the remarkable vision, greets her returning husband, Doctor Paul Giraud (Monte Blue), as "my beloved sheikh." Yet Paul reacts to her passionate kisses with professional concern. Measuring her temperature with a thermometer, he diagnoses her as "too hot." Where such different temperaments and, implicitly, different readings clash, the source of disturbance must be eliminated. Suzanne orders her husband to draw all venetian blinds, thereby also denying film's primary libidinal source, the desire of looking.

At this point, a man's walking cane is introduced into the narrative, from then on setting off all ensuing complications. As a material object, a cane can be carried along, left behind, used as a weapon and a tool. As a rather obvious phallic symbol, it documents the success and failure of male desire. And insofar as it functions as a stand-in for the narrator, the particular cane in *So This Is Paris* also offers a mocking comment on these equations be-

---

[7] Freud, "Creative Writers and Daydreaming," *Standard Edition*, vol. 9, 149.

[8] The scene illustrates quite nicely Tania Modleski's analysis of woman's association with mass culture in *Loving with a Vengeance: Mass-Produced Fantasies for Women* (New York and London: Methuen, 1984).

tween phallus and authorship.[9] Handing this (indeed overdetermined) cane to her husband in a gesture of male empowerment, Suzanne asks him to confront the sheikh, that is, to remove the source of her arousal. Given the genre's inherent preoccupation with the erotic, such denial of desire of course only generates more. On the other side, Paul is received by a scantily clad lady doing a handstand—another comment of skewed perspectives— who turns out to be his old flame Georgette. With much enthusiasm, they reminisce about old days (Paul: "I am married!" Georgette: "Me, too!"). Several times Paul rushes to the window—the site of the cinematic effect— and stages an aggressive confrontation with the sheikh, thereby satisfying his onlooking wife's need for reality, as it were. He returns home without his cane and claims to have broken it on the poor sheikh's head. In accordance with the dramatic rules of the comedy of manners, the exposition ends with a second complication, caused by the even more significant shift from the representation of an illusion (Suzanne's dream) to that of a deception (Paul's staged fight). Reality is not simply a source of misreadings, with the false taken for the real. On the contrary, the false might turn out to be more convincing than the real itself.

After this first act of transgression, the camera returns to the apartment of the Girauds where the absent/present cane consolidates its central position in the narrative. Maurice, now in ordinary street clothes, comes to return the cane and makes clumsy advances toward Suzanne who clearly prefers her visions of the sheikh over the man of flesh and blood. While they make polite conversation in the salon, Giraud rests on the sofa in the adjoining room, "recuperating" from the exhausting fight but also indulging in sweet dreams of Georgette. He briefly wakes up, notices the (undamaged) cane that Suzanne put next to him as a silent accusation, and again falls asleep. The angry wife returns to the room to fetch the cane and hands it back to Lallé as a promise of future intimacies. As he leaves in high spirits, Giraud's nightmare begins. In the following trick sequence—a good opportunity for Lubitsch to demonstrate his skillful use of animation—the miniature cane begins to dance on Paul's nose, attacks his mouth and, in a veritable Freudian climax, disappears in his throat. At this point, the guilty husband awakes with a heavy cough, literally choking on his own lie and the complications of desire.

With the introduction of the four main protagonists, the spatial order of *So This Is Paris* is established. Now the marriage circle begins. One misunderstanding rapidly leads to the next one until the film culminates in a spectacular ball sequence. Working up to this point, all participants, except for the innocent wife, have in the meantime perfected their skills at deceiv-

[9] As the guarantor of dominant discourse, the cane also resembles the finger that is tracing the text in the act of reading.

ing others. The flirtatious Georgette calls Dr. Giraud under the pretense of a medical emergency and arranges a secret rendezvous in a cafe. Rejuvenated by such extramarital excitement, the doctor tries to impress her through reckless driving until his pubescent behavior is stopped by a police officer. Paul is condemned to three days in prison, a sentence that he plans to begin serving after attending the infamous *bal des artistes* with Georgette. Supposedly leaving to see a patient, he puts on his most elegant evening clothes, while Georgette peeks out of the window to receive the signal for their departure. Maurice, on the other hand, pretends a sudden illness and visits Suzanne once Paul and Georgette have left for the ball. Dancing the night away, Paul and Georgette enjoy themselves tremendously. However, Maurice Lallé's compliments are completely lost on Suzanne, as is evidenced by a close-up of her feet moving longingly to the live broadcast from the ball. Only the sudden arrival of a representative of law and order grants Maurice what illegitimacy has so far denied him. Pretending to be Dr. Paul Giraud, he lets himself be arrested, but not without stealing some good-bye kisses from his confused "wife."

Suspicion—which is, after all, only an overdetermined form of interpretation—inspires a devilish plan in Suzanne, who abandons the role of the passive wife and turns herself into a femme fatale. As in the opening sequence, an external stimulus is responsible for her change of mind; this time it belongs to the aural realm. Emanating from the radio in the form of a spoken script, the voice of the ball's master of ceremonies becomes literally "readable" in the moment that he announces Paul and Georgette as the winners of the Charleston contest. Here Suzanne decides to make an example of her philandering husband. Dressed in a beautiful evening gown and with her face hidden behind a domino mask, she rushes to the ball and immediately arouses the interest of the inebriated Paul. For a short time, the roles are reversed and the transgressive qualities associated with the ball, the festival, and the carnival can again come to the fore. But in contrast to earlier films like *The Oyster Princess* or *The Doll*, it takes the external stimuli of liquor and extramarital affairs to achieve this effect. Then the man is allowed to lose control over the field of vision, while the woman takes possession of the look and, by implication, of the narrative. It is not surprising that Paul's loss of control becomes most evident in a close-up of his eye that, after winking at the mysterious lady, develops a terrible twitch. The confrontation of male debauchery and female revenge, it seems, requires the excuse of a physical handicap—Paul's drunkenness—in order not to challenge the opposition of active masculinity and passive femininity. Moreover, the reversal of the traditional power structure needs the temporary suspension of the story in the dance sequence in order not to challenge the narrative hierarchies. In the end, deviation only confirms the validity of the rule.

In light of these implications, the ball sequence occupies a central position in the film. A "technical tour-de-force of expressionistic filmmaking,"[10] in the words of Poague, the sequence bears witness to Lubitsch's experimental side and reveals the strong influence of the German art cinema. This is particularly evident in his use of associative montage. The ball establishes a spatio-temporal framework in which sexual stereotypes and narrative conventions can be abandoned for the sheer spectacle of eroticism. Moreover, the celebration of dance makes possible the probing of the technical and formal limits of cinematic representation. Lubitsch uses close-ups, skewed perspectives, shots from extremely low and high camera angles, rapid editing, quick dissolves, superimpositions, and multiple framing, thus creating a vertiginous kaleidoscope-like effect. As if to underscore the musicality of the sequence, close-ups of dancing legs and ecstatic faces are inserted repeatedly until everything explodes in an epiphany of images.[11] Narrative gives way to spectacle and all filmic means are called upon to enter into the cinema's multifarious productions. Here the display of the most advanced techniques prepares the ground not for a fetishization of cinema's technology but for its utilization in the representation of desire. For a short moment, the spectacle of dancing bodies takes over the frame; for a short moment, another order of representation seems possible. Significantly, the site for such a transgression, the ballroom, is marked as feminine, as is evidenced by the two gigantic pairs of women's legs that frame the orchestra stage—a reminder of the ongoing tension between transgression and containment.

Yet such moments never last. Back home, Suzanne tears the domino mask from her face and confronts her bewildered husband with the fact that she will take control from now on. Her threat triggers the second dream of emasculation, but now seen from the woman's perspective. Again Lubitsch resorts to animation in order to visualize that which finds no place in the registers of mimetic representation. This time it is Giraud who shrinks to miniature size and then jumps around in order to escape Suzanne's vigorous beatings. Once she realizes what her possession of the cane implies (i.e., Lallé's visit), she gives up her claims to revenge and throws the cane into the fire. Precisely because the man's domestication remains an imaginary one, the marital compromise is based on and results in the complete denial of her viewpoint. The next morning, with the Girauds attending to each other's breakfast needs with great tenderness and with Georgette phoning a new admirer, the marriage circle has merely lost

[10] Leland A. Poague, *The Cinema of Ernst Lubitsch: The Hollywood Films* (South Brunswick, N.J.: A. S. Barnes, 1978), 99.

[11] Contemporary reviewers saw this as the film's most powerful element: "No matter how brilliant may be the picture Mr. Lubitsch produces, he succeeds invariably in inserting a transcendental stroke." In *New York Times*, 16 August 1926.

one participant. Despite the reformist gestures, the epilogue confirms the man's authorial position at the center of meaning production. Reading the sensational newspaper story about the arrest of a certain Dr. Paul Giraud, the male reader in/of the ending turns to the camera and remarks that this "shows how much you can believe in the newspapers!" As the corresponding piece to the suggestive opening, *So This Is Paris* closes with an insert of the unfortunate Maurice who, as the member of a chain gang, carries on the burden of truth, as it were. The film returns to the problem of its beginnings: that is, to the uncertainty inherent in all acts of reading.

The relationships among the multiple readers in and of *So This Is Paris* are structured around the notion of sexual difference. The integrating figure here is Suzanne Giraud, who enters the story as a devoted reader of trashy novels but, given her particular disposition, also functions as the substitute reader through whom the film stages its experiments in negative hermeneutics. Isolated by the camera as the object of close scrutiny, Suzanne represents the typical female reader who, because of excessive daydreaming, falls prey to the narrowness of her "horizon of expectation." By identifying the experience of misreading with a woman, the film allows the (male) spectator to assume the opposite position, a position that requires a certain amount of self-criticism yet still guarantees the pleasures that come with male privilege. In short, the woman in *So This Is Paris* comes to function as the reading figure and the figure of reading.

In order to negotiate the critical and the pleasurable aspects of reading, the spectator must assume the position laid out for him in the text. He must become identical with what Iser has defined as the implied reader: "He [the implied reader] embodies all those predispositions necessary for a literary work to exercise its effect—predispositions laid down, not by an empirical outside reality, but by the text itself. Consequently, the implied reader as a concept has his roots firmly planted in the structure of the text; he is a construct and in no way to be identified with any real reader."[12] In *So This Is Paris*, the "implied spectator" is constituted through the calculated shot sequences, the narrow-frame compositions, and the sudden pans and counter-shot, all of which convey a strong sense of control and mastery. What has become known as the famous "Lubitsch touch"—the suggestive elisions, ellipses, and innuendos—refers precisely to this close collaboration of camera and spectator. More than any other director of the classical Hollywood cinema, Lubitsch relies heavily on the active participation of his audiences. Truffaut describes this quality with admiration: "There would be no Lubitsch without an audience—but watch out—the audience is not something apart from his work; it is *with* him in creating,

[12] Iser, *The Act of Reading*, 34.

it is part of the film."[13] This process, however, requires a particular kind of spectator who, if not actually male, must at least assume a male position from which he or she is able to understand and appreciate the film. In trying to define the "Lubitsch touch," Josef von Sternberg chooses his examples accordingly and, unintentionally, reveals Lubitsch's male bias: "The basic idea behind this often amusing contrivance was that no matter what happened, one would always have a twinkle in the eye and never lose his *sang-froid*. For instance, if the wife was caught in bed with a neighbor, his hat would be brushed off, and when escorted to the door he would be asked to call again."[14] What is only alluded to by Sternberg in this brief remark, in fact, describes an attitude that can be found in all the sophisticated comedies.

Similar to the doubling of the female perspective (woman as reading figure and figure of reading), the male perspective also appears doubly, in the figure of Paul Giraud and, less noticeably, in the textual position reserved for the "implied spectator." By identifying with the camera rather than the male protagonist, the spectator accepts moral double standards, self-righteousness, and irresponsible social behavior as signs of a healthy masculinity. Consequently, much of the humor derives from a triangular structure among the narrator/camera, the male spectator, and the woman as the victim of their discriminatory exchanges. In "Jokes and their Relation to the Unconscious," Freud has commented on this constellation and interpreted it as a substitute for sexual fulfillment. Analyzing the obscene joke, he describes how the addressee of the joke, usually another man, assumes the place of the woman, the initial addressee of the sexual advance. Since the obscene for him represents a form of communication between men, Freud concludes: "Generally speaking a tendentious joke calls for three people: in addition to the one who makes the joke, there must be a second who is taken as the object of the hostile or sexual aggressiveness, and a third on whom the joke's aim of producing pleasure is fulfilled."[15] Such eye-winking misogyny, it seems, leaves little room for a female perspective.

As this chapter has shown so far, the actualization of *So This Is Paris* through an "implied spectator" is structured around very traditional notions of sexual difference. Nonetheless, alternative readings are possible,

[13] François Truffaut, "Lubitsch Was a Prince," in *The Films in My Life*, trans. Leonard Mayhew (New York: Simon & Schuster, 1975), 51.

[14] Josef von Sternberg, *Fun in a Chinese Laundry* (New York: Macmillan, 1965), 38.

[15] Freud, "Jokes and Their Relation to the Unconscious," *Standard Edition*, vol. 8, 100. Compare Mary Ann Doane who discusses certain aspects of Freud's work on jokes (e.g., the *Aufsitzer*) in the context of an essay on film and irony, "The Film's Time and the Spectator's Space," in *Cinema and Language*, ed. Stephen Heath and Patricia Mellencamp (Frederick, Md.: University Publications of America, 1983), 35–48.

even from a feminist perspective. Time works in their favor. Since the film, more than sixty years after its release, has lost much of its provocation and appeal (e.g., as an expression of castration anxiety), other modes of actualization can attach themselves to its exaggerated visions of femininity. Through the presence of different spectators—those of the twenties and the nineties—the focus of reading can be shifted from an interpretation based on sexual difference to an interpretation of its main functions.[16] Consequently, the temporal and theoretical displacement makes possible a reassessment (no matter how double edged) of the film's hackneyed plot and trivial characters and exposes to ridicule its signs of misogyny. Reading the film no longer requires the spectator's agreement, neither with a character's moral position nor with the prevalent notions of femininity built into the narrative. Iser has pointed to the meta-discursive potential inherent in every text that is read outside of its original framework of reception: "For the contemporary reader, the reassessment of norms contained in the repertoire will make him detach these norms from their social and cultural context and so recognize the limitations of their effectiveness. For the later reader, the reassessed norms help to re-create that very social and cultural context that brought about the problems which the text itself is concerned with. In the first instance, the reader is affected as a participant, and in the second as an observer."[17] Similarly, the kind of masculinity espoused by *So This Is Paris* (and many other sophisticated comedies) appears so dated that only a retrospective mode of appreciation can do justice to its continuing existence, namely as the irony of an irony. The modern spectator assumes the position of the film's "implied spectator" and simulates cooptation, a liberating move especially for female spectators who will suddenly find themselves in the middle of a playful reenactment of male chauvinism. In that sense, the "Lubitsch touch"—here to be understood as a method of encoding and deciphering—actually contains the plan of its own destruction. With historical distance already providing a powerful incentive for other readings, the concurrent ossification of the genre only contributes

---

[16] Compare Iser, *The Act of Reading*, read against the grain of his gender blindness: "The fecundity of meaning is aesthetic in character. It does not arise solely from the fact that there are many different possibilities from which we choose one and exclude the rest, but also from the fact that there is no frame of reference to offer criteria of right or wrong. This does not imply that the meaning must, consequently, be purely subjective; although it requires the subject to produce and experience it, the very existence of alternatives makes it necessary for a meaning to be defensible and so intersubjectively accessible. The intersubjective communication of a meaning will show up those elements that have been sacrificed, and so through the negativity of one's own processes of meaning assembly, one may again be in a position to observe one's own decisions" (230).

[17] Ibid., 78.

further to the multiplication of distances that leads to the shattering of the film's discursive strategies and its resurrection in the spirit of allegory.[18]

With woman's access to spectatorship only conceivable as a mediated one, the systematic and yet irreverent reappropriation of all available mediations may ultimately turn out to be a very productive strategy for women to gain access to narrative and, thereby, to desire. It could even bring about the often imagined transition from a "negative hermeneutics" (Paul Ricoeur), the belief that there is no universally valid interpretation, to what Naomi Schor has called an "erotics of hermeneutics."[19] From that perspective, every act of close reading interrupts the hermeneutic circle tied around sexual difference.

Filmography

Lady Windermere's Fan (1925). Director: Ernst Lubitsch for Warner Brothers. Scenario: Julien Josephson, based on Oscar Wilde's play *Lady Windermere's Fan* (1882). Photography: Charles J. Van Enger. With Ronald Colman (Lord Darlington), Irene Rich (Mrs. Erlynne), May McAvoy (Lady Windermere), Bert Lytell (Lord Windermere), Edward Martindel (Lord Augustus) et al. Length: 7,816 ft. (2,382 m). Release: 26 Dec. 1925.

Three Women (1924). Director: Ernst Lubitsch for Warner Brothers. Scenario: Hans Kraly, based on the novel *Lillis Ehe* by Iolanthe Marès. Photography: Charles J. Van Enger. With May McAvoy (Jeanne Wilton), Pauline Frederick (Mabel Wilton), Marie Prevost (Harriet), Lew Cody

[18] *So This Is Paris* makes possible such readings, because it possesses a highly conventional narrative structure. In the words of Umberto Eco, the film is an example of a closed text: "Those texts that obsessively aim at arousing a precise response on the part of more or less precise empirical readers . . . are in fact open to any possible 'aberrant' decoding. A text so immoderately 'open' to every possible interpretation will be called a *closed* one." In *The Role of the Reader. Explorations in the Semiotics of Texts* (Bloomington: Indiana University Press, 1979), 8. The textual structure of the closed text, Eco holds, is predicated upon and requires a reading that is fully predetermined. But as the related phenomenon of the cult film demonstrates, its inflexible structure can also generate an array of alternative readings, for instance by sophisticated readers like Eco or by the critical female spectator of the eighties. As examples of the "openness" of closed texts, Eco analyzes the Superman myth and Ian Fleming's James Bond series.

[19] Naomi Schor, "Fiction as Interpretation," in *The Reader in the Text: Essays on Audience and Interpretation*, ed. Susan R. Suleiman and Inge Crosman (Princeton, N.J.: Princeton University Press, 1980), 182. The term is taken from Susan Sontag's polemical call for an erotics of art in her influential essay "Against Interpretation" (1964).

(Edmund Lamont) et al. Length: 7,900 ft. (2,408 m) resp. 8,200 ft. (2,499 m), depending on source. Release: 5 Oct. 1924.

So This Is Paris (1926). Director and producer: Ernst Lubitsch for Warner Brothers. Scenario: Hans Kraly, based on the play *Réveillon* (1872) by Henri Meilhac and Ludovic Halévy. Photography: John Mescall. With Monte Blue (Dr. Paul Giraud), Patsy Ruth Miller (Suzanne Giraud), André Beranger (Maurice Lallé), Lilyan Tashman (Georgette Lallé) et al. Length: 6,135 ft. (1,870 m). Release: 31 July 1926.

Eight

Exploring the Boundaries of Sound: *Monte Carlo*

Monte Carlo—another imaginary place on the Lubitsch map, another place where woman and desire come together in the distance to begin a story and to give a name. Set in the glittering casinos and elegant grand hotels of Monte Carlo, this little-known musical tells the story of the adventurous Countess Helene Mara (Jeanette MacDonald) who chooses the challenges of the unknown over a marriage of convenience and finds true love in the end. In collaboration with script writer Ernest Vajda, Lubitsch again adapted a frivolous Hans Müller play, *Die blaue Küste* (1914, "The Blue Coast"), and with the support of Paramount's leading set designer, Hans Dreier, and cinematographer Victor Milner created a successful musical that received instant recognition for its imaginative sound direction.[1] As contemporary reviews suggest, much of *Monte Carlo*'s appeal stemmed from the distinct, old-fashioned flair surrounding its aristocratic characters, setting, and story and, most of all, from the enormous popularity of Jeanette MacDonald, the female lead. But the film was also praised for its sleek set design and visual finesse, both of which were the speciality of Paramount, then known as the studio of "continental sophistication."

Among the musicals Lubitsch directed for Paramount, *Monte Carlo* stands closest to the streamlined modernity of later films like *Design for Living* or *Angel* and furthest away from the self-reflexive atmosphere of the Warner comedies. The late twenties saw the end of a formative period in

[1] For a contemporary review, see Alexander Bakshy's "*Monte Carlo* and *Animal Crackers*" (1932): "Mr. Lubitsch is out to capture the very spirit of the artificial, conventional musical comedy, with its music and dancing as means of dramatic expression independent of the realistic requirements of the plot." In *American Film Criticism. From the Beginnings to Citizen Kane*, ed. Stanley Kauffmann and Bruce Henstell (New York: Liveright, 1972), 237. As was frequently noted by critics, Jeanette MacDonald, the popular Broadway actress and singer, was largely responsible for the film's lively atmosphere even though she was cast vis-à-vis Jack Buchanan, an English music-hall tenor, and not her usual partner, the French chansonnier Maurice Chevalier. This circumstance prompts MacDonald biographer Lee Edward Stern to note: "a somewhat sprightlier film than the previous year's *The Love Parade*, but still marred by clumsy camera work and, in addition, hampered by the vacuity of its leading man." In *Jeanette MacDonald* (New York: Harven, 1977), 79. Ethan Mordeen even calls Buchanan a "smarmy British wimp [who] . . . has a voice like tapioca pudding on high speed and the most irritating laugh a leading man has ever tried to get away with." In *The Hollywood Musical* (New York: St. Martin's Press, 1981), 38.

film history that had established the rules of storytelling in the cinema. With the advent of sound, a complete reassessment of filmic styles, genres, and techniques was necessary. From the year 1927, the year the *The Jazz Singer* was released, until about 1932, the conditions of film production changed dramatically.[2] While the sound film also led to a process of economic concentration, it introduced a wide range of new artistic possibilities. Techniques previously limited to visual mise-en-scène and visual montage could be expanded to include the aural registers of noise, speech, and music. The aim would be the development of an equally complex auditory field. But more often than not, the "supplement of reality" provided by the sound track necessitated a temporary return to the anthropocentric perspective of the theater and resulted in an impoverishment of the visual field. The increased standardization also put an end to more idiosyncratic approaches to camera movement and editing. Obviously, the human voice and what it signified required a highly normative spatio-temporal order. While the sound film finalized the identification of camera and spectator, the strong emphasis on a coherent narrative left little room for authorial interventions. Similarly, while specific forms of editing (rapid cutting, associative montage) continued to exist in designated sequences, the new rules of continuity editing set the standard against which everything else had to be measured. The shot/reverse-shot pattern represented the most effective means through which the spectator was drawn into this new order and reinstated at the center of meaning production.

Lubitsch began to experiment with image-sound relations while the majority of directors, perhaps with the exception of Lang, Hawks, Mamoulian, Sternberg, and Ford, still struggled with the technological problems of the sound-recording apparatus. He continued to work in the old style, for instance, by shooting long takes without sound and then adding the songs through postsynchronization. As is well known, he used this method for *The Love Parade* and *Monte Carlo*, two musicals that were originally planned as silent films. Rather than subjecting everything to the exigencies of diegetic sound, Lubitsch developed a special interest in the creative possibilities of nondiegetic and offscreen sound. Thus he was immediately drawn to musicals, for only a highly stylized genre such as the musical could provide him with the formal means for such an exploration while at the same time justifying the continuing presence of spectacle.[3] Here differ-

---

[2] See *The Classical Hollywood Cinema: Film Style and Mode of Production to 1960*, ed. David Bordwell, Janet Staiger, and Kristin Thompson (New York: Columbia University Press, 1985), esp. the chapter "The Formulation of the Classical Style," 155–240.

[3] For an insightful discussion of the problem of spectacle and narrative, see Patricia Mellencamp, "Spectacle and Spectator: Looking Through the American Musical Comedy," *Ciné-Tracts* 1, no. 2 (Summer 1977): 27–35. Also compare Theodor Adorno and Hanns Eisler on the film musical: "Therefore the aesthetic divergence of the media [in an alienated society] is

ent traditions not only existed peacefully side by side but also developed a creative momentum of their own. Early film musicals like *Monte Carlo*—other examples include *Hallelujah* (1929, Vidor), *Applause* (1929, Mamoulian), and *Love Me Tonight* (1932, Mamoulian)—bear witness to this difficult negotiation of the old and the new. Because of their strong investment in sound, these films reveal the gains and losses in the transition to sound with particular clarity.[+] As will be argued, *Monte Carlo* conforms to the new order while continuing to pose the threat of difference. By complying with the new spatio-temporal order and by glossing over the gaps and fissures in the narrative, the film's sound track "distracts," as it were, from the authorial interventions that characterize the earlier Lubitsch films and that remain present in the musicals. The auditory field, in a paradoxical way, guarantees the discursiveness of the visual field, even as this precarious balance is in constant danger of falling prey to the unifying power of sound.

Monte Carlo begins on a note of expectancy. The box with wedding rings, the embroidered names of an aristocratic couple, and the rejoicing subjects singing "Day of Days," conjure up images of happiness and bliss. Instead the rolled-out carpet in front of the wedding chapel becomes the lateral plane on which the ensuing drama is made visible through two extensive pans. In a movement from left to right, the first pan follows the groom as he leaves the chapel and joyfully anticipates receiving his bride. Suddenly, a servant arrives with the shocking news of her disappearance. Illustrating this sudden change, a reverse pan, along with a thunderstorm, now follows the groom—protected by lined-up servants with umbrellas—as he runs back up the carpet. Point-of-view shots of pouring rain punctuate the sequence and create an atmosphere of bleakness and ennui, thereby also capturing the mood that makes flight the only option available to the missing bride. Flight from a formal wedding ceremony, and flight from an elderly yet infantile groom, the Count Otto von Liebenheim (Claude Allister), who reacts to the news with a helpless "Papa! Papa!" From his call for paternal authority—the first spoken words in the film—

---

potentially a legitimate means of expression, not merely a regrettable deficiency, that has to be concealed as well as possible. And this is perhaps the fundamental reason why so many light-entertainment pictures that fall far below the pretentious standard of the usual movie seem to be more substantial than motion pictures that flirt with real art. Movie revues usually come closest to the ideal of montage, hence music fulfills its proper function most adequately in them." In Hanns Eisler, *Composing for the Films* (New York: Oxford University Press, 1947), 74. Compare the slightly different German original, Theodor W. Adorno and Hanns Eisler, *Komposition für den Film* (Frankfurt am Main: Suhrkamp, 1975), 21.

[+] Tom Levin has astutely noted: "The history of the development of cinema sound can thus be read as an oscillation between its difference understood as supplement and its difference understood as threat." In "The Acoustic Dimension," *Screen* 25, no. 3 (May–June 1984): 63. For a comprehensive account of the Hollywood musical, also see John Kobal, *Gotta Sing Gotta Dance* (London: Hamlyn, 1970).

the scene cuts directly to the close-up of a locomotive's wheel and the shapely legs of a woman about to jump aboard the train. And with the same vigor, the film returns to the bewildered members of the court society to whom the first solo number, sung by the comic baritone Claude Allister, is addressed. His official statement on the bride's disappearance opens with a tentative *Sprechgesang*, "I Am a Simple-Hearted Soul," but, encouraged by the listeners' rhythmical "ooh"s and "aah"s, closes with the reassuring melody of "She'll Love Me and Like It." The riddle behind this association of sound (the call for the father) and image (the body of the woman) is quickly solved by the ticket collectors on the train: "Listen, here is a puzzle and believe me it's hot. She comes from a wedding, she has nothing on, she has left her husband behind, she has no ticket, she has no idea where she wants to go and she goes to Monte Carlo. Well, how old is her husband?" Answer: "Too old!" (fig. 20).

As the train approaches Monte Carlo with growing speed, the film builds up to a crescendo of sounds and images, thereby celebrating the woman's newly gained freedom. Jeanette MacDonald opens the window of the compartment, raises her voice, and joins in the locomotive's stamping beat and the whistle's shrill *toot-toot*. From the antiphony between female voice and mechanical noise, from the rapid crosscutting between the

"Five more minutes and I would have been married." 1264·89

20. *Monte Carlo*: Jeanette MacDonald, ZaSu Pitts

singer's face and the engine's flying wheels, the film's most famous song, "Beyond the Blue Horizon," arises: "Blow whistle (*toot toot*) blow away / Blow away the past / Go engine (*toot toot*) anywhere / . . . What matters where I go if I am free." Through rhythmical editing, the scene's basic elements—the trinity of woman, nature, and machine—are transformed into a splendid visual spectacle. These provide the appropriate setting for the song's exuberant melody and suggestive lyrics and constitute its emotional reality. While a hilly landscape flies by, the peasants on the fields pick up the soloist's song and respond with the refrain: "Beyond the blue horizon / There lies a beautiful day / Goodbye to things that bore me / My life has just begun / Beyond the blue horizon / Lies a rising sun."[5] Commenting on Lubitsch's innovative use of sound, Kenneth White noted at the time: "The episode in which the engine's flying wheels introduce the dramatic mood of a song Jeanette MacDonald is on the point of singing and musically sustain the visual and auditory effort of swift motion, is nothing short of a masterpiece of sound direction."[6]

As the "Blue Horizon" sequence demonstrates, narrative and spectacle in the Lubitsch musical function as extensions of each other, with the one taking over the role of the other. The songs are an integral part of the narrative, and they establish a connection between the outside world and the inner feelings of a character; hence also the lack of bracketing devices (the story of a stage production, a performer's career). In contrast to many of the early musicals that rely on such devices for a narrative motivation of their song-and-dance numbers, Lubitsch does not distinguish between filmic reality and theatrical performance, for he treats everything as performance. Two factors contributed to this approach: the particular conditions of production in the late twenties and early thirties and the strong influence of other musical traditions on his work. As noted above, Lubitsch directed *Monte Carlo* before the film musical was fully established as a genre. During this transition period, there was still room for the formal explorations of the silent period, as is evidenced by the film's many visual tropes and the calculated use of props. Moreover, Lubitsch found inspiration in the Viennese operetta, which organizes the relationship between narrative and spectacle differently. The influence of operatic traditions can be seen in the antiphonal singing between soloist and chorus which, even with a machine dictating the rhythm, presupposes an insurmountable difference between individual and masses. Such a formal arrangement of voices implies

[5] Fulfilling Lubitsch's personal wish, Jeanette MacDonald sang "Blue Horizon" at his funeral. For a critical assessment of "Beyond the Blue Horizon," compare the opening sequence in René Clair's *Sous les toits de Paris* (1930) in which the inhabitants of a quaint Parisian neighborhood join in the singing from their separate apartments and become a community through the song's lyrics and sweeping melody.

[6] Kenneth White, "The Style of Ernst Lubitsch," *Hound and Horn* 4, no. 2 (1931): 274.

a stronger emphasis on class difference, despite the scene's dynamic quality. The operetta allows for imaginary transgressions in the form of melancholy solos and romantic duets but contains all signs of otherness within its artificial worlds; its world view is largely conservative. The film musical, which has at its disposal the unlimited possibilities of time and space, offers a setting in which the operetta's old-fashioned songs can test their power once again. The old musical styles and the new technology thus join forces to provide continuity both in the formal and thematic sense. The songs become agents of the narrative, linking different locales, initiating communication between characters, and representing those emotions that must be denied in the dialogues. In other words, the songs in the Lubitsch musical uphold the promise of a unified space that has been temporarily abandoned in the transition from the operatic stage to the fragmented world of film.

From their first meeting at the gambling table to their happy reunion at the opera, six songs accompany the growing romantic involvement between Helene Mara and Count Rudolph Farrière (Jack Buchanan). The function of these songs is closely related to the spatial opposition of presence/absence, inside/outside, and, as a comment on their emotional significance, of appearance/truth. When the image vanishes, the song—according to Barthes "a dual posture, a dual production—of language and of music"[7]—remains and represents the image in its absence. Songs establish a connection between shots, follow pans and tilts, and inspire extensive tracking shots. In so doing, they control the changing configurations of sound and image. Securing the primacy of the narrative across time and space, the songs stand in the service of the narrative even when the narrative seems to fall apart. Especially in dramatic situations, they perform the mediating role that has always been part of their social and cultural function.[8] In *Monte Carlo*, and in all other Lubitsch musicals as well, singing is more or less synonymous with the expression of sexual desire and love.

[7] Roland Barthes, "The Grain of the Voice," in *Image Music Text*, trans. Stephen Heath (New York: Hill & Wang, 1977), 181.

[8] What Claudia Gorbman has defined as the function of background music also applies, to a certain degree, to the Lubitsch musicals: "Music in film *mediates*. Its nonverbal and nondenotative status allows it to cross all varieties of 'borders': between levels of narration (diegetic/nondiegetic), between narrating agencies (objective/subjective narrators), between viewing time and psychological time, between points in diegetic space and time (as narrative transitions)" (30). According to Gorbman, background music has two functions, a semiotic one—to avoid uncertain signification and a psychological one—to achieve bonding (*suture*). Responsible for what she calls, therein following Barthes, semiotic *ancrage* (a device against "the terror of uncertain signs"), background music may even be compared to the inter-titles of the silent film: "Music, like the caption, anchors the image in meaning, throws a net around the floating signifier, assures the viewer of a safely channeled signified." In *Unheard Melodies. Narrative Film Music* (Bloomington: Indiana University Press, 1987), 58.

Accordingly, the film's mise-en-scène becomes the stage for a musical seduction. This is most evident in the staging of "Give Me a Moment,
Please," a song that develops as a late-night phone "conversation" between
MacDonald and Buchanan after their first meeting at the gambling table.
The phone rings, Helene picks up the receiver, and a male voice begins to
sing, gradually changing from a cappella singing (reminiscent of the classical recitative) to the assertive, wistful "Give Me a Moment, Please" accompanied by a full orchestra. MacDonald joins in and, after hanging up,
continues the song by herself as she falls asleep. The bonding effect of the
first duet carries over to the next morning when Buchanan encounters a
man in the park who whistles the theme of "Give Me A Moment, Please"
and who turns out to be Helene's hairdresser, Paul (John Roche). Together with Rudolph's friend, the three uniformly dressed men—complete
with walking canes, hats, and galoshes—join forces for a musical trio that
betrays the film's secret motto, the boisterous "Trimmin' the Women."
From their park bench, the film moves to an interior setting where Buchanan, Brooks, and Roche are seated around a coffee table and where they
conclude this hymn to male supremacy while lovingly serving each other
mocha, candy, and liqueur.

In order to be closer to Helene, Rudolph conceals his true identity and
introduces himself as the new hairdresser. As a result of her increasing
losses at the roulette table, she is forced to dismiss most of her servants
and, eventually, uses him as her lackey, chauffeur, hairdresser, and private
secretary. The confusions created by "the suitor-as-employee" motif, a variation of "the prince-as-beggar" motif, lead to many compromising situations, often with strong sexual overtones. Helene, for instance, greets the
new "Paul," as she prefers to call Rudolph, with the following words: "You
are in my employ now . . . you must devote yourself entirely to me." Rudolph, in turn, responds emotionally rather than professionally. Instead of
dressing her hair "à la Marat," he cuts off a little curl and puts it in his
locket. Later she receives a thorough head massage but attributes her feelings of exhilaration to Rudolph's professional skills. Already the sexual references are more than obvious, with Helene exclaiming: "No, no, no . . .
don't do that . . . ah-hh . . . that feels good . . . oh-hh . . . I've never felt
like this before . . . gorgeous . . . of course, you must stay." Finally, the
scene culminates in a tentative confession of love, the duet "Whatever It
Is, It's Grand." Rudolph continues to play the hairdresser, while their desire for each other finds expression in a song that begins very melodically
but, as they become more aware of their feelings, ends with the rhythms of
a fiery bolero. All remaining doubts are eliminated during a later argument
over money and the right hair color. Now in charge of Helene's financial
situation, Rudolph tells her about his secret method at the gambling table:
"I have a system that can't miss. If I happen to be standing beside a bru-

nette I bet on red, if I'm standing next to a redhead I bet on black." When she inquires about his reaction to a blonde such as herself, he quickly changes the original version ("I ask her where she lives") and answers: "I always win." As Rudolph's answer implies, the entire system is based on transferences. A single element is taken from one framework of inscriptions to another and changes their meanings in turn. The hair remains the same but, without significant alterations, a frivolous remark turns into a declaration of love.

The third duet between MacDonald and Buchanan, "Always in All Ways," is based on the same principle of visual separation and aural unification that structures the first one. However, its rendition already stands under the sway of a more bodily principle. Once Buchanan makes his grand entry in tails and the sounds of a waltz set in, the musical seduction of woman and spectator/auditor is complete. To underscore this effect, Lubitsch uses orchestral music in a fashion similar to background music—a very unusual technique for the time. The glissandos, crescendos, and brief repetitions of the song's main theme clearly anticipate the sound effects and the narrative function of background music. Beginning with the singers' exuberant rendition of "Always in All Ways," as a result of which the rhythm changes from a three/four bar to an affirming four/four bar, music accompanies their arrival at the casino as well as their late return to the hotel. The passing of time is indicated by three inserts depicting toy figures in a musical clock. These figures repeat the "Always in All Ways" theme as they each blow the hour: first on a trumpet, then on a tuba, and, with daybreak approaching, on a flute. With the sweeping melodies of the violins punctuated by muted trumpets, music conserves the mood, even after their first good-bye, and even during Helene's personal confessions to her maid. Music prevails as the camera follows the movement of emotions and travels along the hotel front in an elaborate crane shot, linking Mac-Donald's figure at the open bedroom window to the image of Buchanan who, several floors above her, is about to take some of his own money to present it as the new casino winnings. Back in Helene's suite, he hands her a considerable amount of money. The following close-up has the money drop to the ground, while the lovers fall into each other's arms. Then Helene tells him to leave. As if protecting herself against the strong desires that surface with the return of the "Give Me A Moment" theme, she locks the door, puts the key into a drawer, the drawer's key into a box, and the key of the box under her pillow. Separated only by the locked door, Mac-Donald and Buchanan bid each other good-bye by expressing the back and forth of the camera in a similar musical movement between his tentative "Give Me A Moment, Please" to her firm "Always in All Ways."

Songs bring into the open the claims of love. Consequently, it is through language, not song, that the lovers are eventually forced to confront reality.

With the unexpected arrival of Helene's fiancé, Rudolph and Helene begin to talk and, in talking, experience the social barriers between them. For the man, sexual difference is the only acceptable kind of difference. But the woman points to class difference as a major problem in their relationship. Consonant with her role as Countess Helene Mara, she responds to his declaration of love with indignation: "That's what you get for being nice to your servants!" Prepared to teach the countess a lesson, Rudolph continues to court her but only to disappoint all romantic expectations by suddenly dropping her on the sofa. Soon after his angry exit, Helene Mara realizes that she has lost a lover, and not just an employee. She tries to track him down by calling all the city's hair salons. Finally, he agrees to do her hair for a gala evening at the opera. With love and professionalism now reversed, Helene would rather be ugly than share Rudolph with other women customers. Curious about the reasons behind his unexpected kindness, she asks: "You mean I'll be an advertisement for you?" Outraged by Rudolph's "Yes, madame," she continues, "So that all the ladies will come to you?" and decides, after his second "Yes, madame," to mess up her coiffure, exclaiming: "I am going to ruin you."

As in *The Love Parade*, the climax of *Monte Carlo* takes place in a box at the opera. Again the exchanges between characters develop parallel to and as a reflection of the events on the stage. The program lists the eighteenth-century opera *Monsieur Beaucaire* which is summarized by Count Otto as follows: "It's a silly story, only possible with music. Imagine a lady falling in love with her hairdresser . . ." Despairingly, Helene turns her head only to find Rudolph seated in the opposite box. As the analogies between play and reality are developed further by the opera performance, she suddenly realizes her mistakes. The chorus sings "He's a prince!" cut to her astonished face, the lady on the stage sings with tears in her voice "Can you ever . . . ?" and Helene completes the sentence but now addressed to Rudolph: ". . . forgive me?" The man on the stage exits, Helene and her double on the stage sob and, with the voice of male authority, Rudolph decides: "I like happy endings." Like Lubitsch who, in an epilogue, repeats the sweeping melodies of "Beyond the Blue Horizon," this time sung by the happy couple sitting at the window of a train.

The songs in *Monte Carlo*, and the "Always in All Ways" sequence in particular, are masterpieces of sound direction. They stand out through the ease with which sound and image, different locations and events, are brought together to produce a truly cinematic effect. The presentation of the songs is relatively free of the theatricality that characterizes so many early musicals, a result of the technical difficulties in sound recording. Precisely because of its dynamic style Lubitsch's sound direction also establishes the body politics of the sound film. Speaking about the indisputable link between body and voice in the cinema, Mary Ann Doane has described the so-called fantasmic body of the sound film "as a pivot for certain cine-matic practices of representation [that] . . . authorizes and sustains a lim-ited number of relationships between voice and image."[9] Accordingly, the "Always in All Ways" sequence uses the quintessential image of separation, the closed door, in order to bring into play the various effects associated with the fantasmic body. The locked door at the end occasions a forceful demonstration of what Doane has termed voice-off, that is, the voice em-anating from beyond the frame line. Other than the disembodied voice of the voice-over, the voice-off remains part of the mise-en-scène. Because of its presence-to-itself, the voice-off represents a trace of the displaced body and, by confirming the notion of the "just over there," negates the bound-aries of the frame. The locked door only underscores the transgressive quality inherent in the human voice, a reminder both of its origins in the language of desire and its close association with power, including the power of authorship. The "Always in All Ways" sequence explores the emotional side of this double movement, while the telephone scenes em-phasize its humorous potential; note, for instance, Rudolph's suggestive "yes," "no," and "I hope so" during a phone conversation witnessed by Helene. These moments of voluntary and involuntary listening, in turn, draw attention to the close affinities between eavesdropping, the basis of the invocatory drive, and the recurring motif of voyeurism in *Monte Carlo*. The quintessential eavesdropper is, of course, Helene Mara's maid Bertha (ZaSu Pitts), who stands in front of the closed door during the "Whatever It Is, It's Grand" sequence and who responds to MacDonald's ecstatic cries (the head massage) with obvious indignation. Her false conclusions, how-ever, only underscore what the scene already implies.

Film sound always partakes in the hallucination of a unified subject, yet is it through song that the association of body and sound achieves its most provocative effects.[10] For these effects to take place, the process of unifica-tion has to be made difficult or be prevented altogether. The power of an emotion, after all, is often measured best by the problems it encounters. The overcoming of obstacles, of that which at once promises and prevents

---

[9] Mary Ann Doane, "The Voice in the Cinema: The Articulation of Body and Space," *Yale French Studies* 60 (1980): 34. Doane relies heavily on Pascal Bonitzer, *Le regard et la voix* (Paris: Union Générale d'Éditions, 1976).

[10] This calls to mind Stephen Heath's observation "that the sound cinema is the develop-ment of a powerful standard of the body and of the voice as hold of the body in image, the voice literally ordered and delimited as speech for an intelligibility of the body, of people . . . fixed in the order of the narrative and its meanings, its unities and resolutions. In the silent cinema, the body is always pulling towards an emphasis, an exaggeration, a burlesque (the term of an intractable existence); in the sound cinema, the body is smoothed out . . . with the voice as the medium, the expression, of a homogeneous thinking subject—actor and specta-tor—of film." See "Body, Voice," in *Questions of Cinema* (Bloomington: Indiana University Press, 1981), 191.

unification, is the main function of offscreen sound in *Monte Carlo*. These obstacles include framing devices like windows or doors—important props in the Lubitsch universe—and, of course, the frame itself. As song challenges the boundaries of the frame, a new expanded cinematic space develops. Therein lies the transgressive quality of music. Furthermore, the testing of the frame's spatial and the shot's temporal boundaries through songs—again the dynamic of the here and there, the before and after—foregrounds the conditions of meaning production in the cinema. By exceeding the requirements of continuity, Lubitsch's repeated use of onscreen/offscreen sound reveals the presence of a narrator. The effect is not dissimilar to the visual puns known from his silent films. And even as the "acoustic puns" strive to establish, through the assumption of the "just over there," a cinematic space without boundaries, they invariably draw critical attention to their most problematic feature, their foundation upon belief.

In *Monte Carlo*, the play with onscreen/offscreen sound takes two forms. Both forms are based on the absence-presence dichotomy. The first leads to a playful acknowledgment of difference, while the second derives its strongest effects from an effacement of that same difference. Songs, as has been argued above, facilitate transgressions. They help to overcome difference. Thus when differences need to be emphasized, Lubitsch resorts to the less identifiable and, in a way, inferior features of a sound track: noise, or sound effects. Situated at the margins of the narrative, noise tends to blur the boundaries between the animate and inanimate worlds. Neither meaningful nor meaningless, its effects reintroduce a distinctly antihumanist perspective. These different functions attributed to song and noise mirror the distinction between omnipotence and omnipresence made by Nancy Wood in her discussion of early sound film: "Thus, if the position of *omnipresence* afforded by silent cinema's extensive point-of-view cutting and greater depth of focus was temporarily sacrificed in early sound film, this was more than compensated for by the position of *omnipotence* offered the spectator-auditor by a more frequent recourse to the shot/reverse-shot structure and camera movement in the dialogue scene."[11]

For the most part, *Monte Carlo* remains closely aligned with the position of omnipotence from where the distinct elements can be transformed into a meaningful whole. The desire for omnipotence informs all narrative strategies, including the many dialogue scenes. As a film director trained in the silent cinema, however, Lubitsch holds on to the older position of omnipresence through his experiments with offscreen sound. A good example

[11] Nancy Wood, "Towards a Semiotics of the Transition to Sound: Spatial and Temporal Codes," *Screen* 25, no. 3 (May–June 1984): 21. See also her dissertation, "Text and Spectator in the Period of the Transition to Sound," Ph.D. diss., University of Kent: Canterbury, 1983.

is the couple's first encounter at the entrance door of the casino. The entire scene is characterized by intentionally narrow frame compositions and obscured perspectives, as if the world prior to love were only a series of unconnected images. While Rudolph's friend Armand approaches the unknown woman on his behalf, the elegant beau uses the spare moment to slip on his kid gloves in eager anticipation of a conquest. Suddenly a smacking noise emanates from offscreen. The next shot shows the bewildered friend holding his cheek. Then the film cuts to Helene who walks off with indignation, entering the casino by herself. Later in the film, the vague and often ambiguous quality of noise also inspires a number of humorous commentaries. One scene, for instance, focuses on the sound effects created through the opening and closing of a door; another one cuts from a strange hacking sound to the image of a typing secretary. Rather than denying the problem of absence, Lubitsch's conscious use of noise highlights, indeed even celebrates, its very existence. In so doing, he grants the spectator the experience of omnipresence, sometimes even in defiance of the position of omnipotence associated with the protagonists and their love story.

In Lubitsch's silent films and early musicals, music belongs to the group of legitimate transgressions and derives its main function from this association. No matter whether music is performed by musicians in the motion-picture theaters (the piano accompanist, the full symphonic orchestra) or by the musicians depicted on the screen; no matter whether music is continuously present or limited to specific moments in the narrative—its mere presence poses a challenge to the representational order. Music appears on the scene as an extension of the body, an excess of pleasure, a supplement of reality that is capable of defying the laws of filmic realism. Characters, spectators, and the ever-present narrator participate in its functioning, making music both an expression of desire and a desire for expression. Yet it is the problematic position of women within the narrative that facilitates this process.

Already Lubitsch's earliest films use music to challenge the existing order, either directly in the form of live accompaniment or indirectly through specific narrative motifs or through visual spectacle. Since, technically speaking, these films are silent, they must depend on their dance sequences to bring about the musical moment of truth, as it were. These sequences often function as a turning point in the sense of the classical drama, while at the same time anchoring the potentially disruptive use of montage within the narrative. The visualization of music is achieved through shots of ecstatic faces and bodies in motion and, concurrently, through the simulation of rhythm, melody, and polyphony by means of rhythmical editing, camera movement, and special effects. However, as music helps to resolve the dramatic complications, it also makes possible a celebration of its sheer spectatorial qualities. With music dictating the rhythm of editing, the images assume a quality that transports them outside of the spatio-temporal order, beyond the laws of continuity and contiguity. Consequently, the "musical" sequences in the silent films (*Kohlhiesel's Daughters, The Oyster Princess, Passion*) have a tendency to transcend the diegesis and reveal the material conditions of signification in the cinema. In a way, the ecstatic dancers act out what the implied spectators are invited to feel. The visual representation of music through movement initiates, by introducing such analogies, a momentous shift from the epic to the poetic qualities of silent cinema. The story disappears in the background, and the epiphany of music and dance reveals the true powers of camera work, editing, and lighting. As a result of the representation of one art form through another, Lubitsch's German films open up a space for counter-narrative strategies—and for a poetics of film. The basis for such a poetics lies in the filmmaker's awareness of the distinct elements that constitute film as an art form. Its realization, however, depends on the spectator's willingness to appreciate and carry on this self-reflexive move.

For reasons that have to do with a growing concern with questions of morality, music relinquishes its subversive quality, beginning with Lubitsch's American silent comedies. In place of the ecstatic crowds and the playful testing of cinematic means, music becomes increasingly tied to the desire of the individual, a development that in turn strengthens the films' anthropocentric perspective. In *The Marriage Circle*, the seductive Mitzi seats herself at the piano and plays Grieg's famous "I Love You!" while casting meaningful glances toward Franz. But in a realistic assessment of her chances, she finishes the serenade with her own words: "We'll get over it!" The utopian potential inherent in music has given way to blatant erotic innuendoes and a pragmatism that reduces music to a useful auxiliary in a seduction scene. This trend culminates in the film musicals where the musical references become synonymous with sexual desire and romantic love. Even the act of playing music is reduced to blatantly erotic meanings, for instance when the male protagonist of *The Smiling Lieutenant*, Nicki (Maurice Chevalier), brags to his friend Maxi about the various talents of a girlfriend, the violinist Franzi (Claudette Colbert). His proud "She plays the violin" elicits a tentative "Yes?" from Max who, reacting to Nicki's suggestive "I play the piano," only manages to voice a meek "I don't play any instruments."[12] The gradual transformation of music's transgressive qualities into rather hackneyed metaphors of musical eroticism can be seen in another example, the song "Dream Lover" from *The Love Parade*. "Dream lover, fold your arms around me / Dream lover, your romance has found

---

[12] First White Script of 17 January 1931; the scene was later changed because of censorship problems.

me": Queen Louise (Jeanette MacDonald) sings the song for the first time
when she awakens from a pleasant dream. Immediately the ministers of
state and the ladies-in-waiting rush to her bed with concern, and a military
band starts playing Mendelssohn's Wedding March, a not-so-subtle comment on the missing royal husband. "Dream Lover," in the beginning of
the film, evokes a male-female relationship based on true love, and not
reasons of state. MacDonald sings the song for a second time during a
private dinner with the charming Count Alfred (Maurice Chevalier), who
has just returned from Paris. Although the camera is denied access to the
site of their blossoming romance, it participates from afar through the reactions of the spying servants and, most importantly, through the sound
track. The sequence begins with chambermaids and lackeys who peek
through keyholes and glance over bushes, thereby resorting to the most
grotesque body positions. The absence of the couple is further underscored
by the presence of their lapdogs, eating peacefully from one plate. Even
Alfred's declaration of love takes place behind closed doors. Nonetheless,
MacDonald's second rendering of "Dream Lover" leaves no doubt about
its emotional impact. Some time later, she repeats the song in tears while
Alfred, having been reduced to the insignificant role of a prince consort,
prepares for his departure for Paris. The "lover," Queen Louise has to
learn, is no longer a "dream" but a "man" who requires special gestures of
submission. In that sense, *The Love Parade* shows to what degree the function of music had changed since Lubitsch's German films, having turned
from a means of transgression into a conventional metaphor of sexual desire and a measure of woman's domestication.

Last but not least, the many musical references in the Lubitsch films also
point to the close association of music and the feminine that has inspired
opera and operetta from the very beginning and that must be regarded as
a threat and a form of containment.[13] Continuing in this tradition, *Monte*

---

[13] Because the film musical seems to tend toward the side of excess, some caution is advis-
able once again to avoid glorifying the new/old association of music and the feminine, now
resurrected as subversive bliss, regression, as the maternal voice. Warning of such nostalgic
investments, Kaja Silverman writes: "The theoretical and cinematic equation of the maternal
voice with 'pure' sonorousness must therefore be understood not as an extension of its intrin-
sic nature, or of its acoustic function, but as part of a larger cultural disavowal of the mother's
role both as an agent of discourse and as a model for linguistic (as well as visual) identification.
The characterization of the mother's voice as babble or noise is also . . . one of the primary
mechanisms through which the male subject seeks both to recover an imaginary infantile
plenitude, and to extricate himself from the 'afterbirth' of perceptual and semiotic insuffi-
ciency. Last but not least, that characterization contradicts the notion of exteriority which is
implied by the metaphors of enclosure with which it is frequently linked—metaphors such as
'envelope,' 'cobweb,' or 'bath'—and facilitates the alignment of femininity with an unpleasur-
able and disempowering interiority." In Kaja Silverman, *The Acoustic Mirror: The Female Voice
in Psychoanalysis and Cinema* (Bloomington: Indiana University Press, 1988), 100. As examples
of the recent emphasis on female voice, see Julia Kristeva, *Desire in Language: A Semiotic*

Carlo uses its songs to tell a story of romantic love and female surrender but also organizes the different performance styles along the lines of gender. Jeanette MacDonald's singing conforms with operatic traditions that favor a classical voice, sweeping melodies, and expressive lyrics. Conversely, the singing style of the men (especially of Claude Allister with his *Sprechgesang*) stands closer to vaudeville, where speech and song mix more freely and where the high musical standards are deliberately abandoned in favor of humorous exchanges with other performers and the audience. Thus Allister's first solo addresses an actual audience in the film, the court society, whereas MacDonald's only solo in the film is but an expression of her innermost feelings, aimed at the camera.

Commenting on such practices, Carol Flinn has analyzed how the sound film makes use of existent associations between music and the feminine: "Music's relation to psychic activity—however intimate it may be—is a mediated one: its unconscious pleasures actively participate within rigorously organized symbolic systems. . . . For music does have its meanings in cinema, although they may not be inscribed according to the conventions of standard representational practice. Music constantly oscillates between meaning and 'meaninglessness,' representational and nonrepresentational functions, and because of this cannot be claimed that it uniformly or unproblematically inhabits one extreme or the other."[14] Only seemingly outside of representation, music participates in all of its productions, namely by representing the other, the unnameable. Despite the continuous affiliation with dominant discourse, music can therefore be thought of as containing the elements of its own existential insecurity, a quality that marks the sound track as a place for counter-narrative strategies.

This quality inherent in music ultimately saves *Monte Carlo*, in spite of its sentimental story and its rather conventional musical score. As Jeanette MacDonald gives two performances of "Beyond the Blue Horizon," the various layers of the song—the sound of her warm maternal soprano, the emotional power of female confession, the association of woman, nature, and machine, and so forth—reach a point of completion and fullness. On the one hand, the satisfaction of her romantic desire in the final rendition

---

Approach to Literature and Art, trans. Thomas Gora, Alice Jardine, and Leon S. Roudiez (New York: Columbia University Press, 1980), especially Kristeva's notion of the *chora*/womb; Luce Irigaray, *The Sex Which Is Not One*, trans. Catherine Porter (Ithaca, N.Y.: Cornell University Press, 1985); Hélène Cixous and Catherine Clément, *The Newly Born Woman*, trans. Betsy Wing (Minneapolis: University of Minnesota Press, 1986), especially Clément's statement: "First I sense femininity in writing by a privilege of *voice*: *writing and voice* are entwined and interwoven and writing's continuity/voice's rhythm take each other's breath away through interchanging, make the text gasp or form it out of suspenses and silences, make it lose its voice or rend it with cries" (92).

[14] Carol Flinn, "The 'Problem' of Femininity in Theories of Film Music," *Screen* 27, no. 6 (November–December 1986): 72.

of "Beyond the Blue Horizon" gives an unmistakable answer, placing the film firmly on the side of conformism. Yet on the other hand, that moment also brings back the first rendition of "Beyond the Blue Horizon" in which the association of music and the feminine, made possible through the radical expansion of the aural mise-en-scène, brings forth a moment of freedom and bliss—even for the woman.

Filmography

Monte Carlo (1930). Director: Ernst Lubitsch for Paramount. Screenplay: Ernest Vajda, based on the Hans Müller play *Die blaue Küste* (1914) and episodes from the operetta *Monsieur Beaucaire* (1901) by Booth Tarkington and Evelyn Greenleaf. Photography: Victor Milner. Art Director: Hans Dreier. Music: Richard A. Whiting and W. Franke Harling. Lyrics: Leo Robin. With Jack Buchanan (Count Rudolph Farrière), Jeanette MacDonald (Countess Helene Mara), Claude Allister (Duke Otto von Liebenheim), ZaSu Pitts (Bertha, Maid to the Countess), Tyler Brooks (Armand), John Roche (Paul, a hairdresser) et al. Length: 90 min. Songs: "Day of Days," "I'm a Simple Hearted Soul," "She'll Love Me and Like It," "Beyond the Blue Horizon," "Give Me a Moment, Please," "Trimmin' the Women," "Whatever It Is, It's Grand," "Always in All Ways." Release: 4 Sept. 1930.

Nine

The Object, the Image, the Cinema:
Trouble in Paradise

AN exploration of the affinities between late capitalism and cinematic representation—this description applies equally to *Trouble in Paradise* (1932) and its forerunner "The Clerk," Lubitsch's short contribution to the omnibus film *If I Had a Million* (1932). In contrast to *Trouble in Paradise* and its classy setting, the earlier film approaches the Depression from the perspective of ordinary people. Its eight episodes are held together by a fantastic premise: the dying multimillionaire John Glidden (Richard Bennett) decides, much to the chagrin of his greedy lawyers and relatives, to distribute his wealth among a number of people whom he picks at random from the pages of the telephone directory. After an inappropriate first pick (a man named John D. Rockefeller), eight individuals become the recipients of a one-million-dollar check. The different episodes show their reactions to such sudden wealth. The film covers the entire range of possibilities, from liberating orgies of destruction ("The Auto" episode with W. C. Fields) to moralistic "money doesn't bring happiness" parables (the "Three Marines" episode with Gary Cooper). Lubitsch's contribution, however, stands out because he needs only the minimum of filmic means to create the maximum of effects. The episode begins with the close-up of a middle-aged clerk, Phineas V. Lambert (Charles Laughton). A letter is passed to him. Automatically he puts it aside, then stops, opens the letter—and holds his breath. As he rises from his chair, the camera pulls back to show a large office with rows of identical desks and faceless office workers behind them. The clerk walks toward the staircase, climbs several flights of stairs, passes through a number of doors and, finally, reaches the door to the president's office.[1] He stops to rearrange his tie and knocks. A voice—the episode's first spoken words—says "Come in!" The clerk asks "Mr. Brown . . . ," the president replies "Yes . . . ?" and Phineas V. Lambert responds with what

---

[1] A very similar scene takes place at the beginning of *Bluebeard's Eighth Wife* when the employees of a clothing store try to deal with Michael Brandon's eccentric request for a pajama top. The problem is quickly "promoted" from the lower to the higher ranks of the store management, until someone calls the owner who, rising from his bed without pajama pants, takes the receiver and shouts "That is communism!"

is commonly known as a hearty raspberry: " 'Lubitsch touch' *in excelsis*,"[2] as Weinberg succinctly notes.

Trouble in Paradise takes up the investigation of different economies, both cinematic and other, where the "The Clerk" ends. With the credits still running, the title song, sung by a romantic tenor to the lascivious rhythms of a fandango, recommends increased vigilance: "While arms entwine and lips are kissing / But if there's something missing / That signifies trouble in paradise." By focusing on the experience of loss, the song proclaims the failure of the earlier wish dream of pecuniary bliss but, by announcing yet another story of its success, also prepares the ground for its resurrection in the spirit of irony. As if to confirm the song's suggestive lyrics, the film begins with a series of remarkable cinematic deceptions. The voice that gives an a capella rendition of "O Sole Mio!" belongs to a garbageman who uses his gondola to ship away the trash of Venice, that monument to beauty and its transitoriness. Yet his voice is actually that of the legendary Italian tenor Enrico Caruso who, through postsynchronization, has lent his talents to the Venetian garbage collector. Here the influence of Lubitsch's work in the musical is most evident. The same ironic use of music, for instance, can be found at the beginning of *The Love Parade* (the singing servant), and the crane shot along the hotel's exterior recalls a similar one linking Helene and Rudolph's suites in *Monte Carlo*. By using sound-image relations in a highly reflected manner, Lubitsch calls into question the distinction between appearance and reality and initiates a vertiginous play with different levels of filmic reality. That is why the original deception (i.e., the identity of sound and image) must be double-fold. Only an excess of duplicity makes possible the laying bare of deception as the governing principle of cinema, that is, the unmasking of one layer of filmic reality through the means of another, more hidden one. To phrase it differently, the scene grants access to the truth only on the level of representation (the image of the menial laborer vs. the sounds of opera), but not of production (the body of the extra vs. the recorded voice of Caruso). For the sake of the fiction effect, the means of production must remain hidden.

Confronted with such duplicities, the following chapter proposes to read *Trouble in Paradise* on two levels as well. The first part concentrates on the film's plot structure, protagonists, and mise-en-scène and analyzes their participation in an insidious parable of capitalism. The second, more theoretical part tries to shed light on its constituting elements. To that end, it makes use of the psychoanalytic concepts of fetishism and displacement, and Christian Metz's notion of the cinema as an imaginary signifier in par-

[2] Herman G. Weinberg, *The Lubitsch Touch: A Critical Study*, 3d. rev. ed. (New York: Dover, 1977), 148.

ticular. As will be argued, Gaston and Lily's adventures in the high art of theft demonstrate on the level of narrative that which distinguishes Lubitsch as a filmmaker: the deceptive point-of-view shots, the unexpected shot/reverse-shot patterns, the disorienting temporal and spatial ellipses. They lay the foundation for a self-reflective play with shifting signifiers. *Trouble in Paradise* brings out the close affinities between cinema and psychoanalysis, as analyzed by Metz through the figures of metaphor and metonymy. But by retracing the movements of these figures, the film also undermines them in the spirit of irony. Only by paying close attention to this double movement can we learn to understand the kind of "trouble in paradise" in what may well be Lubitsch's most profound film and, even more importantly, come to appreciate its lasting modernity.

The film's musical opening is followed by a series of apparently unconnected images: a man fleeing over a balcony, a suspicious shadow outside, a body lying on the floor, two Italian women at the door. As the incessant ringing of the bell implies: a crime has taken place. Tracking along the nightly exterior of a hotel, the camera moves to another suite of the hotel where the elegant Gaston Monescu (Herbert Marshall) is all dressed up for an intimate dinner. While the waiter awaits last instructions about the menu, Monescu, "the symbiotic twin of Lubitsch himself, the master of manners and social irony,"[3] notes pensively: "Beginnings are always difficult," thus referring both to the staging of a romantic evening and the problems of filmmaking itself. Finally Gaston's guest, Lily (Miriam Hopkins), arrives in a gondola, dressed in a beautiful evening gown. While they exchange witty remarks about the disadvantages of wealth, the place of action shifts to another room in the hotel.[4] A robbery has taken place in suite 253-5-7- and 9, and the representatives of the hotel and the police have gathered to reconstruct the events. As Monsieur Filiba (Edward Everett Horton) tells them, an elegantly dressed man appeared at the door, introduced himself as a doctor, and examined his tonsils—only suddenly to knock him out and disappear with his valuables. The hotel manager translates Filiba's matter-of-fact account for the Italian police officers, who respond to the Italian version with expressions of astonishment and disbelief.

---

[3] Leo Braudy, "The Double Detachment of Ernst Lubitsch," *Modern Language Notes* 98, no. 5 (December 1983): 1076.

[4] Lily introduces herself with one of those anti-Americanisms that appear in many Lubitsch films. Her "You know, when I first saw you, I thought you were an American" first elicits a proud "Thank you" from Gaston but then continues in a truly impertinent direction: "Someone from another world—so entirely different. Oh! One get's so tired of one's own class—princes and counts and dukes and kings!" This exchange of words is missing from most copies. Compare the very similar dialogue between Princess Anna and her father in *The Smiling Lieutenant*. Anna: "Papa, if you don't let me have my lieutenant, do you know what I am going to do?" Father: "What?" Anna: "I am going to marry an American." Father: "My poor child. Does he really mean so much to you?"

The function of the translator, and the nature of translations, is made visible by the camera's panning back and forth between the perplexed victim and the shouting Italians. The pans only mark the distance between the original and the translation and draw attention to the changes (and falsifications) that come with every translation and, more generally, with every creative intervention. In that sense, the scene also comments on Lubitsch's own approach to filmmaking. Continuing in the spirit of the previous scenes, it reveals the conditions under which an event becomes a story, for instance about a mysterious robbery. However insignificant or implausible the story may be, as long as it is presented with conviction, the audience will be satisfied and the purpose of storytelling thus fulfilled. The hotel manager need not even resort to lies; he only has to add something: style. This emphasis on the formal qualities of film also explains Lubitsch's preference for settings that, through their self-imposed boundaries, virtually demand such self-reflexive comments.

With storytelling such an essential part of life, the two main protagonists cannot remain unaffected by its logic. The process of their unmasking begins with a telephone conversation between Lily and a certain Duchess of Chambro. From Lily's society small talk, the scene cuts to an unkempt older woman in pajamas complaining about Lily's dog. Soon afterwards, the romantic dinner culminates in a remarkable declaration of love. Dropping the high-society facade, Lily announces "Baron, you are a crook," but Gaston replies calmly "Countess, you are a thief." Suddenly, he jumps up, locks the door, pulls the curtains and, as if overcome by passion, grabs Lily and shakes her like a wet dog. With much clattering, her loot falls to the ground. As it turns out, a number of precious objects have changed owners during the dinner, including Lily's garter, Gaston's pocket watch, and, of course, the wallet of the gentleman from suite 253-5-7 and 9. The similarities between theft and seduction are developed further as Lily returns the watch rewound and as Gaston begs her to let him keep the garter. At no point do the characters lose their composure. As Frieda Grafe and Enno Patalas note: "Their nobility was fake; yet the noble forms do not lose their value because of that. On the contrary, they reach their full meaning as forms, for they are no longer tied to a specific content. Thus it is clear that forms develop their specific qualities in the relationships between people— most Lubitsch films are based on that premise."[5] Accordingly, Gaston falls in love with the same commitment to form that he shows in his career as an international master thief. And Lily embraces him with the same sense of excitement that she later feels for a string of pearls. While giving new meaning to the popular expression of "stealing one's heart," both characters continue to pay full attention to their meal. The outcome of the eve-

5 Frieda Grafe and Enno Patalas, *Im Off. Filmartikel* (Munich: Hanser, 1981), 69.

ning is only alluded to by a series of dissolves that lead from their passionate embrace at the table to a more intimate scene on the sofa (Gaston: "My
little shoplifter, my sweet little pickpocket!") and that finally results in the
couple's wondrous disappearance "into the air." Only the offscreen sound
of a light switch suggests the scene's continuation elsewhere. What remains
is the image of an empty sofa cast in twilight, an image that, once again,
bears witness to the gains and losses involved in all relationships (fig. 21).
With the singing garbageman, Lubitsch ends the Venice sequence; with
the next scene, the film continues in an entirely different place and time.

To stop somewhere and begin somewhere else: This motto accurately
describes Gaston's criminal method as well as Lubitsch's narrative strategies. The story, too, moves from Venice to Paris without further explanation. Through an elaborate montage sequence (see detailed discussion below) Lubitsch establishes a link between Gaston and Lily and a wealthy
Parisian widow, Mariette Colet (Kay Francis), the owner of a perfume factory. As if continuing the morning after, the next scene shows Gaston and
Lily at breakfast, but a breakfast that takes place one year later. The simple
hotel room suggests financial problems, their nostalgic mood a lack of challenges.[6] The promise of wealth—in the words of Gaston: "Prosperity is
just around the corner!"—enters their lives in the form of a newspaper ad
in which Madame Colet offers a 20,000-franc reward for her lost evening
bag. The bag, of course, is already in Gaston's possession; hence also the
film's alternative title *The Honest Finder*. Against Lily's objections, Gaston
decides to return it, opting for an honest "cash business" because of the
worsened economic situation.

In the entrance hall of Madame Colet's luxurious villa many people have
gathered hoping to be the lucky finder. Among them is a fanatic Bolshevik
who, spurred on by Madame Colet's impatient "Yes"s, talks himself into a
frenzy: "So you lost a handbag, madame? . . . And it had diamonds in the
back? . . . And diamonds in the front? . . . Diamonds all over?" After her
impatient "Well, have you found it?" he finally explodes: "No. But let me
tell you—any woman who spends a fortune in times like these for a handbag—phooey, phooey, and phooey! And as Leo Trotsky said: *Kashdaya
damitchka . . .*"[7] Suddenly Gaston appears and, after silencing the man with

---

[6] In the breakfast scene, Lily is caught off guard as she dunks her roll into the coffee, a
gesture later to be repeated by Madame Colet herself. With this rare exception, dunking remains the trademark of the social climber. Sally Pinkus of *Shoe Salon Pinkus* proudly establishes the tradition in the presence of the elegant Melitta Hervé. While the spoiled millionaire's daughter Claudette Colbert in Capra's *It Happened One Night* (1934) even receives a
lesson by Clark Gable in the high art of dunking 'populist style,' Lubitsch continues to emphasize its petty-bourgeois origins; hence the shock experienced by Kralik and Pirovitsch in
The Shop Around the Corner (1940) when they spy on Klara only to find out that "she dunks."

[7] This brief appearance of a Bolshevik in Paris anticipates the three comrades in *Ninotchka*
(1938).

21. *Trouble in Paradise*: Miriam Hopkins, Herbert Marshall

a few Russian words, begins to practice what the other only preaches. His impeccable manners become the main weapon in a more devious strategy of expropriation. Presenting himself as Monsieur Laval, "a member of the nouveaux poor," Gaston hands over the bag, takes the cash reward—and is immediately hired as Madame's personal secretary. In contrast to the Bolshevik's moralistic diatribe, Gaston's method calls for a dispassionate analysis of class society. Seduction rather than confrontation is his motto. He puts to use the external markers of class (e.g., dress, manners, language) in the cheating of its most affluent members. First he reverses the hierarchy between owner and finder by asking Mariette to present some identification. Then he offers some cosmetic advice on powder shades and lipstick colors, satisfying both her flirtatiousness and her narcissism. Applying the laws of capitalism Gaston undermines the system from within. Conspicuous consumption links him to his victims in behavior and values, and the existence of private property secures his professional career. But while Mariette is left with a free beauty consultation and the prospect of an amorous adventure, Gaston takes complete control over her professional and personal life.

For the remaining part, the Colet villa provides the appropriate backdrop for the film's slippery equations of capitalism and eroticism. The appearance of Madame Colet, as the "other woman," puts an end to the romantic mood of the Venice episode but only in order to confirm once more, in the film's happy ending, the power of love. At the same time, her infatuation with luxury and her complete lack of concern for others make Gaston's and Lily's theft seem morally justified. The Colet villa functions like a display case for the owner and her possessions, a celebration of the spectacle of woman and her equally spectacular mise-en-scène. In that sense, Madame Colet, as the embodiment of commodity fetishism, poses an equal challenge to Gaston's philosophy of expropriation and the principles of filmic representation operative throughout the film.

As the film continues, the desire for the object and the object of desire become almost synonymous. Nowhere is this more evident than when the butler (in an earlier version of the script) tells Mariette's rival suitors, the major (Charles Ruggles) and Monsieur Filiba: "Madame doesn't see visitors today. Her evening bag has been returned, and the nervous tensions before and the relaxing tensions after that were too much tension." Generating endless chains of substitution, the eroticism of wealth leads to a growing romantic involvement between Gaston and Mariette. While she flaunts her femininity, he takes control of the business but is also captivated by her weary sensuality. The process of his empowerment is documented in a series of wipes that, in imitation of an earlier sequence, begins with medium shots of employees and servants who obediently reply "Yes, M'sieu Laval," "Thank you, M'sieu Laval," and "No, M'sieu Laval," and that concludes with the maid's flirtatious "Maybe, M'sieu Laval" and Mariette's joking reprimand, "No, M'sieu Laval, please!" At the end of this montagelike shot sequence, female boss and male employee descend the stairs to join the party guests, and Gaston is officially introduced to the members of Parisian high society. However, the arrival of Lily, who, in the role of an ugly orphan, takes the job of Gaston's assistant secretary, puts an end to these flirtatious moments. Rejecting the kind of sensuous passivity embodied by Mariette, Lily presses for the execution of their initial plan—the robbing of the safe—and, in doing so, reintroduces an element of high drama. Her bouts of jealousy, and the growing tension between the lovers, only underscore the need for a quick solution. Responding to Lily's accusations, Gaston first claims: "So far as I am concerned, her whole sex appeal is in that safe." But when he later notes, "There's more sex appeal coming on the first of the month," the spectators are, like Lily, no longer sure whether the prospect of a full safe may not just be the pretense for a more personal interest in Mariette.

In addition to the complications of the love triangle, Gaston's true identity is about to be discovered by Monsieur Filiba, one of Mariette's elderly suitors and, coincidentally, the victim of the Venice hotel robbery. This dramatic moment is reached when Filiba remembers the circumstances under which he first met Gaston. The mention of the word *doctor* in a casual conversation and the sight of a gondola-shaped ashtray trigger a distinct sensation in his tonsils that brings back the unpleasant memory. Fortunately, Gaston's cool professionalism turns out to be his saving grace. Playing the role of the devoted employee with great efficiency, he uncovers another fraud, the ongoing embezzlement of company money by Mariette's most trustworthy accountant, Adolphe Giron. This knowledge becomes his main weapon against not being uncovered himself. Yet in contrast to the gentlemen's agreement between two profiteers of capitalism, the "embezzlement" of love cannot be calculated as easily. In a highly dramatic moment, Gaston and Lily meet in front of Madame Colet's safe. His warning, "You have to get out of here," elicits only an outraged reply from Lily: "That's what I'm here for—to get out! I want to get away from here, from you—as far as I can and as far as one-hundred thousand francs will take me, sixty-five—ninety-four . . . thirty-five to the left—sixty-three— eight. . . . I wouldn't fall for another man if he were the biggest crook on earth. . . . Seventy-six—eighty-four—fifty-five. . . . What has she got that I haven't got?" Suddenly Mariette returns from a dinner engagement and discovers Gaston and Lily in her private rooms. After a brief exchange of insults, Lily leaves with the money. But Gaston too decides to bid farewell, expressing his regrets but also taking a string of pearls, a present for Lily that Mariette hands him with the composure of a woman of the world: "With the compliments of Colet and Company." The epilogue, then, returns to the spirit of the beginning. Escaping in a taxicab to new adventures, Lily has already taken hold of the pearls and politely exchanges it against the money Gaston has stolen from her. Again their mutual thefts result in a passionate embrace. The social order and the order of narrative have been restored, with Madame Colet protected from a criminal in her own ranks and with the two crooks on their way to new adventures. Both groups of thieves again go their ways, with power remaining in the hands of those who possessed it from the outset but with desire once again free to question its legitimacy.

Almost as an extension of the challenges met by the protagonists, *Trouble in Paradise* poses a challenge to traditional film criticism. Seduced by the film's lighthearted story and the parade of frivolous characters, many critics have failed to see its complexity. That is why critical concepts must (sometimes) be developed through close attention to a particular film, and not their universal applicability. When the analysis of narrative structures and recurring motifs fails, the attention must turn to what is being shown and thus made visible: the lure of the object, the lure of the image, the lure of filmic representation. Short of that, the attempt at extracting a fixed meaning from the film is doomed from the outset, no matter whether one relies on generic, formalist, or sociological categories. For instance, Andrew Bergman's statement that "[a]t the center of all the relationships in *Trouble in Paradise* was a fundamental cynicism"[8] or Richard Koszarski's critique of the many "sex/money metaphors [set] against a background in times so troubled that the true nature of anything is suspect"[9] confuse ironic references to the social conditions with actual social criticism. Even critics who are aware of the film's deceptive involvement with social reality resort to such juxtapositions of superficiality and profundity, while at the same time trying to reclaim Lubitsch for a socially conscious project. But instead of introducing new categories, they either propose new meanings for the old categories or speculate about the director's true intentions. William Paul insists: "There *is* social criticism in *Trouble in Paradise*, but too much of Lubitsch's vision has been distorted to make it fit attitudes imposed on the film."[10] Similarly, Gerald Mast argues that the film's sleek Hollywood façade conceals a trenchant analysis of capitalism in which "Lu-

---

[8] Andrew Bergman, *We're in the Money: Depression America and Its Films* (New York: New York University Press, 1971), 58. Perhaps in anticipation of negative reviews, the trade journal *Film Daily* informed exhibitors shortly after the film's release: "Because of its many touches of dramatic artistry and finesse it is preferably class fare, but in spite of its Lubitschian distinction the story is of a style that should meet with general appreciation." In *Film Daily*, 10 November 1932.

[9] Richard Koszarski, "On *Trouble in Paradise*," *Film Comment* 6, no. 3 (1970): 47.

[10] William Paul, *Ernst Lubitsch's American Comedy* (New York: Columbia University Press, 1983), 42.

bitsch, in the most Marxist way, equates property with theft."[11] In spite of the European setting, *Trouble in Paradise* could thus be interpreted as a comment on the Depression and its devastating impact on American society. Paul and Mast both acknowledge the different layers of meaning in the film, but they continue to insist on referentiality (i.e., social reality) as the ultimate standard of critical evaluation. Here Richard Corliss's "whether Lubitsch and Raphaelson are exposing the dishonesty of romance in Depression-ridden Europe or extolling the romance of dishonesty"[12] introduces a new perspective. His question puts an end to the controversy over referentiality, which invariably introduces moral issues, and draws attention to the film's inherent ambivalence, which is a function of its very material obsession with surfaces.

One could, for instance, approach *Trouble in Paradise* through the notion of style, a critical concept often brought into play when others fail.[13] The term *style* arrests what escapes easy definitions and unites the most disparate formal elements under a very seductive idea, conjuring up images of beauty, grace, and perfection. Its usefulness lies in the way it foregrounds the visual qualities of a film and establishes a connection between questions of textuality and spectatorship. That *Trouble in Paradise* is indeed a highly stylized film and thus susceptible to a "stylistic" reading explains its affinities with camp, that elusive phenomenon described by Susan Sontag through formulations such as "a vision of the world in terms of style," "a consistently aesthetic experience of the world," "a mode of enjoyment, of appreciation—not judgment," "a theatricalization of experience."[14] Distinguished by a love of the unnatural, and therefore highly susceptible to notions like aestheticism and androgyny, camp erodes the moral categories of good and bad, serious and frivolous. In their place, a higher form of morality emerges, one that brings with it an awareness of the transitoriness of all things human.

[11] Gerald Mast, *The Comic Mind: Comedy and the Movies* (Indianapolis: Bobbs-Merrill, 1973), 219. In the words of Mast, Gaston has grasped the secret of capitalism: "Those who are intimidated by the toy's power (the servants and the working class), those who are incensed by the toy's beautiful possessions (the frantic Marxist who hurls his 'phooeys' at Madame Colet with impunity), have already lost to the toy. To beat the toy, Monescu (with Lubitsch as his ally) merely knocks the workings out of it" (219).

[12] Richard Corliss, *Talking Pictures: Screen Writers in the American Cinema 1927–73* (Woodstock, N.Y.: Overlook Press, 1974), 166.

[13] Richard Corliss, for instance, uses the distinction between "the Stylists" and "the Authors/Auteurs" to count Lubitsch's collaboration with Sam Raphaelson among the Stylists. He writes: "Whatever the secret, the Stylists seemed effortlessly able to establish an aura without sending a message—a triumph of sociable context over social content" (163). By subscribing to the auteurist distinction between "metteur-en-scène" and "auteur," Corliss situates his definition of style within a rather traditional approach to the problem of evaluation.

[14] Susan Sontag, "Notes on 'Camp,'" in *Against Interpretation* (New York, Farrar, Straus & Giroux, 1966) 279, 287, 291, and 290.

Seen in this light, *Trouble in Paradise* does not just tell a story about crooks: it also represents a marvelous piece of fraud in itself. On the surface, there are hints of social consciousness. The film shows how rich people continue with their self-complacent life-styles while others—those at the margins of the story and those in the contemporary audience—suffer under the economic depression. Its characters include a silly old fool like Filiba, who rents a hotel suite with four rooms, or a vain woman like Madame Colet, who buys a diamond-studded handbag just for fun. By contrast, Gaston's strategies reach beyond the requirements of the narrative and utilize the critical potential of editing and mise-en-scène. In so doing, he functions as an indispensable mediator between the filmmaker and his audience and a central metaphor for the production of meaning in the cinema. Gaston makes his living by adjusting to the economic conditions; that is, he steals from those who commit similar offenses but act under the protection of the law. The material resources available to this modern-day Robin Hood may be limited to his knowledge of manipulating others. Yet he manages to confuse them so profoundly that they are no longer able to distinguish between reality and its simulation. For Gaston, and for Lubitsch as well, economic necessity and aesthetic production must therefore be seen as functions of each other.

These secret affinities between narrative ellipsis and the act of theft have been commented upon by Grafe and Patalas. Quoting the French critic Roger Leenhardt, they write: "Film, Leenhardt said, is the art of ellipsis. What else is theft, fraud, and swindle? The elimination of links, the production of feigned, that is, of merely external connections between initially separate elements: such is the art of the cineaste and the imposter, such is the nature of their respective means of expression. The slowness of the iris, then, comes as a blessing to both."[15] Aware of these gaps in the systems of representation, Gaston uses them for his own purposes. He resorts to the promotional effects of advertising and employs all the tricks of the classical Hollywood cinema, even endowing them with a new, additional level of artificiality. Accurately calculating the requirements of time and space, Gaston operates with the same apparent ease that the dream factory pretends to have: never at work, always with the loot already in his pockets. In so doing, he takes advantage of the self-delusions of a class society that, behind its flawless surface, is narcissistic and morally depraved but that, because of these qualities, must also allow intruders like Gaston Monescu (or Mrs. Erlynne of *Lady Windermere's Fan*) to get away. As the film's ending indicates, capitalism's encounter with its mirror reflection in the figure of Gaston proves how bourgeois society deals with the most difficult crises and how it emerges from such situations triumphantly. Of course, the film

---

[15] Grafe and Patalas, *Im Off. Filmartikel*, 70.

must not be confused with social reality. Every calculated shot, pan, or cut defies such an impulse. *Trouble in Paradise* develops analogously to the social conditions. But that also is the reason that there is sometimes "trouble in paradise."

Given this very materialistic story about thieves and imposters, meaning in *Trouble in Paradise* seems both contingent upon and deferential to the materiality of the cinema apparatus. The film's subversive qualities originate in its self-conscious exhibition of the means of production. Through costume and set design, including their mutual exchangeability, a system of references is set up for the rituals of production and consumption to take place. Acting styles, rather than characterization, become an integral part of this equation. The foregrounding of the filmic means, both in the sense of techniques and actual materials, is possible only because plot construction and characterization follow the rules of the sophisticated comedy to the point of depletion. The love triangle among Lily, Gaston, and Mariette repeats a standard constellation in which two women are pitted against each other. Their rivalry underscores the man's central position and, more generally, provides a steady supply of dramatic situations. By adopting this triangular structure, Lubitsch accepts basic assumptions of the genre as well, including its association with an explicitly male perspective. However, he remains surprisingly indifferent to the customary lessons of morality—an "omission" that distinguishes *Trouble in Paradise* from the endearing humanism of many other sophisticated comedies.

This double strategy is evident in the casting of the characters. Herbert Marshall, with his suave appearance, blasé British accent, and understated manners the embodiment of the perfect gentleman, stands between the dark, sultry Kay Francis and the blond Miriam Hopkins. His reserved acting finds a counterpoint in the sharp-tongued and slightly ordinary Hopkins, together with Myrna Loy and Carole Lombard one of the leading actresses of the sophisticated comedy. While Marshall's camaraderie with Hopkins eventually triumphs as the more satisfying form of love between the sexes, precisely because it includes friendship, his relationship with the ladylike Francis thrives on the problem of sexual difference. The similar performance styles of Marshall and Francis—both actors use a minimum of gestures and movements—suggest from the outset that their desire cannot be fulfilled, despite the erotic attraction between them. By contrast, Miriam Hopkins is Gaston's partner on the level of the narrative, and his antagonist on the level of acting. Thus her character is able to satisfy both aspects of their relationship, the desire for similarity and the desire for difference. The love triangle among the main characters is mirrored in a comic subplot that situates Kay Francis between two legendary comic actors, Edward Everett Horton and Charles Ruggles, who play her elderly suitors. As their behavior changes from male rivalry to the involuntary solidarity of losers, they act out all the misunderstandings that the main protagonists try to hide. Reminiscent of the hilarious male couples of slapstick comedy, Horton and Ruggles represent an earlier tradition of the comic and, in so doing, function like a comic mirror, a distancing device, inside the film itself.

Trouble in Paradise shows convincingly how props and interiors become an integral part of the narrative, sometimes even dominating events or characters. Set designer Hans Dreier, who was trained in the Bauhaus tradition, had already collaborated with Lubitsch on *Forbidden Paradise* and would continue to do so throughout his years at Paramount. As the studio's supervising art director from 1923 to 1950, Dreier was largely responsible for Paramount's famous visual style and exerted a strong influence comparable only to Cedric Gibbons's position at MGM. His work for Sternberg may have been characterized by a low-key and heavily shadowed visual style, but for Lubitsch, Dreier created pure "icing-sugar frivolities."[16]

In *Trouble in Paradise*, the elegant Art Deco sets perform functions generally not associated with set design. Caught in an ongoing communication with the protagonists, they assume the role of a mold and a mirror. The environment controlled by Madame Colet, in particular, renders visible the story's other site, that which becomes representable only in the form of material objects. From smooth surfaces revealing all shades of white, from spacious lines and curves collapsing in "meaninglessness," to typographic details, ornamental patterns, and precious materials, set design at once determines and reflects the experiences made within and vis-à-vis the film. From tables, chairs, lamps, clocks, lighters, and tableware to the smallest details of cabinetmaking, the film's material ingredients participate in an ongoing celebration of form. This process begins with the close-up of the stylish Art Deco logo of Colet & Cie. and, from then on, brings the entire film under the spell of beautiful commodities. Like Gaston and his ploys, the beautiful objects/images appeal to the spectators and draw them into their circle of deceit. But while they are successful in their attempt to win them over to the world of imaginary gratifications, they also reproduce the anxieties that are part of every story of seduction. By average moral standards, the beautiful objects and the equally beautiful filmic images resemble illusionists, and sometimes even imposters, who derive their great powers from society's obsession with appearances. But by the standards of the film, they also function as agents in a secret scheme that brings this condition into the light of its own self-critical appreciation. Frieda Grafe has characterized this obsession with surfaces as the distinguishing mark of all Lubitsch films: "Lubitsch furnishes all his films with the exter-

[16] *The Art of Hollywood. Fifty Years of Art Direction*, ed. John Hambley and Patrick Downing (London: Thames Television, for the Victoria and Albert Museum, 1979), 38.

nal signs of industrial production. Appealing to an audience of consumers, they are full of advertisement; they aim at the gaze. That is probably the reason why Zukor made him head of production at Paramount. A realistic misunderstanding of his films: to think of him as a business man and of his cinematic sense as business sense."[17]

In *The Imaginary Signifier*, Christian Metz defines the cinema as a technique of the imaginary that is characteristic of a specific historical epoch (capitalism) and state of society (industrial civilization). Its functioning as a technology and discursive practice, he claims, is based on disavowal: "The fiction film is the film in which the cinematic signifier does not work on its own account but is employed entirely to remove the traces of its own steps . . ."[18] Thus Metz demands to disengage the cinema from the imaginary and to claim it for the symbolic, a project that requires a more rigorous investigation of the cinema as a signifying practice. It is with such intentions that, for the remaining part of the chapter, the notions of fetishism, displacement, and repetition will be introduced in order to demystify specific moments in *Trouble in Paradise* that stand out because of their self-reflexivity.

Not surprisingly, it is here that psychoanalysis enters the scene. Psychoanalysis not only attempts to explain the movement between different levels of representation as they manifest themselves in dreams, jokes, or certain physical symptoms. It also relates these movements to the problem of desire and representation as such. Therein lies the usefulness of psychoanalytic concepts for *Trouble in Paradise*. To begin with, the film's central motif of theft must be seen in close relation to the experience of absence and presence that marks the beginning of an important phase in early childhood. Discussing the child's reaction to the mother's absence, Freud writes: "The child has a wooden reel with a piece of string tied around it. . . . What he did was to hold the reel by the string and very skilfully throw it over the edge of his curtained cot, so that it disappeared into it, at the same time uttering his expressive 'o-o-o-o' [e.g. the German word *fort*, gone]. He then pulled the reel out of the cot again by the string and hailed its reappearance with a joyful 'da' ['there']. This, then, was the complete game—disappearance and return."[19] Freud interprets the child's game as a

[17] Grafe, "Was Lubitsch berührt," in Prinzler and Patalas, *Lubitsch*, 84.

[18] Christian Metz, *The Imaginary Signifier. Psychoanalysis and the Cinema*, trans. Celia Britton, Annwyl Williams, Ben Brewster, and Alfred Guzzetti (Bloomington: Indiana University Press, 1982), 40.

[19] Freud, "Beyond the Pleasure Principle," *The Standard Edition*, vol. 18, 15. The description of this scene has inspired Jacques Lacan to elaborate on some of its implications: "This reel is not the mother reduced to a little ball by some magical game worthy of the Jivaros—it is a small part of the subject that detaches itself from him while still remaining his, still retained. This is the place to say, in imitation of Aristotle, that man thinks with his object. It is with his object that the child leaps the frontiers of his domain, transformed into a well, and begins

cultural achievement that is absolutely necessary, for its teaches him how to allow his mother to disappear, finding comfort in the knowledge of her return.

Precisely this play with absence and presence links the motif of theft to a general investigation of filmic representation and, more specifically, to the questionable status of the object/image. Apart from the obvious similarities between the act of theft and the image of the empty frame, these moments of loss point to difference as that principle through which meaning manifests itself. For instance, the first encounter between Gaston and Mariette is punctuated by a series of point-of-view shots, by what could be called an "absence/presence game." Like Freud's child and the cot, Mariette twice loses his image from her field of vision, only to each time reclaim it with the next shot. The "game" begins with a medium shot of Mariette, who is distracted by a phone conversation, and continues with her point-of-view, resulting in a disorienting, meaningless image. Gaston, the intended recipient of the look, is no longer there. But already the next shot, by simulating a slight turn of the head, a slight shift in perspective, reaffirms his presence to the mise-en-scène. As Mariette's second point-of-view shot proves, Gaston has only changed his position in the room to admire a valuable Chinese vase. Shortly thereafter, Mariette looks for her checkbook and, at the end of an identical series of shots, again loses and regains Gaston, this time discovering him in her former secretary's bedroom.

As these examples suggest, the problem of point-of-view is closely related to that of control. Narrative mastery requires, from characters as well as spectators, an acute awareness of the existence of others (including his or her erratic movements) and a basic understanding of the laws of perspective, both in a spatial and critical sense. In the scene described above, the camera, therein following Freud's example, uses Mariette playfully to test the parameters of this double condition. Here the experience of absence and presence is constitutive of and remains limited to the relationship between characters. However, as the earlier example of the Venetian sofa demonstrates (occupied sofa/dissolve/empty sofa), the absence/presence game can also involve the narrator, represented by the camera, and a character or an object—in this case, the sofa from which Gaston and Lily magically disappear. No matter what kind of participants are involved and no matter what constellations are achieved, only the dominating presence of

---

the incantation. If it is true that the signifier is the first mark of the subject, how can we fail to recognize here—from the very fact that this game is accompanied by one of the first oppositions to appear—that it is in the object to which the opposition is applied in act, the reel, that we must designate the subject. To this object we will later give the name it bears in the Lacanian algebra—the *petit a.*" See "Tuché and Automaton," in *The Four Fundamental Concepts of Psycho-Analysis,* ed. Jacques-Alain Miller, trans. Alan Sheridan (New York: W. W. Norton, 1981), 62.

the camera seems to guarantee the success of the absence/presence game. In that, it is aided by the principle of repetition. As Freud has pointed out in his remarks on repetition compulsion, repetition is closely linked to castration and disavowal. Yet Lubitsch uses repetition in such a way that it allows the spectator to detach him or herself from the narrative and to take pleasure in the process of meaning production itself—an essential precondition for irony and parody.[20]

From the play with presence and absence (possession/theft) and from the obsession with material objects (set design), a direct line leads to the notion of fetishism. The fetish, according to Freud, is "a substitute for the woman's (the mother's) penis that the little boy once believed in and—for reasons familiar to us—does not want to give up." It becomes both "a token of triumph over the threat of castration and a protection against it."[21] Apart from its hidden ties to the technology of cinema which always lurk under the surface, fetishism in *Trouble in Paradise* influences the constitution of more specific configurations, including framing and camera movement. Metz writes: "Cinema with directly erotic subject matter deliberately plays on the edges of the frame and the progressive, if need be incomplete revelations allowed by the camera as it moves, and this is no accident. Censorship is involved here: censorship of films and censorship in Freud's sense. Whether the form is static (framing) or dynamic (camera movements), the principle is the same; the point is to gamble simultaneously on the excitation of desire and its nonfulfillment. . . . The way the cinema, with its wandering framings (wandering like the look, like the caress), finds the means to reveal space has something to do with a kind of permanent undressing, a generalized strip-tease, a less direct but more perfected striptease, since it also makes it possible to dress space again, to remove from view what it has previously shown, to *take back* as well as to retain . . ."[22]

---

[20] *Trouble in Paradise* contains a number of similar scenarios of repetition, including one between Gaston and Mariette. Here Gaston tries to persuade Mariette to attend a dinner engagement so that he can rob the safe and disappear forever. He does so by staging a conflict between sexual desire and social etiquette as a result of which Mariette repeatedly changes her mind—until she decides to leave precisely because of Gaston's advances. The resulting misunderstandings culminate in the question whether she still needs her car or not. Time and again, Gaston and Mariette emerge from their rooms—he from his office, she from his office, she from her bedroom, he from her bedroom—and every time they confront the man servant with a new decision. As a result, the voluminous man has to walk up and down the stairs several times.

[21] Freud, "Fetishism," *The Standard Edition*, vol. 21, 153 and 154. Discussing *Desire*, John Belton provides an accurate description of such fetishistic scenarios: "Lubitsch's sophisticated wit irreverently jokes with traditional notions of morality and, at the same time, denies the essential humanity of his characters, identifying them with objects or with artificial surfaces and textures in their environment." In *The Hollywood Professionals: Howard Hawks, Frank Borzage, Edgar G. Ulmer* (London: Tantivy, 1974), 75.

[22] Metz, *The Imaginary Signifier*, 77.

Precisely these scenarios of cinematic fetishism, as it were, come to the fore in the film's explicitly erotic situations and its unabashed commodity fetishism.

The scandal of absence and the comforts of fetishism structure Gaston and Madame Colet's first romantic evening, which takes place without the couple, as it were (fig. 22). Lubitsch refers the spectator to several close-ups of clocks that, while marking the passage of a long night, are overlaid with muffled bits of offscreen dialogue. These clocks fulfill three equally important functions: as the keepers of time, they document the flow of the narrative. As stand-ins for the absent characters, they become the primary means of displacement, thereby also initiating the presence/absence game. And as beautiful objects, they satisfy the desire for visual pleasure in a way that makes the couple's absence both disturbing and gratifying. The sequence begins with the close-up of an Art Deco clock (5:00 P.M.) on Gaston's office desk announcing, with the gentle ringing of its chimes, the end of the working day. A little later (5:12 P.M.) Mariette enters the office and innocuously asks for the typing services of Lily who, of course, has already left. The following close-up of the same clock, now cast in twilight (9:05 P.M.), is briefly disturbed by the ringing of a telephone (of course, Lily!). Again a little later (10:50 P.M.), one hears the offscreen voices of Gaston and Mariette bidding each other good night. However, the next dissolve to the angular clock on the living-room mantel (11:00 P.M.) contradicts such declarations. Only the setting has changed, not the situation. While the invisible characters praise each other's dancing skills, the camera pans to the side and reveals two half-empty champagne glasses. With the low sounds of the hall clock (2:00 A.M.), Lubitsch finally grants access to the sight of the romantic couple as they face each other in the hall, separated only by the clock's erect shape. Dressed in elegant evening clothes, Gaston and Mariette stand at the half-open doorways of their bedrooms and, after several longing glances, close, indeed even lock, all doors to further involvement. While the true nature of their relationship remains outside of the frame, subject only to the imagination, its limitations are more than alluded to in a previous shot sequence. Here Mariette's suggestive remark "We have weeks . . . months . . . years" inspires a series of medium shots that suggest the opposite, thereby also revealing her susceptibility to fantasy and self-deceit (fig. 23). Every word is accompanied by a new shot of the embracing couple: first as a reflection in a round mirror ("weeks"), then in another mirror ("months"), and, finally, as a shadow falling onto the bed ("years"). Significantly, the romantic image never appears directly but is reflected by and contained within the world of objects (the mirrors, the bed). Mariette and Gaston, as the scene implies, desire each other in their shared desire for the object and the self. Thus the film's story can only reach

22. *Trouble in Paradise*: The clock sequence

23. *Trouble in Paradise*: Kay Francis, Herbert Marshall

a satisfactory ending by emphasizing the difference between the love of things and the love of people.

Trouble in Paradise not only contains a number of paradigmatic scenes of cinema but also foregrounds the conditions under which these take place. The dynamics of fetishism compel an originally undifferentiated eroticism toward the substitute satisfaction provided by beautiful consumer objects. In so doing, fetishism becomes the last stage in a chain of displacements. Displacement, then, can be seen as the film's driving force and structuring principle. Freud defines it as a shift in the cathexis from one representation to an associated one, or a replacement of a former by a latter.[23] Metz elaborates on this point in regard to the cinema: "Displacement substitutes one object for another: in so doing it separates them, but it also tends to assimilate them, to *identify* them, to see them as equivalents, all the more completely the more primary it is (= the *total* charge is then transported). For Freud identification was a kind of condensation. Displacement of course refuses this identification at the very moment it outlines it (points to it): a refusal—a flight—which sets it in motion, which pushes it on, which makes it a displacement (whereas condensation accepts the identification, and establishes it). Displacement keeps us a good distance away from the truth of the unconscious, it proceeds via substitutes."[24]

In special moments, the workings of displacement draw attention to the ongoing negotiation between representation and narration, between distance and involvement. One such moment is the second meeting of Gaston and Filiba. While Filiba tries to remember when and where he has met the man before, Gaston subtly directs his mental and emotional energies in other directions. Confronted with the question "Have you ever been in Venice?" he replies with a torrent of questions that reduce Filiba to confused "no"s. With Gaston's last question, he assumes control of the situation: "Have you ever been in Vienna? . . . Amsterdam? . . . Constantinople? . . . You've never been in Constantinople? . . . But you have been in Venice. . . . And let me tell you, Venice can't compare with Constantinople." To the sound of Turkish background music, the topic of conversation turns to harems; suddenly whispered recommendations are given and Gaston is saved. His success, and that of the film as a whole, is founded upon the diversion of psychic energies, a process in which the experience of displeasure (the tonsils) is magically transformed into the confession of an erotic fantasy. Only later, in Gaston's absence, is Filiba able to trace back the displacements to their point of origin. This moment of recognition is

---

[23] For a definition of condensation and displacement, see Freud, "The Interpretation of Dreams," *The Standard Edition*, vols. 4 and 5.

[24] Metz, *The Imaginary Signifier*, 269. For a discussion of displacement/metonymy and condensation/metaphor, see the chapter "Metaphor/Metonymy, or the Imaginary Referent," 149–314.

triggered by a synaesthetic experience, the hearing of the word *doctor*, the sight of a gondola-shaped ashtray, and a sudden sensation in his tonsils.

For the most part, the film's figures of speech—for what else are these chains of displacement?—are integrated in the flow of the narrative. However, *Trouble in Paradise* contains one remarkable sequence: the transition from Venice to Paris where the figures of speech take over the filmic reality, as it were. Meaning is shifted from one image to the next, a process that seems to confirm, like the art of advertising itself, the utter conventionality and, hence, total availability of all signs and images. It is within the framework of a radio advertisement that the strategies of fetishism and displacement join forces with those of metonymy, traditionally a figure of copresence and substitution and, according to Metz, one of the fundamental principles of cinematic representation. Such deviation from the norm is only possible because the sequence performs an important narrative function, that is, of establishing a link between different locales and of introducing a new narrative element. The triangulation of desire can begin.

The sequence opens with the sound of Morse-code signals and a view of the Eiffel Tower at night, a well-known image that is instantly put into question through the radio rays emanating from its top (fig. 24). Through Lubitsch's deceptive play with sound-image relations, animation techniques, and audience expectations, a landmark such as the Eiffel Tower is transformed into another, equally codified image, namely the trailer for a newsreel. The next groups of shots each represent a specific narrative or formal unit, yet they all attest to the underlying principle of transition and transience: on the one hand, Gaston and Lily's move from Venice to Paris and, on the other, the fleeting trajectory of meaning in the cinema. As a reflection on its media consciousness, the sequence continues with a radio announcer who relates the latest news about the master thief Monescu, "the man who robbed the Peace Conference yesterday." Then a second announcer takes over the microphone, presenting his hymn to the perfumes of Colet & Cie: "Remember, it doesn't matter what you say, it doesn't matter how you look, it's how you smell." After that, Lubitsch unleashes the sheer power of associations: cut to a retail store with the company's logo, cut to a kiosk advertisement, cut to two flashing neon signs, cut to two beautiful models in profile, with perfume bottles in their hands. Cut to a long shot of the Art Deco factory building and a medium shot of the factory gate from which joyful workers emerge, much in the style of socialist realist documentaries. Dissolve to the interior of the boardroom where Madame Colet is about to advise the board of directors not to reduce workers' salaries in spite of falling profits. As if to highlight this eccentric decision, the camera in the next scene follows her on a shopping spree. She ends up buying a beautiful diamond-studded evening bag for 125,000 francs—simply because, according to her logic, another one for

24. *Trouble in Paradise*: The Colet advertisements

3,000 francs seemed outrageously expensive. Structured through diagonal and vertical wipes, the next part assembles snapshots from Madame Colet's daily life. It begins with shop proprietors and servants who respond to her offscreen voice with repeated "yes"s or "no"s. The rhythmical sound of her "No, no, François. I tell you no!" facilitates the transition to two longer scenes with Filiba and the major whose proposals she rejects with equal determination. However, the next series of shots already reunites the strange trio for a visit to the opera. To the sound of the soprano's "I love you," the leaves of the conductor's musical score are turned over in time-lapse photography, the key shifts from major to minor, and the soprano continues without interruption "I hate you!" (here the chorus responds: "She hates him!"). At this point, the sequence comes to a close, having exhausted the means of cinematic representation beyond the call of duty. Through montage, a connection has been established between the love story of two master thieves and their new victim. The suspicious opera glasses aimed at Madame Colet's precious bag, after all, lead back to Gaston, who, from the perspective of his orchestra seat, glances into her box. The intricate trajectory of disparate meanings has reached its goal. Time has passed, and meaning has been passed on.

Given its surprising degree of self-reflexivity and given the semiotic instability that befalls all its images, *Trouble in Paradise* remains a surprisingly modern film.[25] Resisting the call for external referents (the author, social reality), the film relies on the subversive potential of various cinematic strategies. And instead of denying the reality of commodification, the film reveals its secret mechanisms while at no moment jeopardizing the pleasures offered by the sophisticated comedy as a genre of blissful abandon. Through the fractured perspectives of irony, highest conventionality is transformed into subversive energy. Siegfried Kracauer may have once written: "The international recognition of the Lubitsch film rests on the fact that he accommodates the needs of consumers who are connected to

---

[25] Because of its affinities with the allegorical impulse, *Trouble in Paradise* may even be situated within a postmodern aesthetic. Identifying film as the primary vehicle for modern allegory, Craig Owens has characterized the allegorical impulse through the absence, even conscious rejection, of the original text. As is evidenced by its fragmented, incomplete, and synthetic appearance, modern allegory acquires its imagery through appropriation, recycling, and a constant reading through other texts. Delineating the allegorical impulse in postmodern thought, Owens writes: "Allegory first emerged in response to a similar sense of estrangement from tradition; throughout its history it has functioned in the gap between a present and a past which, without allegorical reinterpretation, might have remained foreclosed." See "The Allegorical Impulse: Towards a Theory of Postmodernism," in *Art After Modernism: Rethinking Representation*, ed. and introduction Brian Wallis, forward Marcia Tucker (New York: The New Museum of Contemporary Art, 1984), 203. Owens's term "to confiscate" clearly recalls the thieves of *Trouble in Paradise*.

each other not in reality but only through its denial."[26] However, his statement is put into perspective by a most remarkable piece of dialogue between Gaston and Mariette at the end of *Trouble in Paradise*. Here Mariette's observation "You are crazy about me, monsieur" first elicits an equally cool "I see through all of your tricks" from him. But Gaston finally surrenders to her much more significant insight: "Maybe, but you fall for all of them." And precisely that identity of knowing and not knowing remains the secret of *Trouble in Paradise*.

Filmography

If I Had a Million (1932). Episode: "The Clerk," shot for Paramount. With Charles Laughton (Phineas V. Lambert). Total length of the film: 73 min. Release: 2 Dec. 1932. The Lubitsch episode was added after the film's completion; it replaced "The Condemned Man," an episode that had received negative audience reactions.

Trouble in Paradise. Director: Ernst Lubitsch, for Paramount. Screenplay: Samson Raphaelson, based on the play *The Honest Finder* by Aladar Laszlo. Photography: Victor Milner. Art Director: Hans Dreier. Costumes: Travis Banton. With Miriam Hopkins (Lily), Kay Francis (Mariette Colet), Herbert Marshall (Gaston Monescu), Charles Ruggles (The major), Edward Everett Horton (François Filiba) et al. Length: 83 min. Release: 8 Nov. 1932. The screenplay has been published in *Three Screen Comedies by Samson Raphaelson*, intr. Pauline Kael (Madison: University of Wisconsin Press, 1983), 53–159.

[26] Siegfried Kracauer, *The Smiling Lieutenant* (1931), reprinted in Kracauer, *Kino. Essays Studien Glossen zum Film*, ed. Karsten Witte (Frankfurt am Main: Suhrkamp, 1974), 192.

Afterword _____

THIS study has followed a double strategy: it has provided a comprehensive overview of the early work of Lubitsch and it has offered a number of close textual readings, each within a specific historical and theoretical conjuncture. The first part has tried to reconstruct the framework in which Lubitsch's stories, themes, and styles developed. While paying attention to the external influences (studio politics, collaborators, artistic influences) that contributed to the formation of his directorial style, the introductory part also focused on a more hidden problematic. As has been argued, the classical narrative cinema introduced strategies of cinematic representation that were distinctly different from the silent cinema, especially in its use of mise-en-scène. Since the early silent cinema must be regarded as the dominating influence on Lubitsch's work, his films can be seen as an ongoing negotiation between an earlier and later "paradigm" of cinematic representation. Terms like *narrative*, *spectacle*, and *visual pleasure* are crucial for identifying these differences. Thus it is through the notion of a gradual "paradigm shift," as it were, that specific visual and narrative styles in the Lubitsch film have been examined for how they articulate this problematic and how their visual and narrative strategies bear witness to a growing standardization in the cinema, both in the formal and critical sense.

Passions and Deceptions has shown how the early Lubitsch films rely on a complicated system of differences, involving narrative elements as well as cinematic representation itself. The foregrounding of formal aspects, this strong emphasis on style, explains their intellectual appeal but also accounts for their emotional detachment. Understanding this self-reflexive quality, however, makes necessary a reassessment of traditional notions of identity (form-content, author-work, production-reception) and a full acknowledgment of difference as one of the basic "ingredients" of cinematic representation. Difference in this context means both a particular thematic complex, involving questions of sexual and cultural difference, and a discursive means through which relations in the cinema are established. As this study has argued, the early Lubitsch films thrive on such differences. They are most convincing when they play with various levels of difference, for instance pitting against each other the morality of the narrative and the immorality of representation. Lubitsch's obsession with difference is the basis for the changing subject-object relationships, the triangulation of desire among looking, dancing, and consumption, and, most of all, the position of ironic detachment assumed by the camera/narrator. In fact, irony—by marking a position both inside and outside of the narrative—can be described as a way of dealing with difference in a productive way. Irony knows of the different perspectives on reality and the different layers of truth, and it accepts deception, fraud, and dishonesty as integral parts of the human condition. Since no longer in control of reality or the truth, irony allows for a more tolerant and enlightened view of human nature.

While difference in the Lubitsch films appears in many ways, most critics have focused on the function of sexual difference, and the representation of women in particular. Consequently, Lubitsch has been accused of male chauvinism, and his films have been scrutinized for their liberal or cynical attitude toward sexuality, depending on the argument. What has been neglected, however, is how Lubitsch uses the all-important distinction between "narrating" and "showing" sexuality as a point of departure for other investigations. This instrumental approach to sexual difference also explains the discrepancy between his daring stories and the absence of a sensuous, eroticized atmosphere. Sexual difference in the early Lubitsch films, then, functions above all as a theoretical model through which to come to terms with difference in general: as a philosophical problem, a precondition of aesthetic experience, and a fundamental aspect of life.

As the first films to focus on sexual difference, *The Oyster Princess*, *The Doll*, and *The Mountain Cat* profited undoubtedly from the fact that the problem of femininity, the linchpin of signification, was again subject to redefinition. For a brief moment the imagination was free to explore new roles and new identities. The women protagonists in the films, as well as the women in the audience, were granted access to narrative mastery and visual pleasure, though only within the clear boundaries of particular genres. For only in the context of comedy, fantasy, and the grotesque could sexual difference still be treated as a game. The association of woman, narrative, and spectacle is essential for the functioning of this game, and the formulation of a critical perspective in particular. The theoretical implications of this association, however, are still subject to debate. For instance, a reexamination of the changing function of spectacle within the registers of the comic and the fantastic might reveal other forces operating against the Oedipal claim. A greater awareness of the tension between narrative and spectacle, and between competing registers of visual pleasure, might lead to more productive encounters between the discourses of film history and film theory. And finally, closer attention to the function of femininity in the early cinema might shed more light on a certain "repetition compulsion" by means of which the individual's attachment to earlier stages of infantile narcissism seeks fulfillment within that pleasure machine called cinema.

The problem of sexual difference carries over into the sound film. As has been argued, Lubitsch uses the musicals to redefine difference in visual and aural terms and, moreover, to renegotiate the relationship of narrative and spectacle along these lines. Thus the communication between the sexes and the classes in *Monte Carlo* becomes inextricably linked to song which brings together music and language to establish the body—the origin of the singing voice—as the ultimate site of truth. To rephrase it in filmic terms, the songs challenge the boundaries between offscreen and on-screen space while at the same time drawing attention to the frame as the threshold of all negotiations. As a result, continuity is maintained where it is threatened and the claims of true love are protected when they are endangered. Physical and emotional reality become extensions of each other. By appealing to the desire for presence, the songs contribute to the hallucination of a unified subject. At the center of this process stands again the woman: as visual spectacle, as narrative agent, and as voice. However, this association of woman and voice remains haunted by ambivalences, that is, of being a product of woman's repression and a manifestation of female desire.

With sexual difference functioning as a matrix, all other systems of difference are distributed accordingly. As a rule, Lubitsch uses class difference and cultural difference as a way of intensifying the difference between the sexes. His references to the discourses of class and nationality remain strictly individualistic, as is evidenced by the strong erotic attraction between members of the aristocracy and the middle class, and the unavoidable clashes between European and American cultures. These three systems of difference—gender, class, and nationality—mark the early Lubitsch film as a configuration rather than a set of fixed meanings. Specific genres may favor specific combinations (e.g., the musicals: European/aristocratic/female vs. American/middle-class/male), but their implications are often corrected or annulled through more disturbing constellations on the level of mise-en-scène, editing, and camera work. The result is always an intriguing play with difference, affecting every aspect of the film's textual and contextual existence.

Two strategies stand out in this exploration of difference: the recurring investigation of objects in the filmic mise-en-scène and the self-reflective approach to the materials of cinema. The first strategy involves the themes of consumerism and conscious consumption, the other focuses more on Lubitsch's approach to set design and, ultimately, his calculated use of filmic means like mise-en-scène, camera work, and editing. Both, however, are linked to the question of femininity, with woman as the modern consumer and the center of the cinematic spectacle. This triangulation among the woman, the object, and the "materials" of cinema can be found in the German period films as well as in the American comedies of the early thirties. As *Passion* and *Deception* show, Lubitsch's historicizing of style, rather than his stylization of history, relies on the same material ingredients that can be found in other films: the comical, the double entendre, the ellipsis, the significant detail—disturbances that unmask those in power but that, in the context of cinematic representation, also rely on their continuing existence. As Lubitsch's authorial interventions drive a wedge between the intimate scenes and the mass spectacles, forever depriving the period film of full closure, they draw attention to the more disquieting struggle between narrative and spectacle. While woman, as the object of the male gaze, propels the narrative toward its tragic but conclusive ending, history assumes its rightful position through set design and mise-en-scène. To be sure, this history is, and always has to be, synonymous with the history of domination, for only the abuses of power justify the monumental architecture, the luxurious interiors, and the grandiose mass ceremonies. But, at the same time, the reduction of history to its spectacular elements also points toward something outside of narrative. Thus it is as spectacle, a mode potentially disruptive of the classical order of representation, that history becomes both instrumental and excessive and assumes, in this double function, its real significance. Not unlike the camera's shifting focus, the center of meaning production in the period film moves back and forth between surface and background, that is, between the narrative of the individual and the spectacle of the masses, or, to rephrase it in conceptual terms, between eroticism and historicism. Similar processes take place in *Trouble in Paradise*, but within a distinctly modern framework. Here play with presence and absence becomes a primary figure for representing difference: as difference between the sexes, the classes and, last but not least, between the discourses of authenticity and simulation. *Trouble in Paradise*, in this regard, takes part in the celebration of the commodity and the destruction of its aura. It does so for the purpose of its resurrection as the object of visual pleasure, that is, a pleasure without possessions but also with unlimited powers. The film's spectacular Art Deco sets and the use of theft as a metaphor of capitalism and the cinema bear witness to this process.

The play with difference, as it has been described thus far, requires the visible presence of a camera/narrator and the active involvement of spectators. Lubitsch's concept of spectatorship shifts the attention from the film as a product to the film as a production; hence the strong emphasis on looking as a narrative motif. The problem of spectatorship expresses itself in triple form: through the spectators in the film whose reactions are built into the narrative and visual structure; through the historical spectator who represents the then-contemporary concerns; and through the modern spectator who approaches the film from the fractured perspectives of the nineties, for instance as a movie buff, film critic, or feminist scholar. Consequently, the "modernity" of a Lubitsch film depends to a large degree on the kind of relationships, and the kind of exchanges, that can take place among these three groups of spectators. As the close readings have suggested, the conflation between textual and historical spectator often played a role in studio politics and the definition of national identity (*Passion*). From today's perspective, the contrast between textual and modern spectator can also produce very liberating effects (*So This Is Paris*). Depending on the particular film, the identities and nonidentities among various spectators establish a network of relations and references that inevitably draws attention to their invisible counterpart: the author/narrator.

The problem of spectatorship and the presence of different spectators also lies at the core of *So This Is Paris*. In this film Lubitsch explores the different interpretative strategies that take place in and vis-à-vis a film. These involve the acts of (mis)reading performed by the woman character, the visual positioning of woman as the fulcrum of interpretation, the presence of the implied (male) spectator of the twenties and, finally, the radically different readings brought to bear on the film by critical (female) spectators of the nineties. Thus *So This Is Paris* makes it possible to assess the challenges posed by woman as reader and by a reading "through woman." The implications of such reading scenarios, both in the context of Lubitsch scholarship and feminist film criticism, are still difficult to assess. For instance, it has been argued that female spectatorship in the cinema always requires a moving back and forth between masculine and feminine positions. The ability to assume different positions is crucial in the construction of female subjectivity, but it also accounts for woman's exclusion from the center of meaning production. Interpretation, including the kinds of readings afforded by the cinema, could therefore be regarded as a feminizing activity, for it involves acts of transgression and simulation traditionally associated with the feminine. Thus *So This Is Paris* may be described as both a manifestation of sexism and a model for turning sexism into a parody of itself.

Behind the obsession with style and behind the conspiracy between camera and spectator, irony emerges as the governing principle that organizes all systems of difference, including those of gender, class, and nationality. As a position or perspective chosen by the author/narrator, irony originates in an experience of social and cultural exclusion that finds expression in emotional detachment. In the spaces of the films, however, irony becomes the structuring device through which the exigencies of narrative, mise-en-scène, camera work, and editing can be brought together in a meaningful way. Some of these elements relate directly to irony (e.g., the irreverent movements of the camera, the revealing shot sequences), while others are merely colored by its suggestions. In all cases, irony remains omnipresent as well as omnipotent: questioning the images, unmasking the characters, subverting the stories, while at all times safeguarding the pleasures of cinema.

As has been argued, irony, eroticism, and conservatism in the early Lubitsch film must be seen as reflections of and reflections on each other. Previous criticism has treated these elements separately and with little regard for their discursive function, thus reading Lubitsch's conservatism as bad politics and his eroticism as sexism. Given the omnipresence of irony, however, Lubitsch's conservatism really speaks of an acceptance of life as it is, that is, a critique of reality without the desire for change. The intellectual nature of this critique results from a melancholic acceptance of powerlessness. Similarly, the emphasis on eroticism reflects a strong desire for life that transgresses the standards of morality but can only express itself through intellectual means. No longer experienced directly, it requires the analyzing forces of reason to preserve its utopian qualities. As a result, Lubitsch's irony must be seen as a form of self-reflection, a discourse about cinema through the means of cinema. Editing and camera work, in particular, provide him with the means to disrupt the flow of the story and draw attention to the artificiality of all filmic techniques and effects. The ironic elements in the narrative itself, and their ironic representation, contribute to this discursive quality; hence the need for distinguishing between various levels of narration and representation. It remains open to debate whether this irony still carries within itself the utopian potential of integrating difference, and is thus capable of returning the simulations of reality to their original source, or whether reflection has to content itself with the irreversible fragmentation of modern consciousness. Possible answers not only depend on the specific film that motivates such questions; they also depend on the specific configurations among historical, textual, and modern spectators in which irony, as a practice of criticism and a criticism of practice, is able to prosper and flourish.

Select Bibliography

Arnheim, Rudolf. *Kritiken und Aufsätze zum Film*. Edited by Helmut H. Diederichs. Munich: Carl Hanser, 1977.

Baxter, John. *The Hollywood Exiles*. New York: Taplinger, 1976.

————. *Hollywood in the Thirties*. New York: A. S. Barnes, 1968.

Balázs, Béla. *Schriften zum Film*. Vol. 1. Edited by Helmut H. Diederichs, Wolfgang Gersch, and Magda Nagy. Munich: Carl Hanser, 1982.

Barry, Iris. *Let's Go to the Pictures*. London: Chatto and Windus, 1926.

Belach, Helga. *Henny Porten: Der erste deutsche Filmstar 1890–1960*. Berlin: Haude and Spener, 1986.

Bergman, Andrew. *We're in the Money: Depression America and Its Films*. New York: New York University Press, 1971.

Bond, Kirk. "Ernst Lubitsch." *Film Culture* 63/64 (1977): 139–53.

Braudy, Leo. "The Double Detachment of Ernst Lubitsch." *Modern Language Notes* 95, no. 5 (December 1983): 1071–84.

Brennicke, Ilona, and Joe Hembus. *Klassiker des deutschen Stummfilms 1910–1930*. Munich: Wilhelm Goldmann, 1983.

Byron, Stuart, and Elisabeth Weis, eds. *The National Society of Film Critics on Movie Comedy*. New York, Grossman, 1977.

Carringer, Robert, and Barry Sabath. *Ernst Lubitsch—A Guide to References and Resources*. Boston: G. K. Hall, n.d.

Cahiers du Cinéma 198 (February 1968): 10–45 and 68–71.

Corliss, Richard. *Talking Pictures: Screenwriters in the American Cinema 1927–73*. Woodstock, N.Y.: Overlook Press, 1974.

Davidson, David. "The Importance of Being Ernst: Lubitsch and *Lady Windermere's Fan*." *Film/Literature Quarterly* 11, no. 2 (1983): 120–31.

Durgnat, Raymond. *The Crazy Mirror: Hollywood Comedy and the American Image*. New York: Horizon Press, 1970.

Eisenschitz, Bernard. "Lubitsch (1892–1947)." In *Anthologie du Cinéma*. Paris: L'Avant-scène du cinéma, 1968.

Eisner, Lotte. *The Haunted Screen*. Translated from the French by Roger Greaves. Berkeley: University of California Press, 1973.

Everson, William K. *American Silent Film*. New York: Oxford University Press, 1978.

Fink, Guido. *Ernst Lubitsch*. Florence: La nuova Italia, 1977.

Fraenkel, Heinrich. *Unsterblicher Film*. Munich: Kindler, 1956.

Gad, Urban. *Der Film. Seine Mittel—seine Ziele*. Translated from the Danish by Julia Koppel. Berlin: Schuster and Loeffler, 1921.

Grafe, Frieda, and Enno Patalas. *Im Off. Filmartikel*. Munich: Carl Hanser, 1981.

Gregor, Ulrich, and Enno Patalas. *Geschichte des Films*. Vol. 1. Reinbek: Rowohlt, 1976.

Griffith, Richard, and Arthur Mayer. *The Movies.* Rev. ed. New York: Simon & Schuster, 1970.

Hanisch, Michael. *Auf den Spuren der Filmgeschichte: Berliner Schauplätze.* Berlin: Henschel, 1991.

Haskell, Molly. *From Reverence to Rape: The Treatment of Women in the Movies.* 2d. ed. Chicago: University of Chicago Press, 1987.

Horak, Jan-Christopher. "Ernst Lubitsch and the Rise of Ufa, 1917–1922." M.A. thesis, Boston University, 1975.

Hubert, Ali. *Hollywood—Legende und Wirklichkeit.* Leipzig: E. A. Seemann, 1930.

Huff, Theodore. "An Index to the Films of Ernst Lubitsch." *Sight and Sound Index Series* 9 (January 1947).

Huie, William O., Jr. "Style and Technology in *Trouble in Paradise*: Evidence of a Technicians' Lobby?" *The Journal of Film and Video* 39, no. 2 (Spring 1987): 37–51.

Ihering, Herbert. *Von Reinhardt bis Brecht. Eine Auswahl der Theaterkritiken.* Edited by Rolf Badenhausen. Reinbek: Rowohlt, 1967.

Isaacs, Neil D. "Lubitsch and the Filmed-Play Syndrome." *Literature/Film Quarterly* 3 (Fall 1975): 299–308.

Jacobs, Lewis. *The Rise of the American Film: A Critical History.* New York: Teachers College Press, 1968.

Kalbus, Oskar. *Vom Wesen deutscher Filmkunst.* Vol. 1. Altona-Bahrenfeld: Zigaretten-Bilderdienst, 1935.

Kaminsky, Stuart. *American Film Genres: Approaches to a Critical Theory of Popular Film.* Dayton, Ohio: Pflann, 1974.

Kaplan, E. Ann. "Lubitsch Reconsidered." *Quarterly Review of Film Studies* 6, no. 3 (Summer 1981): 305–12.

Knowles, Eleanor. *The Films of Jeanette MacDonald and Nelson Eddy.* New York: A. S. Barnes, 1975.

Koszarski, Richard. *Hollywood Directors 1914–40.* New York: Oxford University Press, 1976.

Kracauer, Siegfried. *From Caligari to Hitler: A Psychological History of the German Cinema.* Princeton, N.J.: Princeton University Press, 1977.

———. *Kino. Essays Studien Glossen zum Film.* Edited by Karsten Witte. Frankfurt am Main: Suhrkamp, 1974.

———. *Das Ornament der Masse.* Mit einem Nachwort von Karsten Witte. Frankfurt am Main: Suhrkamp, 1977.

Kurtz, Rudolf. *Expressionismus und Film.* Berlin: Lichtbild-Bühne, 1926.

Lejeune, C. A. *Cinema.* London: Alexander Maclehose, 1931.

Lubitsch, Ernst. "Comparing European and American Methods." *Film Daily,* 6 May 1923.

———. "Der deutsche Film in 1921: Neue Aufgaben der Produktion." *Der Film* 2, 8 January 1921.

———. "Deutsche Filme und die Welt." *Film-Kurier* 155, 5 July 1921.

———. "Film-Internationalität." In *Das deutsche Lichtbildbuch: Filmprobleme von gestern und heute,* edited by Heinrich Pfeiffer. Berlin: A. Scherl, n.d.

———. "Lubitsch contra Ewers . . ." *Lichtbild-Bühne* 52, 25 December 1920.

————. "Lubitsch Praises Griffith." *Film Daily*, 5 January 1922.

————. "My Two Years in America." *Motion Picture* (December 1924).

————. "Unsere Chancen in Amerika." *Lichtbild-Bühne* 56, 17 May 1924.

————. "Wie mein erster Großfilm entstand." *Lichtbild-Bühne*, Luxusnummer "30 Jahre Film" (1924).

————. "Ernst Lubitsch." *Wir über uns selbst*. Edited by Hermann Treuner. Berlin: Sibyllen Verlag, 1928.

MacDonald, Dwight. "Notes on Hollywood Directors" (1933). Reprinted in *Dwight MacDonald on Movies*. Englewood Cliffs, N.J.: Prentice-Hall, 1969.

McCaffrey, Donald. *The Golden Age of Sound Comedy*. South Brunswick, New York: 1973.

McVay, Douglas. "Lubitsch—The American Silent Films." *Focus on Film* 32 (April 1979).

Mast, Gerald. *The Comic Mind: Comedy and the Movies*. Indianapolis: Bobbs-Merrill, 1973.

————. *The Movies in Our Midst: Documents in the Cultural History of Film in America*. Chicago: University of Chicago Press, 1982.

Mills, Robert William. "The American Films of Ernst Lubitsch—A Critical History." Ph.D. diss., University of Michigan, 1976.

Mordden, Ethan. *The Hollywood Musical*. New York: St. Martin's Press, 1981.

Morek, Curt. *Sittengeschichte des Kinos*. Dresden: Paul Aretz, 1926.

Negri, Pola. *Memoirs of a Star*. Garden City, N.Y.: Doubleday, 1970.

Paolella, Roberto. "Ernst Lubitsch, regista del tempo perduto," *Bianco e nero* (Jan. 1958): 1–19.

Parish, James Robert. *The Jeanette MacDonald Story*. New York: Mason/Charter, 1976.

Paul, William. *Ernst Lubitsch's American Comedy*. New York: Columbia University Press, 1983.

Pickard, Roy. *The Hollywood Studios*. London, Tantivy, 1978.

Poague, Leland A. *The Cinema of Ernst Lubitsch: The Hollywood Films*. South Brunswick, N.J.: A. S. Barnes, 1978.

Porges, Friedrich. *Geschichte des Films*. Basel, 1946.

Pratt, George C. *Spellbound in Darkness: A History of the Silent Film*. Rev. ed. Greenwich, Ct.: New York Graphic Society, 1973.

Prinzler, Hans Helmut, and Enno Patalas, eds. *Lubitsch*. Munich: C. J. Bucher, 1984.

Riess, Curt. *Das gab's nur einmal*. 2 vols. Munich: Hanser, 1977.

Ringgold, Gene, and Dewitt Bodeen. *Chevalier: The Films and Career of Maurice Chevalier*. Secaucus, N.J.: Citadel Press, 1973.

Robinson, David. *Hollywood in the Twenties*. London: Methuen, 1973.

Rosen, Marjorie. *Popcorn Venus: Women, Movies and the American Dream*. New York: Coward, McCann and Goeghegan, 1973.

Rotha, Paul. *The Film Till Now*. Rev. and enl. ed. New York: Funk and Wagnalls, 1949.

Roud, Richard, ed. "Ernst Lubitsch." In *Cinema: A Critical Dictionary. The Major Film-makers*. Vol. 1. New York: The Viking Press, 1980.

Sachs, Hanns. "Film Psychology: *Drei Frauen*, by Lubitsch." *Close Up* (November 1928): 14–15.

Sarris, Andrew. *The American Cinema. Directors and Direction 1929–68*. New York: Dutton, 1968.

———. "Lubitsch in the Thirties." *Film Comment* (Winter 1971–72): 54–57 and (Summer 1972): 20–21.

Schebera, Jürgen. *Damals in Neubabelsberg: Studios, Stars und Kinopaläste im Berlin der zwanziger Jahre*. Leipzig: Edition Leipzig, 1990.

Schuman, Peter, and Werner Dütsch, eds. *Retrospektive Ernst Lubitsch*: Broschüren der Internationalen Filmfestspiele Berlin, 1968.

Seeßlen, Georg. *Klassiker der Filmkomik*. Reinbek: Rowohlt, 1980.

Stern, Ernst. *My Life, My Stage*. Translated from the German by Edward Fitzgerald. London: Victor Gollancz, 1951.

Tannenbaum, Eugen. "Der Großfilm." In *Der Film von morgen*, edited by Hugo Zehder. Dresden/Berlin: Rudolf Kaemmerer, 1923.

Toeplitz, Jerzy. *Geschichte des Films*. Vol. 1. Translated from the Polish by Lilli Kaufmann. Munich: Rogner and Bernhard, 1977.

Truffaut, François. "Lubitsch Was a Prince." In *The Films in My Life*, translated by Leonard Mayhew. New York: Simon & Schuster, 1975:

Urgiß, Julius. "Ernst Lubitsch: Künstlerprofile VI." *Der Kinematograph*, 30 August 1916.

Verdone, Mario. *Ernst Lubitsch*. Lyon: Serdoc, 1964.

Von Sternberg, Josef. *Fun in a Chinese Laundry*. New York: Macmillan, 1965.

Vitoux, Frédéric. "Ernst Lubitsch, le maître." *Positif* 137 (April 1972): 57–63.

Weinberg, Herman G. *The Lubitsch Touch: A Critical Study*. 3d. rev. ed. New York: Dover, 1977.

White, Kenneth. "The Style of Ernst Lubitsch." *Hound and Horn* 4, no. 2 (January–March 1931): 173–76.

Whittemore, Don, and Philip Alan Cecchettini, eds. *Passport to Hollywood. Film Immigrants: Anthology*. New York: McGraw-Hill, 1976.

Wollenberg, H. H. "Ernst Lubitsch." *Penguin Film Reviews* 7 (September 1948): 61–67.

———. *Fifty Years of German Film*. London: Falcon Press, 1948.

———. "Two Masters: Ernst Lubitsch and Sergei M. Eisenstein," *Sight and Sound* (Spring 1948): 46–48.

Zglinicki, Friedrich von. *Der Weg des Films*. Hildesheim/New York: 1979.

Other sources cited include (in alphabetical order): *Film Daily, Film-Kurier, Lichtbild-Bühne, Motion Picture Herald, Moving Picture Chronicle, Moving Picture World, Nation, News Telegram, New York, Das Tage-Buch, Variety, Variety Weekly*.

Index